Comp
Symb

SHEFFIELD HALLAM UNIVERSITY
LEARNING CENTRE
WITHDRAWN FROM STOCK

Brian Harvey

Computer Science Logo Style

SECOND EDITION

Volume 1
Symbolic Computing

The MIT Press
Cambridge, Massachusetts
London, England

For information on program diskettes for PC and Macintosh, please contact the Marketing Department, The MIT Press, 55 Hayward Street, Cambridge, Massachusetts, 02142.

Drawings on pages 53 and 169 by James Brzezinski. Photograph of U.C. Berkeley on page 234 by Dennis Galloway, courtesy of the Public Information Office, University of California. Photographs of Stanford University on page 235 courtesy of the News and Publications Service, Stanford University.

This book was typeset in the Baskerville typeface.

Library of Congress Cataloging-in-Publication Data

Harvey, Brian, 1949–
Computer Science Logo Style / Brian Harvey. — 2nd ed.
p. cm.
Includes indexes.
Contents: v. 1. Symbolic computing. — v. 2. Advanced techniques — v. 3. Beyond programming.
ISBN 0–262–58151–5 (set : pbk. : alk. paper). — ISBN 0–262–58148–5 (v. 1 : pbk. : alk. paper). — ISBN 0–262–58149–3 (v. 2 : pbk. : alk. paper). — ISBN 0–262–58150–7 (v. 3 : pbk. : alk. paper)
1. Electronic digital computers–Programming. 2. LOGO (Computer programming language) I. Title.
QA76.6.H385 1997
005.13′3—dc20 96–35371
CIP

Contents

Order Form for Diskettes for
Computer Science Logo Style, second edition
Brian Harvey

The Logo Programs from all three volumes of *Computer Science Logo Style, second edition,* along with Berkeley Logo are available on diskettes in both PC and Macintosh versions. The PC diskette has a DOS version of Berkeley Logo; the Macintosh diskette has a Macintosh version of Berkeley Logo. The programs require about 2 Mb of disk space; 2 Mb of RAM is recommended for running the programs.

These programs are available over the internet, free of charge. They can be found at **anarres.cs.berkeley.edu** in the directory **pub/ucblogo**. The files are **blogo.exe** for DOS machines, **ucblogo.sea.hqx** for Macintosh, and **ucblogo.tar.Z** for Unix. Instructions for getting the files, installing them, and running them are given in Appendix A of Volume 1 of the book.

Order Form

Please send

_____ copies of the Macintosh version of the programs and Logo interpreter ISBN 0-262-58085-3 (HARD2M)

_____ copies of the IBM-compatible PC version of the programs and Logo interpreter ISBN 0-262-58084-5 (HARD2I)

$ _____ Amount ($10.00 per copy U.S. dollars)

$ 3.50 Postage for first copy for shipment via first-class mail within North America or Airmail Letter Rate outside North America

$ _____ Add $0.75 for each additional copy to North American addresses
Add $2.00 for each additional copy outside North America

$ _____ Canadians customers add 7% GST

$ _____ Total

❒ Check or money order enclosed ❒ Purchase order attached

❒ MasterCard ❒VISA ❒ AmEx

Card Number ______________________________ expiration date__________

Ship to: Name____

Address____

____

City/State/Postal Code______________________________

Purchase Order Number_____________________________

Special Instructions_________________________________

____

Send orders to:

The MIT Press
55 Hayward Street
Cambridge, MA 02142 U. S. A.

Toll-free telephone number: 1-800-356-0343
FAX number: 617-625-6660
Internet e-mail address: mitpress-orders@mit.edu

Appendices

Preface

This book isn't for everyone.

Not everyone needs to program computers. There is a popular myth that if you aren't "computer literate," whatever that means, then you'll flunk out of college, you'll never get a job, and you'll be poor and miserable all your life. The myth is promoted by computer manufacturers, of course, and also by certain educators and writers.

The truth is that no matter how many people study computer programming in high school, there will still be only a certain number of programming jobs. When you read about "jobs in high-tech industry," they're talking mostly about manufacturing and sales jobs that are no better paid than any other manufacturing jobs. (Often, these days, those jobs are exported to someplace like Taiwan where they pay pennies a day.) It's quite true that many jobs in the future will involve *using* computers, but the computers will be disguised. When you use a microwave oven, drive a recently built car, or play a video game, you're using a computer, but you didn't have to take a "computer literacy" course to learn how. Even a computer that looks like a computer, as in a word processing system, can be mastered in an hour or two.

This book is for people who are interested in computer programming because it's fun.

The Intellectual Content of Computer Programming

When I wrote the first edition of this book in 1984, I said that the study of computer programming was intellectually rewarding for young children in elementary school, and for computer science majors in college, but that high school students and adults studying on their own generally had an intellectually barren diet, full of technical details of some particular computer brand.

At about the same time I wrote those words, the College Board was introducing an Advanced Placement exam in computer science. Since then, the AP course has become popular, and similar official or semi-official computer science curricula have been adopted in other countries as well. Meanwhile, the computers available to ordinary people have become large enough and powerful enough to run serious programming languages, breaking the monopoly of BASIC.

So, the good news is that intellectually serious computer science is within the reach of just about everyone. The bad news is that the curricula tend to be imitations of what is taught to beginning undergraduate computer science majors, and I think that's too rigid a starting point for independent learners, and especially for teenagers.

See, the wonderful thing about computer programming is that it *is* fun, perhaps not for everyone, but for very many people. There aren't many mathematical activities that appeal so spontaneously. Kids get caught up in the excitement of programming, in the same way that other kids (or maybe the same ones) get caught up in acting, in sports, in journalism (provided the paper isn't run by teachers), or in ham radio. If schools get too serious about computer science, that spontaneous excitement can be lost. I once heard a high school teacher say proudly that kids used to hang out in his computer lab at all hours, but since they introduced the computer science curriculum, the kids don't want to program so much because they've learned that programming is just a means to the end of understanding the curriculum. No! The ideas of computer science are a means to the end of getting computers to do what you want.

Computer Science Apprenticeship

My goal in this series of books is to make the goals and methods of a serious computer scientist accessible, at an introductory level, to people who are interested in computer programming but are not computer science majors. If you're an adult or teenaged hobbyist, or a teacher who wants to use the computer as an educational tool, you're definitely part of this audience. I've taught these ideas to teachers and to high school students. What I enjoy most is teaching high school freshmen who bring a love of programming into the class with them—the ones who are always tugging at my arm to tell me what they found in the latest *Byte.*

I said earlier that I think that for most people programming as job training is nonsense. But if you happen to be interested in programming, studying it in some depth can be valuable for the same reasons that other people benefit from acting, music, or being a news reporter: it's a kind of intellectual apprenticeship. You're learning the discipline of serious thinking and of taking pride in your work. In the case of computer programming, in particular, what you're learning is *mathematical* thinking, or *formal* thinking. (If you like programming, but you hate mathematics, don't panic. In that case it's not really mathematics you hate, it's school. The programming you enjoy is much more like real mathematics than the stuff you get in most high school math classes.) In these books I try to encourage this sort of formal thinking by discussing programming in terms of general rules rather than as a bag of tricks.

When I wrote the first edition of this book, in 1984, it was controversial to suggest that not everyone has to learn to program. I was accused of elitism, of wanting to keep computers as a tool for the rich, while condemning poorer students to dead-end jobs. Today it's more common that I have to fight the opposite battle, trying to convince people why *anyone* should learn about computer programming. After all, there is all that great software out there; instead of wasting time on programming, I'm told, kids should learn to use Microsoft Word or Adobe Illustrator or Macromind Director. At the same time, kids who've grown up with intricate and beautifully illustrated video games are frustrated by the relatively primitive results of their own first efforts at programming. A decade ago it was thrilling to be able to draw a square on a computer screen; today you can do that with two clicks of a mouse.

There are two reasons why you might still want to learn to program. One is that more and more application programs have programming languages built in; you can customize the program's behavior if you learn to speak its "extension" language. (One well-known example is the Hypertalk extension language for the Hypercard program; the one that has everyone excited as I'm writing this is the inclusion of the Java programming language as the extension language for the Netscape World Wide Web browser.) But I think a more important reason is that programming—learning how to express a method for solving a problem in a formal language—can still be very empowering. It's not the same kind of fast-paced fun as playing a video game; it feels more like solving a crossword puzzle.

I've tried to make these books usable either with a teacher or on your own. But since the ideas in these books are rather different from those of most computer science curricula, the odds are that you're reading this on your own. (When I published the first edition, one exception was that this first volume was used fairly commonly in teacher training classes, for elementary school teachers who'd be using Logo in their work.)

About the Second Edition

Three things have happened since the first edition of these books to warrant a revision. The first is that I know more about computer science than I did then! In this volume, the topics of recursion and functional programming are explained better than they were the first time; there is a new chapter on higher order functions early in the book. There are similar improvements in the later volumes, too.

Second, I've learned from both my own and other people's experiences teaching these ideas. I originally envisioned a style of work in which high school students would take a programming course in their first year, then spend several years working on independent projects, and perhaps take a more advanced computer science class senior year. That's why I put all the programming language instruction in the first volume and all the project ideas in the second one. In real life, most students don't spread out their programming experience in that way, and so the projects in the second volume didn't get a chance to inspire most readers. In the second edition, I've mixed projects with language teaching. This first volume teaches the core Logo capabilities that every programming student should know, along with sample projects illustrating both the technical details and the range of possibilities for your own projects. The second volume, *Advanced Techniques,* teaches more advanced language features, along with larger and more intricate projects.

Volume three, *Beyond Programming,* is still a kind of sampler of a university computer science curriculum. Each chapter is an introduction to a topic that you might study in more depth during a semester at college, if you go on to study computer science. Some of the topics, like artificial intelligence, are about programming methods for particular applications. Others, like automata theory, aren't how-to topics at all but provide a mathematical approach to understanding what programming is all about. I haven't changed the table of contents, but most of the chapters have been drastically rewritten to improve both the technical content and the style of presentation.

The third reason for a second edition of these books is that the specific implementations of Logo that I used in 1984 are all obsolete. (One of them, IBM Logo, is still available if you try very hard, but it's ridiculously expensive and most IBM sales offices seem to deny that it exists.) The commercial Logo developers have moved toward products in which Logo is embedded in some point-and-click graphical application program, with more emphasis on shapes and colors, and less emphasis on programming itself. That's probably a good decision for their purposes, but not for mine. That's why this new edition is based on Berkeley Logo, a free implementation that I developed along with some of my students. Berkeley Logo is available for Unix systems, DOS machines, and Macintosh, and the language is exactly the same on all platforms. That means I don't have to clutter the text with footnotes like "If you're using this kind of computer, type that instead."

Why Logo?

Logo has been the victim of its own success in the elementary schools. It has acquired a reputation as a trivial language for babies. Why, then, do I use it as the basis for a series of books about serious computer science? Why not Pascal or C++ instead?

The truth is that Logo is one of the most powerful programming language available for home computers. (In 1984 I said "by far the most powerful," but now home computers have become larger and Logo finally has some competition.) It is a dialect of Lisp, the language used in the most advanced research projects in computer science, and especially in artificial intelligence. Until recently, all of the *books* about Logo have been pretty trivial, and they tend to underscore the point by strewing cute pictures of turtles around. But the cute pictures aren't the whole picture.

What does it mean for a language to be powerful? It *doesn't* mean that you can write programs in a particular language that do things you can't do in some other language. (In that sense, all languages are the same; if you can write a program in Logo, you can write it in Pascal or BASIC too, one way or another. And vice versa.) Instead, the power of a language is a way of measuring how much the language helps you concentrate on the actual problem you wanted to solve in the first place, rather than having to worry about the constraints of the language.

For example, in C, Pascal, Java, and all of the other languages derived originally from Fortran, the programmer has to be very explicit about what goes where in the computer's memory. If you want to group 20 numbers together as a unit, you must "declare an array," saying in advance that there will be exactly 20 numbers in it. If you change your mind later and want 21 numbers, too bad. You also have to say in advance that this array will contain 20 integers, or perhaps 20 numbers with fractions allowed, or perhaps 20 characters of text—but not some of each. In Logo the entire process of storage allocation is *automatic;* if your program produces a list of 20 numbers, the space for that list is provided with no effort by you. If, later, you want to add a 21st number, that's automatic also.

Another example is the *syntax* of a language, the rules for constructing legal instructions. All the Fortran-derived languages have a dozen or so types of instructions, each with its own peculiar syntax. For example, the BASIC `PRINT` statement requires a list of expressions you want printed. If you separate expressions with commas, it means to print them one way; if you separate them with semicolons, that means something else. But you aren't allowed to use semicolons in other kinds of statements that also require lists of expressions. In Logo there is only one syntax, the one that invokes a procedure.

It's not an accident that Logo is more powerful than Pascal or C++; nor is it just that Logo's designers were smarter. Fortran was invented before the mathematical basis of computer programming was well understood, so its design mostly reflects the capabilities (and the deficiencies) of the computers that happened to be available then. The Fortran-based languages still have the same fundamental design, although some of its worst details have been patched over in the more recent versions like Java and C++. More powerful languages are based on some particular mathematical model of computing and use that model in a consistent way. For example, APL is based on the idea of matrix manipulation; Prolog is based on predicate calculus, a form of mathematical logic. Logo, like Lisp, is based on the idea of composition of functions.

The trouble is that if you're just starting this book, you don't have the background yet to know what I'm talking about! So for now, please just take my word for it that I'm not insulting you by asking you to use a "baby" language. After you finish the book, come back and read this section again.

A big change since 1984 is that Logo is no longer the only member of the Lisp family available for home computers. Another dialect, Scheme, has become popular in education. Scheme has many virtues in its own right, but its popularity is also due in part to the fact that it's the language used in the best computer science book ever written: *Structure and Interpretation of Computer Programs,* by Harold Abelson and Gerald Jay Sussman with Julie Sussman (MIT Press/McGraw-Hill, 1985). I have a foot in both camps, since I am co-author, with Matthew Wright, of *Simply Scheme: Introducing Computer Science* (MIT Press, 1994), which is sort of a Scheme version of the philosophy of this book.

The main difference between Scheme and Logo is that Scheme is more consistent in its use of functional programming style. For example, in Scheme, every procedure is what Logo calls an operation—a procedure that returns a computed value for use by some other procedure. Instead of writing a program as a sequence of instructions, as in Logo, the Scheme programmer writes a single expression whose complexity takes the form of composition of functions.

The Scheme approach is definitely more powerful and cleaner for writing advanced projects. Its cost is that the Scheme learner must come to terms from the beginning with the difficult idea of function as object. Logo is more of a compromise with the traditional, sequential programming style. That traditional style is limiting, in the end, but people seem to find it more natural at first. My guess is that ultimately, Logo programmers who maintain their interest in computing will want to learn Scheme, but that there's still a place for Logo as a more informal starting point.

Hardware and Software Requirements

The programs in this series of books are written using Berkeley Logo, a free interpreter that is available on diskette from the MIT Press or on the Internet. (Details are in Appendix A.) Berkeley Logo runs on Unix systems, DOS machines, and Macintosh.

Since Berkeley Logo is free, I recommend using it with this book, even if you have another version of Logo that you use for other purposes. One of the frustrations I had in writing the first edition was dealing with all the trivial ways in which different Logo dialects differ. (For example, if you want to add 2 and 3, can you say `2+3`, or do you have to put spaces around the plus sign? Different dialects answer this question differently.) Nevertheless, the examples in this first volume should be workable in just about any Logo dialect with some effort in fixing syntactic differences. The later volumes in the series, though, depend on advanced features of Berkeley Logo that are missing from many other dialects.

The Berkeley Logo distribution includes the larger programs from these books. When a program is available in a file, the filename is shown at the beginning of the chapter. (There are only a few of these in the first volume, but more in later volumes.)

Words of Wisdom

The trick in learning to program, as in any intellectual skill, is to find a balance between theory and practice. This book provides the theory. One mistake would be to read through it without ever touching a computer. The other mistake would be to be so eager to get your hands on the keyboard that you just type in the examples and skip over the text.

There are no formal exercises at the ends of chapters. That's because (1) I hate a school-like atmosphere; (2) you're supposed to be interested enough already to explore on your own; and (3) I think it's better to encourage your creativity by letting you invent your own exercises. However, at appropriate points in the text you'll find questions like "What do you think would happen if you tried thus-and-such?" and suggestions for programs you can write. These questions and activities are indicated by this symbol: ☞ (the finger of fate). You'll get more out of the book if you take these questions seriously.

If you're not part of a formal class, consider working with a friend. Not only will you keep each other from handwaving too much but it's more fun.

Acknowledgments

The people who read and commented on early drafts of this book include Hal Abelson, Sharon Yoder, Michael Clancy, Jim Davis, Batya Friedman, Paul Goldenberg, Tessa Harvey, Phil Lewis, Margaret Minsky, and Cynthia Solomon. I am especially grateful to Paul Goldenberg and Cindy Carter for their professional, financial, and emotional support during the months I spent as a guest in their home while working on this project, keeping them from their own work and tying up Paul's computer equipment. This book wouldn't exist without them. Special mention also goes to Hal Abelson, without whose support this book wouldn't have found a publisher.

The main ideas in this book, and some of the specific examples, first surfaced in the form of self-paced curriculum units for a programming class at the Lincoln-Sudbury Regional High School, in Sudbury, Massachusetts. Alison Birch, Larry Davidson, and Phil Lewis were my colleagues there. (So, later, was Paul.) All of them helped debug the curriculum by finding mistakes and by pointing out the parts that were correct but incomprehensible. Larry, especially, was my mentor and untiring collaborator, helping me survive my first real teaching job, even though he had his own work and wasn't officially part of the computer department at all. I'm also grateful to the many students who served as guinea pigs for the curriculum, and to David Levington, then the district superintendent, who was generous with equipment and with administrative freedom in support of an untested idea.

My work at Lincoln-Sudbury would not have been possible without the strong support of computer scientists at the Massachusetts Institute of Technology, especially but not only the ones at the Logo Laboratory. Equipment grants from the Digital Equipment Corporation and from Atari, Inc., were also crucial to this work.

And thanks, also, to my faculty supervisors in the Graduate Group in Science and Mathematics Education, at the University of California at Berkeley, for their patience and understanding while I worked on this instead of my thesis.

Second Edition

In 1992 one of my then-undergraduate students, Matt Wright, suggested that we collaborate on a textbook for Berkeley's introductory programming course for non-majors. The book would use Scheme, the same language used in our first course for students in the computer science major, but would be based on the ideas in the first edition of this book. The result of that collaboration, *Simply Scheme,* was published in 1994.

In writing *Simply Scheme,* Matt and I reconsidered every detail of the presentation used in *Computer Science Logo Style.* We added a greater emphasis on higher order functions, and we completely reorganized the chapters on recursion. Large example programs were added to the text, along with suggestions for student projects.

Most of the changes in this second edition were inspired by the work that Matt and I did together for the Scheme book. In a few cases I have lifted entire paragraphs from it! Matt also read early drafts of some of the new chapters in this edition, and this text benefits from his comments.

Berkeley Logo, the interpreter used in this edition, is a collective effort of many people, both at Berkeley and across the Internet. My main debt in that project is to three former students: Dan van Blerkom, Michael Katz, and Doug Orleans. At the risk of missing someone, I also want to acknowledge substantial contributions by Freeman Deutsch, Khang Dao, Fred Gilham, Yehuda Katz, George Mills, Sanford Owings, and Randy Sargent.

Computer Science Logo Style
Symbolic Computing

1 Exploration

The name Logo comes from the Greek word *logos,* which means "word." In contrast to earlier programming languages, which emphasized arithmetic computation, Logo was designed to manipulate language—words and sentences.

Like any programming language, Logo is a general-purpose tool that can be approached in many ways. Logo programming can be understood at different levels of sophistication. It has been taught to four-year-olds and to college students. Most of the books about Logo so far have been introductory books for young beginners, but *this* book is different. It's for somewhat older learners, probably with some prior computer experience, although not necessarily Logo experience.

This book was written using the Berkeley Logo dialect, a version of Logo that's available at no cost for PCs, Macintoshes, and Unix systems. Recent commercial Logo dialects have emphasized the control of real-time animation, robotics, and other such application areas, somewhat at the expense of more traditional Logo features designed to be useful in the development of larger and more complex programs. Berkeley Logo follows the traditional design, so you may miss some "bells and whistles" that you associate with Logo from elementary school. In fact, we'll hardly do any graphics in this book!

Some of the details you'll have to know in order to work with Logo depend on the particular kind of computer you're using. This book assumes you already know some things about your computer:

- How to turn on your computer and start Logo
- How to type a command, ending with the RETURN key
- How to use control keys to correct typing mistakes
- How to use a text editing program

These points I've listed aren't actually part of the Logo *language* itself, but they're part of the Logo programming *environment.* Appendix A has a brief guide to some of these machine-specific aspects, but if you've never used a computer before at all, start by working with some application programs to get the feel of the machine.

On the other hand, I'd like to pretend that you know nothing about the Logo language—the primitive procedures, the process of procedure definition, and so on—even if you've really used Logo in elementary school. The reason for this pretense is that I want you to think about programming in what will probably be a new way. The *programs* may not be new to you, but the *vocabulary* with which you think about them will be. I'm warning you about this ahead of time because I don't want you to skip over the early chapters, thinking that you already know what's in them.

Okay, it's time to start Logo running on your computer. You should then see a screen that says something like

```
Welcome to Berkeley Logo version 3.3
?
```

The question mark is Logo's *prompt.* When you see the question mark, it means that the computer is prepared for you to type in a Logo *instruction* and that Logo will carry out the instruction as soon as you finish it.

Getting Acquainted with Logo...

Right now, type this instruction:

```
repeat 50 [setcursor list random 75 random 20 type "Hi]
```

Remember that square brackets `[]` are different from parentheses `()`. Also remember that it's important to put spaces between words. However, it doesn't matter whether you use `UPPER CASE` or `lower case` letters in the words that Logo understands.

If all goes well, Logo will cheerfully greet you by scattering `His` all over the screen. If all doesn't go well, you probably misspelled something. Take a look at what you typed, and try again.

Afterward, you can clear the screen by typing `cleartext` or its abbreviation `ct`.

... in Two Senses

I thought it would be appropriate to start exploring Logo by having it say hello. You and Logo can get acquainted as you would with another person.

But, of course, the point of the exercise is to get acquainted with Logo in a more serious sense too. You're seeing what a Logo instruction looks like and a little bit about what kinds of things Logo can do. In this first chapter the kind of acquaintance I have in mind is relatively superficial. I'm trying to get across a broad sense of Logo's flavor rather than a lot of details. So I'm not explaining completely what we're doing here. For that reason, the second chapter will repeat some of the same activities, but I'll give a more detailed discussion there.

Perhaps you've made Logo's acquaintance before, probably through the medium of turtle graphics. In that first introduction you may have explored Logo's ability to manipulate text as well as graphics. But maybe not. Writing a book like this, it's not easy for me to carry on a conversation with someone I haven't met, so in this introduction I may be saying too much or too little for your individual situation. I hope that by the second chapter you and the other readers will all be ready for the same discussion.

If you haven't used Logo before, or if you've used only the part of Logo that has to do with turtles, look at the instruction I asked you to type earlier. Think about the different parts of that instruction, the words like `repeat` and `random` and `setcursor`. Try to figure out what each one means. Then see if you can figure out an experiment to decide if you've understood each word correctly! Later, we'll go over all these details and you'll learn the "official" explanations. But the kind of experimenting I'm suggesting isn't pointless. This kind of exploration may raise questions in your mind, not just about the meanings of the Logo words but about how they're connected together in an instruction, or about *why* a word means just what it does rather than something a little different.

Another Greeting

Here is a somewhat less "scatterbrained" greeting instruction:

```
repeat 20 [repeat random 30 [type "Hi] print []]
```

Try that one. Compare it to the one we started with. Which do you like better? Do you prefer random scattering, or orderly rows? Perhaps this question will teach you something about your own personality!

Fooling Around

Then again, maybe you think this is all silly. If so, I'd like to try to convince you that there are some good, serious reasons for you to take a lighthearted approach to computer programming, no matter how serious your ultimate goals may be.

There are two aspects to learning how to program in a language like Logo. One aspect is memorizing the vocabulary, just as in learning to speak French. If you flip through the reference manual that came with your Logo,* you'll find that it's a sort of dictionary, translating each Logo word into a bunch of English words that explain it. But the second aspect is to learn the "feel" of Logo. What kinds of problems does Logo handle particularly well? What are the examples of programming *style* that correspond to the idioms of a human language? What do you do when something doesn't work?

It is by fooling around with Logo that you learn this second aspect of the language. Starting with the second chapter of this book, we'll be going through plenty of dry, carefully analyzed fine points of Logo usage. But as we progress, you should still be fooling around, on the computer, with the ideas in the chapters.

In fact, I think that that kind of intellectual play is the best reason for learning about computer programming in the first place. This is true whether you are a kid programming for the fun of it or an adult looking for a career change. The most successful computer programmers aren't the ones who approach programming as a task they have to carry out in order to get their paychecks. They're the ones for whom programming is a joyful game. Just as a baseball diamond is a good medium in which you can exercise your body, the computer is a good medium in which you can exercise your mind. That's the real virtue of the computer in education, not anything about job training or about arithmetic drill.

A Slightly Longer Conversation

The Logo words such as `print` and `random` are the names of *procedures,* little pieces of computer program that are "specialists" in some particular task. We are now going to add to Logo's repertoire by inventing a new procedure named `hi`. At the question mark prompt, start by typing this:

* If you're using Berkeley Logo, it's in a file named `usermanual` (or `userman.ual` if you're using a DOS machine) that should be installed along with the Logo program. The Berkeley Logo reference manual is also an appendix to Volume 2 of this series.

```
to hi
```

The word `to` here is short for "here's how to." The name is intended to suggest the *metaphor* that what you're doing when you write computer programs is to *teach* the computer a new skill. Metaphors like this can be very helpful to you in understanding a new idea. (Just ask any English teacher.) I'll point out other metaphors from time to time.

Logo should have responded to this instruction by printing a different prompt character. Instead of the question mark, you should now see a greater-than sign (>) at the beginning of the line:

```
? to hi
>
```

(Whenever I show an interaction with the computer in this book, I'll show the part that you're supposed to type in **`boldface`**; what the computer prints in response is in `lightface`. But I won't use boldface when I'm only showing what you type and not a complete interaction.) This new prompt means that Logo will not immediately carry out whatever instructions you type; instead Logo will remember these instructions as part of the new procedure `hi`. Continue typing these lines:

```
print [Hi. What's your name?]
print sentence [How are you,] word first readlist "?
ignore readlist
print [That's nice.]
end
```

Again, be careful about the spaces and punctuation. After the last line, the one that just says `end`, Logo should go back to the question mark prompt. Now just type

```
hi
```

on a line by itself. You can carry on a short conversation with this program. Here's what happened when I tried it.

```
? hi
Hi. What's your name?
Brian Harvey
How are you, Brian?
I'm fine.
That's nice.
```

If something unexpected happens when you try it, perhaps you made a typing mistake. If you know how, you can fix such mistakes using the Logo editor. If not, you'll have a chance to review that process later, but for now, just start over again but give the procedure a different name. For example, you can say

```
to hi2
```

for the second version of `hi`.

☞ This program pretends to be pretty smart. It carries on a conversation with you in English. But of course it isn't really smart. If you say "I feel terrible" instead of "I'm fine," the procedure cheerfully replies "That's nice" anyway. How else can you mess up the program? What programming tools would you need to be able to overcome the "bugs" in this program?

(When a paragraph starts with this symbol ☞ it means that the paragraph asks you to invent something. Often it will be a Logo program, but sometimes, as in this case, just answers to questions. This is a good opportunity to take a break from reading, and check on your understanding of what you've read.)

A Sneaky Greeting

This chapter started as a sort of pun in my mind—the one about getting acquainted. How should I have Logo introduce itself? I'm still playing with that idea. Here's another version.

```
to start
cleartext
print [Welcome to Berkeley Logo version 3.3]
type "|? |
process readlist
type "|? |
wait 100
print [Ha, ha, fooled you!!]
end

to process :instruction
test emptyp :instruction
iftrue [type "|? | process readlist stop]
iffalse [print sentence [|I don't know how  to|] first :instruction]
end
```

The vertical bars are used to tell Logo that you want to include space characters within a word. (Ordinarily Logo pays no attention to extra spaces between words.) This is the sort of grubby detail you may not want to bother with right now, but if you are a practical joker you may find it worth the effort.

A Quiz Program

Before we get on to the next chapter, I'll just show you one more little program. Try typing this in. As before, you'll see greater-than prompts instead of question marks while you're doing it.

```
to music.quiz
print [Who is the greatest musician of all time?]
if equalp readlist [John Lennon] [print [That's right!] stop]
print [No, silly, it's John Lennon.]
end
```

You can try out this procedure by typing its name as an instruction.*

☞ If you don't like my question, you could make up your own procedures that ask different questions. Let's say you make up one called `sports.quiz` and another called `history.quiz`, each asking and answering one question. You could then put them all together into one big quiz like this:

```
to total.quiz
music.quiz
sports.quiz
history.quiz
end
```

Saving Your Work

If you do write a collection of quiz procedures, you'll want to save them so that they'll still be available the next time you use Logo. Certainly you'll want to save the work you

---

* It has been suggested by some reviewers of the manuscript that there may be younger readers who don't know who John Lennon is. Well, he's the father of Julian Lennon, an obscure rock star of the '80s, and he used to be in a rock group called the Quarrymen. If you have trouble with some of the cultural references later in the book you'll have to research them yourself.

do in later chapters. You can ask Logo to record all of the definitions you've made as a *workspace* file using the `save` command. For example, if you enter the instruction

```
save "mystuff
```

you are asking Logo to write a disk file called `mystuff` containing everything you've defined. (The next time you use Logo, you can get back your definitions with the `load` command.)

Don't get confused about the difference between a *procedure* name and a *workspace* name. Logo beginners sometimes think that `save` saves only a single procedure, the one whose name you tell it (in this example, a procedure named `mystuff`). But the workspace file named `mystuff` will actually contain *all* the procedures you've defined. In fact, you probably don't have a procedure named `mystuff`.

The format for the name of a disk file will depend on the kind of computer you're using, whether you're writing to a hard disk or a floppy disk, and so on. Just use whatever file name format your system requires in other programs, preceded by the quotation mark that tells Logo you're providing a word as the input to the `save` command.

About Chapter 2

In this chapter the emphasis has been on *doing* things. You've been playing around with some fairly intricate Logo instructions, and if you don't understand everything about the examples, don't let that worry you.

Chapter 2 has the opposite emphasis. There is very little to do, and the examples will seem quite simple, perhaps even insultingly simple! But the focus of the chapter is on *understanding* those simple examples in great detail.

Logo deserves its reputation as an easy-to-learn language, but it is also a very sophisticated one. The ease with which Logo can be learned has lured many people into sloppy thinking habits that make it hard for them to grow beyond the most trivial programming. By studying examples that seem easy on the surface, we can start exploring *below* the surface. The important questions will not be ones like "what does `print` do," but instead ones like "what is going on *inside* the Logo interpreter when I type `print`?"

Later chapters will strike more of a balance between things to do and things to think about. If the pace seems slow in chapter 2, glance back at the table of contents to reassure yourself about how much territory we'll cover before the end of the book. Then keep in mind that you'll need the ideas from chapter 2 in order to understand what comes later.

No Exercises

This is the point in the chapter where you might be expecting a set of exercises: Problem 1.1, get the computer to print your name.

There aren't any exercises—but not because you shouldn't try using Logo at this point. The reason is that part of the challenge is for *you* to invent things to try, not just rely on me for your ideas. In each chapter there will be some sample procedures to illustrate the new information in the chapter. You should try to invent programs that use those ideas.

But I hope it's clear by now that I don't want you to do this with a sense of duty. You should play with the ideas in each chapter only to the extent that it's interesting and mind-stretching for you to do so.

In this chapter I really haven't yet told you any of the rules for putting together Logo instructions. (I'll do that in Chapter 2.) So you shouldn't get discouraged or feel stupid if you don't get very far, right now, in playing with Logo. It will be a few more chapters before you should expect to feel really *confident* about undertaking new projects of your own. But you won't break anything by trying now. Go ahead, fool around!

2 Procedures

Logo is one of the most powerful programming languages around. In order to take advantage of that power, you must understand Logo's central ideas: *procedures* and *evaluation.* It is with these ideas that our exploration of Logo programming begins.

Procedures and Instructions

In response to Logo's question-mark prompt, type this instruction:

```
print 17
```

Logo will respond to this instruction by printing the number 17 and then printing another question mark, to indicate that it's ready for another instruction:

```
? print 17
17
```

(Remember, the things in **`boldface`** are the ones *you* should type; what's in `lightface` is what the computer prints.)

This instruction doesn't do much, but it's important to understand how it's put together. The word `print` is the name of a *procedure,* which is a piece of a computer program that has a particular specialized task. The procedure named `print`, for example, has the task of printing things on your screen.

If you have previously used some other programming language, you may be accustomed to the idea of different *statement types* making up the repertoire of the language. For example, BASIC has a `print` statement, a `let` statement, an `input` statement, etc. Pascal has an assignment statement, an `if` statement, a `while` statement, etc. Each kind of statement has its own *syntax,* that is, its own special punctuation and organization. Logo is very different. It does not have different kinds of instructions; *everything* in Logo is done by the use of procedures. If Logo is your first programming language, you don't have to worry about this. But for people with previous experience in another language, it's a common source of misunderstanding.

When you first start up Logo, it "knows" about 200 procedures. These initial procedures are called *primitive* procedures. Your task as a Logo programmer is to add to Logo's repertoire by defining new procedures of your own. You do this by putting together procedures that already exist. We'll see how this is done later in this chapter.

The procedure `print`, although it has a specific task, doesn't always do *exactly* the same thing; it can print anything you want, not always the number 17. (You've seen several examples in Chapter 1.) This may seem like an obvious point, but later you will see that the *flexibility* of procedures is an important part of what makes them so powerful. To control this flexibility, we need a way to tell a procedure exactly what we want it to do. Therefore, each procedure can accept a particular number of *inputs.* An input is a piece of information. It can be a number, as in the example we're examining, but there are many other kinds of information that Logo procedures can handle. The procedure named `print` requires one input. Other procedures will require different numbers of inputs; some don't require any.

Technical Terms

In ordinary conversation, words such as *instruction* and *procedure* have pretty much the same meaning—they refer to any process, recipe, or method for carrying out some task. That's not the situation when we're talking about computer programming. Each of these words has a specific technical meaning, and it's very important for you to keep them straight in your head while you're reading this chapter. (Soon we'll start using more words, such as *command* and *operation,* which also have similar meanings in ordinary use but very different meanings for us.)

An *instruction* is what you type to Logo to tell it to do something. `Print 17` is an example of an instruction. We're about to see some more complicated instructions, made up of more pieces. An instruction has to contain enough information to specify *exactly* what you want Logo to do. To make an analogy with instructing human beings, "Read Chapter 2 of this book" is an instruction, but "read" isn't one, because it doesn't tell you what to read.

A *procedure* is like a recipe or a technique for carrying out a certain kind of task. `Print` is the name of a procedure just as "lemon meringue pie" is the name of a recipe.

(The recipe itself, as distinct from its name, is a bunch of instructions, such as "Preheat the oven to 325 degrees.") A procedure contains information about how to do something, but the procedure doesn't take action itself, just as a recipe in a book can't bake a pie by itself. Someone has to carry out the recipe. In the Logo world something has to *invoke* a procedure. To "invoke" a procedure means to carry it out, to do what the procedure says. Procedures are invoked by instructions. The instruction you gave just now invoked the procedure named `print`.

If an instruction is made up of names of procedures, and if the procedures invoked by the instruction are made up of more instructions, why doesn't the computer get caught in a vicious circle, always finding more detailed procedures to invoke and never actually doing anything? This question is a lot like the one about dictionaries: When you look up the definition of a word, all you find is more words. How do you know what *those* words mean? For words in the dictionary this turns out to be a very profound and difficult question. For Logo programming the answer is much simpler. In the end, your instructions and the procedures they invoke must be defined in terms of the primitive procedures. Those procedures are not made up of Logo instructions. They're the things that Logo just knows how to do in the first place.

Evaluation

Now try this instruction:

```
print sum 2 3
```

If everything is going according to plan, Logo didn't print the words "`sum 2 3`"; it printed the number 5. The input to `print` was the expression `sum 2 3`, but Logo *evaluated* the input before passing it to the `print` procedure. This means that Logo invoked the necessary procedures (in this case, `sum`) to compute the value of the expression (5).

In this instruction the word `sum` is also the name of a procedure. `Sum` requires two inputs. In this case we gave it the numbers 2 and 3 as inputs. Just as the task of procedure `print` is to print something, the task of procedure `sum` is to add two numbers. It is the result of this addition, the *output* from `sum`, that becomes the *input* to `print`.

Don't confuse *output* with *printing*. In Logo the word "output" is one of those technical terms I mentioned before. It refers to a value that one procedure computes and hands on to another procedure that needs an input. In this example `sum` outputs the number 5 to `print`, but `print` doesn't output anything to another procedure. When print prints the 5, that's the end of the story. There are no more procedures waiting for inputs.

See if you can figure out what this instruction will do before you try it:

```
print sum 4 product 10 2
```

Here are the steps Logo takes to evaluate the instruction:

1. The first thing in the instruction is the name of the procedure `print`. Logo knows that `print` requires one input, so it continues reading the instruction line.
2. The next thing Logo finds is the word `sum`. This, too, is the name of a procedure. This tells Logo that the *output* from `sum` will be the *input* to `print`.
3. Logo knows that `sum` takes two inputs, so `sum` can't be invoked until Logo finds `sum`'s inputs.
4. The next thing in the instruction is the number 4, so that must be the first input to `sum`. This input, too, must be evaluated. Fortunately, a number simply evaluates to itself, so the value of this input is 4.
5. Logo still needs to find the second input to `sum`. The next thing in the instruction is the word `product`. This is, again, the name of a procedure. Logo must carry out that procedure to evaluate `sum`'s second input.
6. Logo knows that `product` requires two inputs. It must now look for the first of those inputs. (Meanwhile, `print` and `sum` are both "on hold" waiting for their inputs to be evaluated. `print` is waiting for its single input; `sum`, which has found one input, is waiting for its second.) The next thing on the line is the number 10. This number evaluates to itself, so the first input to `product` is 10.
7. Logo still needs another input for `product`, so it continues reading the instruction. The next thing it finds is the number 2. This number evaluates to itself, so the second input to `product` has the value 2.
8. Logo is now ready to invoke the procedure `product`, with inputs 10 and 2. The output from `product` is 10 times 2, or 20.
9. This output, 20, is the value of the second input to `sum`. Logo is now ready to invoke `sum`, with inputs 4 and 20. The output from `sum` is 24.
10. The output from `sum`, 24, is the input to `print`. Logo is now ready to invoke `print`, which prints 24. (You were only waiting for this moment to arise.)

That's a lot of talking about a pretty simple instruction! I promise not to do it again in quite so much detail. It's important, though, to be able to call upon your understanding of these details to figure out more complicated situations later. Using the output from one procedure as an input to another procedure is called *composition of functions.*

Some people find it helpful to look at a pictorial form of this analysis. We can represent each procedure as a kind of tank, with input hoppers on top and perhaps an output pipe at the bottom. (This organization makes sense because gravity will pull the information downward.) For example:

`Print` has one input, which is represented by the hopper above the tank. It doesn't have an output, so there is no pipe coming out the bottom. `Sum` has two inputs, shown at the top, and an output, shown at the bottom.

We can put these parts together to form a kind of "plumbing diagram" of the instruction:

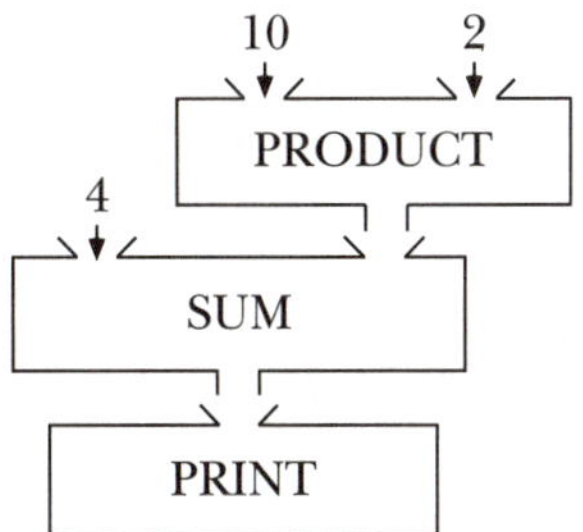

In that diagram the output pipes from one procedure are connected to the input hoppers of another. Every pipe must be connected to something. The inputs that are explicitly given as numbers in the instruction are shown with arrows pointing into the hoppers.

You can annotate the diagram by indicating the actual information that flows through each pipe. Here's how that would look for this instruction:

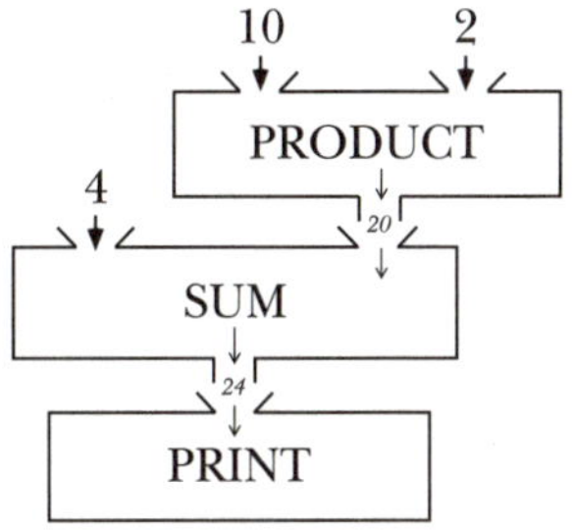

By the way, I've introduced the procedures `print`, `sum`, and `product` so casually that you might think it's a law of nature that every programming language must have procedures with these names. Actually the details of Logo's repertoire of primitive procedures are quite arbitrary. It would be hard to avoid having a way to add numbers, but it might have been named `plus` or `add` instead of `sum`. For some primitives there are additional arbitrary details; for noncommutative operations such as `remainder`, for example, the rule about which input comes first was an arbitrary choice for Logo's designers. (☞ Experiment with `remainder` and see if you can describe it well enough that someone else can use it without needing to experiment.) I am making a point of the arbitrary nature of these details because people who are learning to program sometimes think they're doing badly if they don't *figure out* how a primitive procedure works in advance. But these rules aren't things you work out; they're things someone has to tell you, like the capital of Kansas.

Error Messages

We've observed that Logo knows in advance how many inputs a particular procedure needs. (`Print` needs one; `sum` and `product` each need two.) What if you give a procedure the wrong number of inputs? Try this:

```
print
```

(That is, the word `print` as an instruction all by itself, with no input.) You should see something like this:

```
? print
Not enough inputs to print
```

This gentle complaint from Logo tells you two things. First, it indicates the general *kind* of thing that went wrong (not enough inputs to some procedure). Second, it names the *particular* procedure that complained (`print`). In this case it was pretty obvious which procedure was involved, since we only used one procedure. But try this:

```
? print remainder product 4 5
Not enough inputs to remainder
```

In this case Logo's message is helpful in pinpointing the fact that it was `remainder`, not `print` or `product`, that lacked an input.

The reason I'm beating this error message to death is that one of the most common mistakes made by beginning programmers is to ignore what an error message says. Some people get very upset at seeing this kind of message and just give up without trying to figure out the problem. Other people make the opposite mistake, breezing past the message without taking advantage of the detailed help it offers. Some smart people at M.I.T. put a lot of effort into designing Logo's error messages, so please pay attention to them.

What if you give a procedure too many inputs? Try this:

```
? print 2 3
2
You don't say what to do with 3
```

(The exact text of the message, by the way, may be slightly different in some versions of Logo.) What happened here is that Logo carried out the instruction `print 2`, and then found the extra number `3` on the line. It would have been okay if we'd done something with the 3:

```
? print 2 print 3
2
3
```

It's okay to have more than one instruction on the same line, as long as they are complete instructions.

Commands and Operations

What's a "complete instruction"? Before I can answer that question, you have to understand that in Logo there are two kinds of procedures: commands and operations.

An *operation* is a procedure that computes a value and outputs it. `Sum` and `product` are operations, for example.

A *command* is a procedure that does *not* output a value but instead has some *effect* such as printing something on the screen, moving a turtle, or making a sound. `Print`, then, is a command. Some commands have effects that are not apparent on the outside but instead change something inside the computer that might become important later in the program.

A complete instruction consists of the name of a command, followed by as many expressions as necessary to provide its inputs. An *expression* is something like `sum 3 2` or 17. Operations are used to construct expressions. More formally, an expression is one of two things: either an explicitly provided value such as a number, or else the name of an operation, followed by as many expressions as necessary to provide its inputs. For example, the expression sum 3 2 consists of the operation name sum followed by two expressions, the number 3 and the number 2. Numbers are the only values we've seen how to provide explicitly, but that's about to change.

Words and Lists

So far, our examples have been about numbers and arithmetic. Many people think that computers just do arithmetic, but actually it's much more interesting to use computers with other kinds of information. You've seen examples of text processing in Chapter 1, but this time we're going to do it *carefully!*

Suppose you want Logo to print the word Hello. You might try this:

```
? print Hello
I don't know how  to Hello
```

Logo interpreted the word Hello as the name of a procedure, just as in the examples with print sum earlier. The error message means that there is no procedure named hello in Logo's repertoire.

When Logo is evaluating instructions, it always interprets unadorned words such as print or sum or hello as names of procedures. In order to convince Logo to treat a word simply as itself, you must type a quotation mark (") in front of it:

```
? print "Hello
Hello
```

Here is why the quotation mark is used for this purpose in Logo: In computer science, to *quote* something means *to prevent it from being evaluated.* (Another way to say the same thing is that *the thing evaluates to itself* or that its value *after* evaluation is the same as what it is *before* evaluation.) For example, we have already seen that in Logo, numbers are automatically quoted. (It doesn't hurt to use the quotation mark with numbers, however.

```
? print sum "2 "3
5
```

Logo is perfectly happy to add the quote-marked numbers.)

(People who have programmed in some other language should note that quotation marks are not used in pairs in Logo. This is not just an arbitrary syntactic foible; it reflects the fact that a Logo *word* is a different idea from what would be called a *character string* in other languages. I urge you not only to program in Logo but even to think in Logo terminology.)

What if you want to print more than one word? You can combine several words to form a *list.* The easiest way to do this is to enclose the words in square brackets, which tells Logo to quote the list. That is, a list in brackets evaluates to the list itself:

```
? print [How are you?]
How are you?
```

(If square brackets quote a list, what does it mean to evaluate a list? Well, every instruction line you type to Logo is actually a list, which is evaluated by invoking the procedures it names. Most of the time you don't have to remember that an instruction is a list, but that fact will become very useful later on.)

The list in the example above contains three *members.* In this example each member is a word. For example, the first member is the word `How`. But the members of a list aren't required to be words; they can also be lists. The fact that a list can have another list as a member makes lists very flexible as a way of grouping information. For example, the list

```
[[cherry vanilla] mango [root beer swirl]]
```

contains three members. The first and third members are themselves lists, while the second member is the word `mango`. A list like this can be represented using a *tree diagram:*

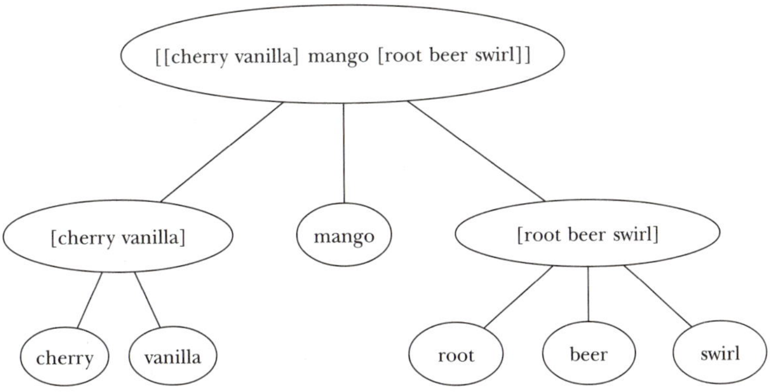

This diagram has the name "tree" because it resembles an upside-down tree, with a trunk at the top and branches extending downward. Often a tree diagram is drawn with only the *leaves* labeled—the words that make up the smallest sublists:

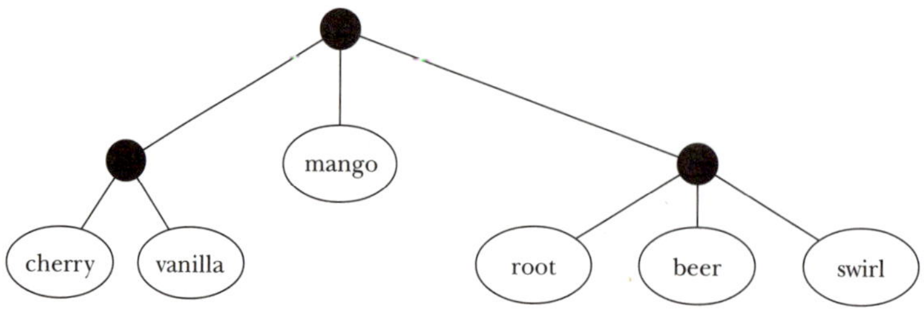

Keep in mind that the square brackets in Logo serve two purposes at once: they *delimit* a list—that is, they show where the list begins and ends—and they also *quote* the list, so that Logo's evaluator interprets the list as representing itself and not as requesting the invocation of procedures. The brackets surround the list; they are not *part of* the list. (Similarly, the quotation mark that indicates a quoted word is not part of the word.)

Words and lists are the two kinds of information that Logo can process. (Numbers are a special case of words.) The name I'll use for "either a word or a list" is a *datum.** A list of words, such as `[How are you?]`, is called a *sentence* or a *flat list.* (It's called "flat" because the tree diagram only has one level, not counting the "root" at the top.) The name "sentence" is meant to suggest that flat lists are often, although not always, used to represent English sentences. A sentence is a special kind of list, just as a number is a special kind of word. We'll see other kinds of lists later.

How to Describe a Procedure

My high school U.S. history teacher was very fussy about what he considered the proper way to color in outline maps. He would make us do them over if we used colors or shading techniques he didn't like. We humored him because he was a very good teacher in other ways; for example, he gave us original historical documents to read instead of boring textbooks.

I hope you will humor me when I tell you that there is a right way and a wrong way to talk about procedures. If I were teaching you in person, I'd be very understanding

* Later we'll use a third kind of datum, called an "array."

about mistakes in your *programs,* but I'd hit you over the head (gently, of course) if you were sloppy about your *descriptions.*

Here is an example of the wrong way: "`Sum` adds up two numbers." It's not that this description isn't true but that it's inadequate. It leaves out too much.

Here is an example of the right way: "`Sum` is an operation. It has two inputs. Both inputs must be numbers. The output from `sum` is a number, the result of adding the two inputs."

Here are the ingredients in the right way:

1. Command or operation?
2. How many inputs?
3. What *type* of datum must each input be?
4. If the procedure is an operation, what is its *output?* If a command, what is its *effect?*

Another example: "The command `print` has one input. The input can be any datum. The effect of `print` is to print the input datum on the screen."

Manipulating Words and Lists

Logo provides several primitive operations for taking data apart and putting data together. Words come apart into *characters,* such as letters or digits or punctuation marks. (A character is not a third kind of datum. It's just a word that happens to be one character long.) Lists come apart into whatever data are the *members* of the list. A sentence, which is a list of words, comes apart into words.

`First` is an operation that takes one input. The input can be any nonempty datum. (In a moment you'll see what an empty datum is.) The output from `first` is the first member of the input if the input is a list, or the first character if the input is a word. Try these examples:

```
? print first "Hello
H
? print first [How are you?]
How
```

`Butfirst` is also an operation that takes one input. The input can be any nonempty datum. The output from `butfirst` is a list containing all but the first member of the input if the input is a list, or a word containing all but the first character of the input if it's a word:

```
? print butfirst "Hello
ello
? print butfirst [How are you?]
are you?
```

Notice that the `first` of a list can be a word, but the `butfirst` of any datum is always another datum of the same type. Also notice what happens when you take the `butfirst` of a datum with only one thing in it:

```
? print butfirst "A

? print butfirst [Hello]

?
```

In each case Logo printed a blank line. In the first case that blank line represents an empty word, a word with no characters in it. The second blank line represents an empty list, a list with no members. You can indicate the empty word in an instruction by using a quotation mark with a space (or the RETURN key to end the instruction) after it. To indicate an empty list, use brackets with nothing inside them:

```
? print " print []


?
```

Do you understand why it doesn't make sense to use the empty word or the empty list as input to `first` or `butfirst`? Try it and see what happens.

You should also notice that the list `[Hello]` is not the same as the word `"Hello`. They look the same when you print them, but they act differently when you take their `first` or `butfirst`.

There are also primitive operations `last` and `butlast`. I'm sure you'll have no trouble guessing what they do. Try them out, then practice describing them properly.

This is probably a good place to mention that there are *abbreviations* for some Logo primitive procedures. For example, `bf` is an abbreviation for `butfirst`. `Pr` is an abbreviation for `print`. There isn't any abbreviation for `first`.

If you want to extract a piece of a word or list that isn't at the beginning or end, you can use the more general operation `item` with two inputs: a positive integer to indicate which member to select, and a word or list. For example:

```
? print item 3 "Yesterday
s
? print item 2 [Good Day Sunshine]
Day
```

`First`, `last`, `butfirst`, `butlast`, and `item` are taking-apart operations, or *selectors*. Logo also provides putting-together operations, or *constructors*.

`Sentence` is a constructor. It takes two inputs, which can be any data at all. Its output is always a list.

Describing the output from `sentence` is a little tricky because the same procedure serves two different purposes. The first purpose is the one suggested by its name: constructing sentences. If you use only words and sentences (flat lists) as inputs, then the output from `sentence` is a sentence concatenating (stringing together) the words contained in the inputs. Here are some examples:

```
? print sentence "hello "goodbye
hello goodbye
? print sentence [this is] [a test]
this is a test
? print sentence "this [is one too]
this is one too
? print sentence [] [list of words]
list of words
```

On the other hand, `sentence` can also be used to append two lists (flat or not). With lists as inputs, the output from `sentence` is a list in which the *members* of the first input and the *members* of the second input are concatenated:

```
? print sentence [[list 1a] [list 1b]] [[list 2a] [list 2b]]
[list 1a] [list 1b] [list 2a] [list 2b]
? print sentence [flat list] [[not flat] [list]]
flat list [not flat] [list]
```

In the second example the output is a list with four members: two words and two lists.

Using a word as input to `sentence` is equivalent to using a list with that word as its single member. `Sentence` is the only primitive operation that treats words the same as single-word lists; you've seen from the earlier examples that `first` and `butfirst` treat the word `hello` and the list `[hello]` differently.

Another constructor for lists is `list`. Its inputs can be any data; its output is a list whose members are the inputs—not the members of the inputs, as for `sentence`.

```
? print list [this is] [a test]
[this is] [a test]
? print list "this [is one too]
this [is one too]
? print list [] [list of words]
[] [list of words]
```

`Word` is an operation that takes two inputs. Both inputs must be words. (They may be the empty word.) The output from `word` is a word formed by concatenating the characters in the input words:

```
? print word "hello "goodbye
hellogoodbye
? print word "now "here
nowhere
? print word "this [is a test]
word doesn't like [is a test] as input
```

Selectors and constructors can be composed, in the same way we composed `sum` and `product` earlier. See if you can work out what this example will do before you try it with the computer:*

---

* The tilde (~) at the end of the first line is the notation used by Berkeley Logo to indicate that this and the following line should be understood as a single, long instruction line. It's somewhat analogous to the way a hyphen (-) is used in English text when a single word must be split between two lines. Berkeley Logo will also continue an instruction to the next line if a line ends inside parentheses or brackets, so another way to indicate a long instruction line is to enclose the entire instruction in parentheses, like this:

```
(print word word last "awful first butfirst "computer
   first [go to the store, please.])
```

Other Logo dialects have other rules for line continuation. (In some dialects everything you type is automatically taken as one big line, so you don't have to think about this.) In the book, I'll indent continuation lines, as above, to make it quite clear that they are meant to be part of the same instruction as the line above. But Logo doesn't pay attention to the indentation.

```
print word word last "awful first butfirst "computer ~
   first [go to the store, please.]
```

Here is how I'd analyze it.

- The input to `print` is the output from `word`.
- The first input to `word` is the output from `word`.
- The first input to (the second) `word` is the output from `last`.
- The input to `last` is the quoted word `awful`.
- The output from `last` is the word `l`, which becomes the first input to the second `word`.
- The second input to the second `word` is the output from `first`.
- The input to `first` is the output from `butfirst`.
- The input to `butfirst` is the quoted word `computer`.
- The output from `butfirst` is the word `omputer`, which becomes the input to `first`.
- The output from `first` is the word `o`, which becomes the second input to the second `word`.
- The output from the second `word` is the word `lo`, which becomes the first input to the first `word`.
- The second input to (the first) `word` is the output from (the second) `first`.
- The input to `first` is the sentence `[go to the store, please.]`.
- The output from `first` is the word `go`, which becomes the second input to the first `word`.
- The output from `word` is the word `logo`, which becomes the input to `print`.
- Finally, `print` prints the word `logo`.

And here is the plumbing diagram:

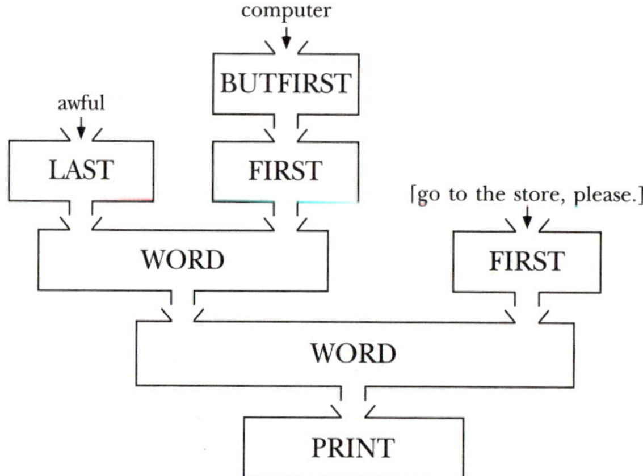

☞ If you made it through that, you should find it easy to predict what these instructions will do:

```
print butlast "tricky
print butlast [tricky]
print se bl "farm bl bl bl "output
print first butfirst "hello
print first butfirst [abc def ghi]
(print word bl "hard word bl bl first [very hard]
   last first [extremely hard])
```

Remember that numbers are words, so you can combine arithmetic operations with these word and list operations:

```
? print word sum 2 3 product 2 3
56
? print sum word 2 3 product 2 3
29
? print sentence sum 2 3 word 2 3
5 23
```

`Count` is an operation that takes one input. The input can be any datum. The output from `count` is a number, indicating the length of the input. If the input is a word, the output is the number of characters in the word. If the input is a list, the output is the number of members in the list.

```
? print count "hello
5
? print count [hello]
1
? print count "
0
? print count []
0
? print word count "hello count "goodbye
57
? print sum count "hello count "goodbye
12
```

Print and Show

Because lists are often used to represent English sentences in conversational programs like the hi procedure of Chapter 1, print prints only the members of a list, without enclosing brackets. This behavior could be confusing if a list contains only one member:

```
? print [aardvark]
aardvark
? print "aardvark
aardvark
```

There is no visible difference between a word and a one-word list. But the two values are actually quite different, as we can see if we use them as inputs to first:

```
? print first [aardvark]
aardvark
? print first "aardvark
a
```

The first of a sentence is its first word, even if it has only one word, but the first of a word is its first letter.

To help distinguish words from lists, Logo has another printing command called show that displays brackets around lists:

```
? show [aardvark]
[aardvark]
? show "aardvark
aardvark
? show sentence [this is] [an example]
[this is an example]
? show list [this is] [an example]
[[this is] [an example]]
```

Use `print` if your program wants to carry on a conversation with the user in English. Use `show` if you are using lists to represent some structure other than a sentence.

Order of Evaluation

You may hear people say something like this: "Logo evaluates from right to left." What they mean is that in an instruction such as

```
print first butfirst butfirst [print the third word]
```

Logo first evaluates

```
butfirst [print the third word]
```

and next evaluates

```
butfirst [the third word]
```

and then

```
first [third word]
```

and finally

```
print "third
```

In other words, the procedures named toward the right end of the instruction line must be invoked *before* Logo can know the appropriate input values for the procedures farther to the left.

This right-to-left idea can be a useful way of helping you understand evaluation in Logo. But you should realize that it's not quite true. It only works out that way if the instruction line contains only one instruction and each procedure used in that instruction takes only one input. If you look back at one of the examples in which two-input procedures such as `word` or `sum` are used, you'll see that Logo really does read the instruction line from left to right. And if there are two instructions on the same line, the one on the left is evaluated first.

The reason for the seeming right-to-left evaluation is that Logo can't *finish* evaluating a procedure invocation until it has collected and evaluated the inputs to the procedure. But Logo *starts* evaluating an instruction line by looking at the first word on the line. In the example just above, the evaluation of `first` and `butfirst` is *part of* the evaluation of `print`.

Special Forms of Evaluation

So far, the evaluation process has been very uniform. Logo looks at the first word of an instruction and interprets that word as the name of a procedure. Logo knows how many inputs each procedure requires. It then evaluates as many expressions as necessary to assign values to those inputs. The expressions are evaluated the same way: Logo looks at the first word... and so on.

Although this evaluation process is perfectly general, Logo also provides a couple of special forms of evaluation to make certain things easier to type. (The computer science terminology for such a special case is a "kludge." The letter "u" in this word is pronounced as in "rude," not as in "sludge.")

One special case is that Logo provides *infix arithmetic* as well as the *prefix arithmetic* we've used so far. That is, you can say

```
print 2+3
```

instead of

```
print sum 2 3
```

When you use infix operations, the usual rules of precedence apply: multiplications and divisions are done before additions and subtractions unless you use parentheses. In other words, `2+3*4` (the asterisk represents multiplication) means `2+(3*4)`, while `2*3+4` means `(2*3)+4`. You should take note that this issue of precedence doesn't arise when prefix operations are used.

☞ For example, look at these expressions:

```
sum 2 product 3 4
product sum 2 3 4
sum product 2 3 4
product 2 sum 3 4
```

Each of these indicates precisely what order of operations is desired. The first, for example, is equivalent to `2+3*4`. Try converting the others to infix form. Which ones require parentheses?

The second special form of evaluation is that certain primitive procedures can be given extra inputs, or fewer inputs than usual, by using parentheses around the procedure name and all its inputs. Here are some examples:

```
? print sum 2 3 4
5
You don't say what to do with 4
? print (sum 2 3 4)
9
? show (list "one)
[one]
? show (list)
[]
```

`Sum`, `product`, `word`, `list`, `sentence`, and `print` can be used with any number of inputs.

By the way, it is always permitted to enclose a procedure name and its inputs (the correct number of them!) in parentheses, even when it's not necessary, to make the instruction more readable. One of the earlier illustrations, for example, might be easier to read in this form:

```
print word (word (last "awful) (first butfirst "computer)) ~
   (first [go to the store, please.])
```

Notice that Logo's placement of parentheses is different from the function notation used in algebra. In algebra you say $f(x)$. In Logo you would express the same idea as `(f x)`.

Writing Your Own Procedures

With these tools, you are ready to begin writing new procedures. Type this:

```
to hello
```

To is a command, but it's a very special one. It's the only one that does not evaluate its inputs. Remember earlier when we said

```
print Hello
```

and Logo complained that it didn't know how to Hello? Well, to doesn't make that kind of complaint. Instead it prepares to have you *teach it how* to hello. (That's why to is called to!) What you should see on the screen is something like this:

```
? to hello
>
```

Instead of a question mark, Logo has printed a greater-than symbol as the prompt. This special prompt warns you that whatever instructions you type won't be carried out immediately, as usual. Instead Logo remembers what you type as part of the procedure named hello. Continue like this:

```
> print "Hello
> print [This is Logo speaking.]
> print [What's new?]
> end
?
```

The word end isn't the name of a procedure. It's a special signal to Logo that you're finished defining the procedure hello.*

Now you can try out your new procedure:

```
? hello
Hello
This is Logo speaking.
What's new?
```

---

* Why can't we simply think of end as the name of a procedure, just as print is? This is a minor point, but one that you can use to test your understanding of what's going on while you are defining a procedure. When you see the greater-than prompt, Logo *does not evaluate* the lines you type. It simply remembers those lines as part of the procedure you're defining. If end were a procedure, it wouldn't be evaluated right away, just as those print instructions aren't evaluated right away. It, too, would be remembered as part of the definition of hello. Instead, typing end has an *immediate* effect: It ends the procedure definition and returns to the question-mark prompt that allows interactive evaluation.

You can also examine the procedure itself by asking Logo to print it out. The command po (for Print Out) takes one input, a word or a list. The input is either the name of a procedure (if a word) or a list of names of procedures. The effect of po is to print out the definition(s) of the procedure(s) named by the input. Here is an example:

```
? po "hello
to hello
print "Hello
print [This is Logo speaking.]
print [What's new?]
end
?
```

Unlike to, but like all other Logo procedures, po *does* evaluate its input. That's why the word hello must be quoted in this example.

In a procedure definition the line starting to is called the *title line.* The lines containing instructions are, naturally, called *instruction lines.* We won't have many occasions to talk about the line containing only the word end, but just in case, we'll call it the *end line.*

The command pops (for Print Out ProcedureS) takes no inputs. Its effect is to print out the definitions of all the procedures you've defined. The command pots (for Print Out TitleS) also takes no inputs and prints out only the title lines of all the procedures you've defined.

Some writers and teachers reserve the word "procedure" to refer only to ones you write yourself, such as hello. They use the word "primitive" as a noun, to mean things like print and butfirst. They say things like "Logo instructions are made up of procedures and primitives." This is a big mistake. The procedures you write are *just like* the procedures Logo happens to know about in the first place. It's just that somebody else wrote the primitive procedures. But you use your own procedures in exactly the same way that you use primitive procedures: you type the name of the procedure and Logo evaluates that name by invoking the procedure. It's okay to say "Last is a primitive" as an abbreviation for "Last is a primitive procedure," as long as you know what you're talking about.

☞ Try defining more procedures. You'll find that you don't have quite enough tools yet to make your procedures very interesting; the main problem is that yours don't take inputs, so they do exactly the same thing every time you use them. We'll solve that problem in the next chapter.

Editing Your Procedures

As you may remember from earlier experiences, Logo includes an *editor,* a program that allows you to make corrections to a procedure you've defined. You can also use the editor to write procedure definitions in the first place. The editor works slightly differently in each version of Logo, so you should consult the manuals for your own computer (or Appendix A, for Berkeley Logo) to review the details.

By the way, when you're learning about the `edit` command, don't forget that it can accept a list of procedure names as input, not only a single word. By listing several procedures in the input to `edit`, you can have them all visible at once while you're editing, and you can copy instructions from one to another. This is a powerful capability of the Logo editor, which beginners often neglect.

Once you've gotten familiar with the Logo editor, you'll probably find yourself wanting to use it all the time, and you'll rarely choose to define a procedure by invoking `to` directly. (Don't get confused about that last sentence; of course you type `to` when you're using the editor, but you don't type it as a command to the Logo interpreter in response to a question mark prompt.) The editor makes it much easier to correct typing mistakes. Nevertheless, if you need to define a short procedure in the middle of doing something else, you may occasionally find it simpler to use `to` rather than wait for an editor to start up.

Syntax and Semantics

Except for the special case of `to`, all Logo instructions follow the same rules about the meaning of punctuation and about which subexpression provides an input to which procedure call. These are called *syntax* rules. The rules pay no attention to what any particular procedure means, or what inputs might or might not be sensible for that procedure; those aspects of a program are called its *semantics,* which is a fancy word for "meaning." You might say that Logo's plumber, the part of Logo that hooks up the plumbing diagrams, doesn't know anything about semantics. So, for example, if you make a mistake like

```
print item [john paul george ringo] 2
```

and get a Logo error message, you might feel that it's obvious what you meant—and it would be, to another person—and so Logo should have figured it out and done the right thing. But computers aren't as smart as people, and so you can rely only on Logo's syntax rules, not on the semantics of your program, to help Logo make sense of what you write.

To illustrate the difference between syntax and semantics, we'll start by examining the following Logo instruction:

```
? print word sum 2 4 "es
6es
```

Here's its plumbing diagram:

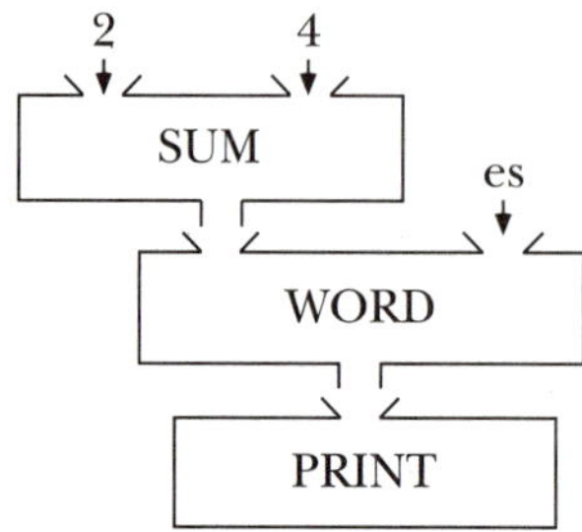

The connections in a plumbing diagram depend only on the numbers of inputs and outputs for each procedure used. Logo "connects the plumbing" *before* invoking any of the procedures named in the instruction. The plumbing is connected regardless of whether the specified inputs actually make sense to the procedures in question. For example, suppose we make a slight change to the instruction given just now:

```
print sum word 2 4 "es
```

The only change is that `word` and `sum` have been interchanged. Since these are both two-input operations, the shape of the plumbing diagram is unchanged.

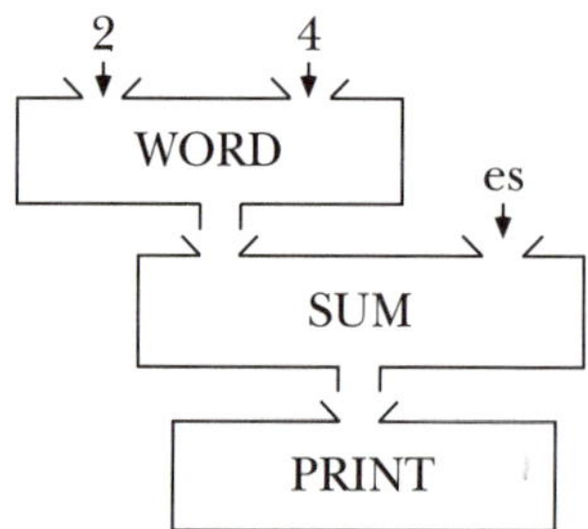

The plumbing connections are syntactically fine, so Logo can work out which expression provides the input to which procedure call. However, when Logo gets around to invoking the procedure `sum` with inputs `24` and `es`, an error message will result because the second input isn't a number. This is a *semantic* error.

By contrast, the following instruction shows a *syntactic* error, in which Logo is unable to figure out a plumbing diagram in which all the pieces connect up.

```
print word sum 2 "es
```

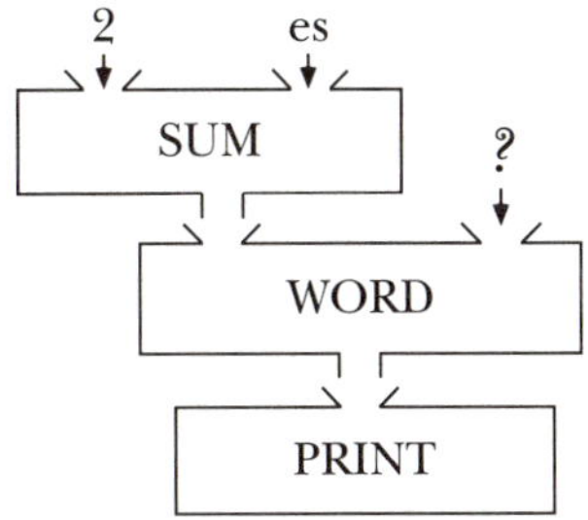

The question mark in the diagram indicates a missing input. In this example, the programmer intended the word `es` to be the second input to `word`; from the programmer's point of view, it is a number, the desired second input to `sum`, that's "really" missing. But Logo doesn't know about the programmer's intentions, and Logo's plumber follows uniform rules in deciding which input goes with which procedure call.

The rule is that Logo starts by looking for an input to `print`. The first thing it finds is `word`, so the output from `word` is hooked up to the input for `print`. Now Logo is looking for two inputs to `word`. The next thing it finds is `sum`, so the output from `sum` is hooked up to the first input for `word`. Now Logo is looking for two inputs to `sum`, and the syntax rules say that Logo must find those two inputs before it can continue with the still-pending task of finding a second input for `word`. Logo's plumber isn't smart enough to say, "Hey, here's a non-number as input to `sum`, and I happen to remember that we still need another input for `word`, so that must be what the programmer meant."

There are really only two kinds of plumbing errors. In the one shown here, too few expressions are included in the instruction, so that the message `not enough inputs` results. The other error is that too many expressions appear inside the instruction. This may result in the message `you don't say what to do with` something, or, if the extra expressions are within parentheses, by `too much inside ()'s`.

Parentheses and Plumbing Diagrams

Parentheses can be used in a Logo instruction for three reasons: for readability, to show the precedence of infix operators, or to include a nonstandard number of inputs for certain primitives. In all three cases, the syntax rule is that everything inside the parentheses must form one single complete expression. In plumbing diagram terms, this means that the stuff inside the parentheses must correspond to a subdiagram with no inputs and with exactly one output (unless an entire instruction is parenthesized, in which case the diagram will have no outputs):

```
print (word "a "b "c)
```

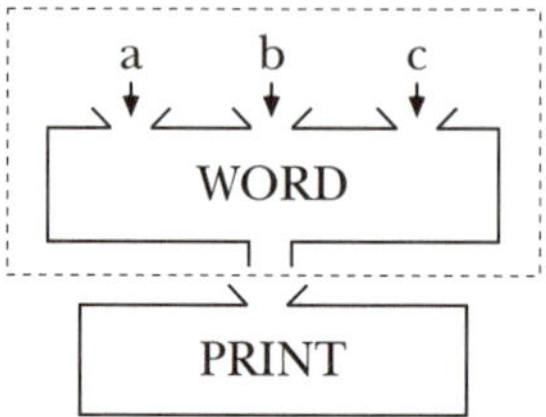

The dotted rectangle indicates the subdiagram corresponding to the expression inside the parentheses. That rectangle has no inputs; there are three inputs *within* the rectangle, but in each case the source of the input and the recipient of the input are both inside. There is no recipient inside the rectangle that needs a source from outside. The rectangle has one output; the entire expression within the rectangle provides the input to `print`.

The mathematical function notation $f(x)$ used in algebra often tempts beginning Logo programmers to write the above example as

```
print word ("a "b "c)           ; (wrong)
```

but by thinking about the plumbing diagram we can see that that would not put one single expression inside the parentheses:

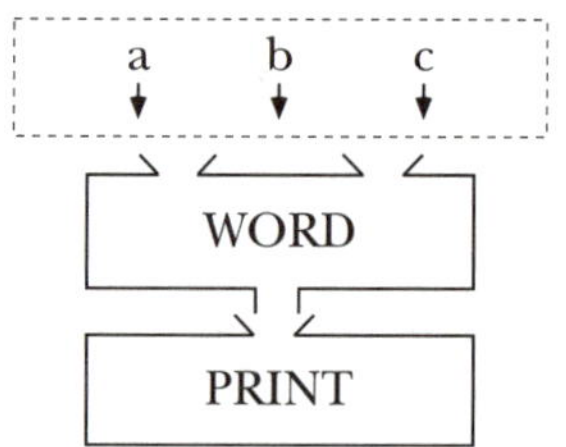

The part of the instruction inside the parentheses is trying to provide three outputs, not just one. This violates the rules. Also, since the word `word` isn't inside the parentheses, that procedure follows its ordinary rules and expects only two inputs.

Nonsense Plumbing Diagrams

To emphasize the point that the plumbing diagram depends only on the number of inputs expected by each procedure, and not on the purpose or meaning of the procedure, we can draw plumbing diagrams for nonsense instructions using unknown procedures. The rule of this game is that each procedure name includes a number indicating how many inputs it accepts. For example, `garply2` is a procedure that requires two inputs. If a procedure can accept extra inputs when used with parentheses, we put an `x` after the number; `baz3x` ordinarily takes three inputs, but can be given any number of inputs by using parentheses around the subexpression that invokes it.

```
john2 "paul george2 ringo0 "stu
```

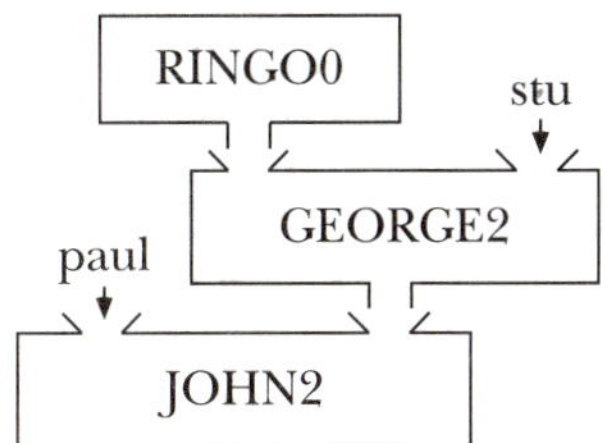

We don't have to know what any of these procedures do. The only information we need is that some words in the instruction are quoted, while others are names of procedures that take a known number of inputs. This is a syntactically correct instruction because each procedure has been given exactly as many inputs as it requires.

☞ Try these:

```
baz3x 1 2 foo3x foo3x 4 5 6 (foo3x 7) 8
baz3x 1 [2 foo3x foo3x 4 5 6 (foo3x 7)] 8
if2 test3 [a b] [c d] [e f] [g h]
if2 try0 [foo3x 8 9]
```

3 Variables

In the last chapter I suggested that you would find yourself limited in writing new procedures because your procedures don't take inputs, so they do exactly the same thing every time you use them. In this chapter we'll overcome that limitation.

User Procedures with Inputs

As a first example I'm going to write a very simple command named `greet`, which will take a person's name as its one input. Here's how it will work:

```
? greet "Brian
Hello, Brian
Pleased to meet you.
? greet "Emma
Hello, Emma
Pleased to meet you.
```

This procedure will be similar to the `hello` command in the last chapter, except that what it prints will depend on the input we give it.

Each time we *invoke* `greet`, we want to give it an input. So that Logo will expect an input, we must provide for one when we *define* `greet`. (Each procedure has a definite number of inputs; if `greet` takes one input once, it must take one input every time it's invoked.) Also, in order for the instructions inside `greet` to be able to use the input, we must give the input a *name.* Both of these needs are met in the `to` command that supplies the title line for the procedure:

```
? to greet :person
```

You are already familiar with the use of the `to` command, the need for a word like `greet` to name the procedure, and the appearance of the greater-than prompt instead of the question mark. What's new here is the use of `:person` after the procedure name. This addition tells Logo that the procedure `greet` will require one input and that the name of the input will be `person`. It may help to think of the input as a container; when the procedure `greet` is invoked, something (such as the word `Brian` or the word `Emma`) will be put into the container named `person`.

Why is the colon used in front of the name `person`? Remember that the inputs to `to`, unlike the inputs to all other Logo procedures, are *not* evaluated before `to` is invoked. Later we'll see that a colon has a special meaning to the Logo evaluator, but that special meaning is *not* in effect in a title line. Instead, the colon is simply a sort of mnemonic decoration to make a clear distinction between the word `greet`, which is a *procedure* name, and the word `person`, which is an *input* name. Some versions of Logo don't even require the colon; you can experiment with yours if you're curious. (By the way, if you want to sound like a Logo maven, you should pronounce the colon "dots," as in "to greet dots person.")

To see why having a name for the input is helpful, look at the rest of the procedure definition:

```
> print sentence "Hello, thing "person
> print [Pleased to meet you.]
> end
?
```

You already know about `print` and `sentence` and about quoting words with the quotation mark and quoting lists with square brackets. What's new here is the procedure `thing`.

`Thing` is an operation. It takes one input, which must be a word that's the name of a container. The output from `thing` is whatever datum is in the container.

The technical name for what I've been calling a "container" is a *variable*. Every variable has a *name* and a *thing* (or *value*). The name and the thing are both *parts of* the variable. We'll sometimes speak loosely of "the variable `person`," but you should realize that this *is* speaking loosely; what we should say is "the variable named `person`." `Person` itself is a *word*, which is different from a variable.

When I type the instruction

```
greet "Brian
```

the Logo interpreter starts with the first word on the line, `greet`. As usual, Logo takes this to be the name of a procedure. Logo discovers that `greet` requires one input, so it continues to the next thing on the line. This is a quoted word, `"Brian`. Since it's quoted, it requires no further interpretation. The word `Brian` itself becomes the input to `greet`.*

Logo is now ready to invoke `greet`. The first step, before evaluating the instruction lines in `greet`, is to create a variable to hold the input. This variable is given the word `person` as its *name,* and the word `Brian` as its *thing.* (Please notice that I don't have to know the name of `greet`'s input in order to use it. All I have to know is what *type of thing*—a person's name—`greet` expects as its input. What are the names of the inputs to a primitive like `sentence`? We don't know and we don't need to know.)

Logo now evaluates the first instruction in `greet`. The process is just like the ones we went through in such detail in Chapter 2. In the course of this evaluation Logo invokes the procedure `thing` with the word `person` as its input. The output from `thing` is the thing in the variable named `person`, namely the word `Brian`. That's how the word `Brian` becomes one of the inputs to `se`. Here's a plumbing diagram.

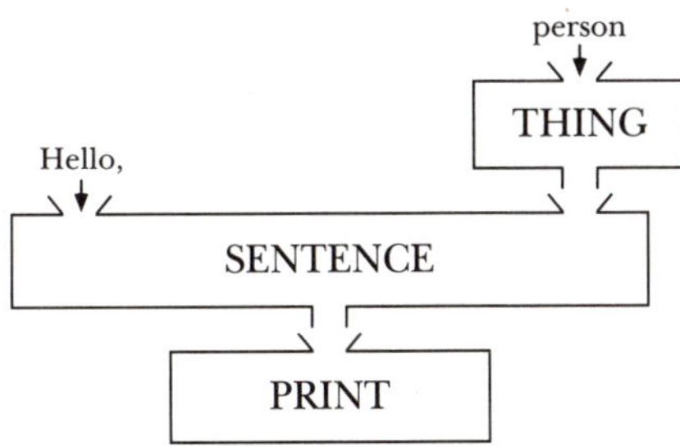

* While reading the definition of `greet`, it's easy to say "the input is `person`"; then, while reading an invocation of `greet`, it's easy to say "the input is `Brian`." To avoid confusion between the input's name and its value, there are more precise technical terms that we can use when necessary. The name of the input, given in the title line of the procedure definition, is called a *formal parameter.* The value of the input, given when the procedure is invoked, is called an *actual argument.* In case the actual argument is the result of a more complicated subexpression, as in the instruction

```
greet first [Brian Harvey]
```

we might want to distinguish between the *actual argument expression,* `first [Brian Harvey]`, and the *actual argument value,* which is the word `Brian`.

What Kind of Container?

One of the favorite activities that Logo experts use to while away the time when the computer is down is to argue about the best metaphor to use for variables. A variable is a container, but what kind of container?

One popular metaphor is a mailbox. The mailbox has a *name* painted on it, like "The Smiths." Inside the mailbox is a piece of mail. The person from the Post Office assigns a *value* to the box by putting a letter in it. Reading a letter is like invoking `thing` on the mailbox.

I don't like this metaphor very much, and if I explain why not, it may help illuminate for you some details about how variables work. The first problem is that a real mailbox can contain several letters. A variable can only contain *one* thing or value. (I should say "one thing at a time," since we'll see that it's possible to replace the thing in a variable with a different thing.)

Another problem with the mailbox metaphor is that to read a letter, you take it out of the mailbox and tear it open. Then it isn't in the mailbox any more. When you invoke `thing` to look at the thing in a variable, on the other hand, it's still in the variable. You could use `thing` again and get the same answer.

There are two metaphors that I like. The one I like best won't make sense for a while, until we talk about scope of variables. But here is the one I like second best: Sometimes when you take a bus or a taxi, there is a little frame up in front that looks like this:

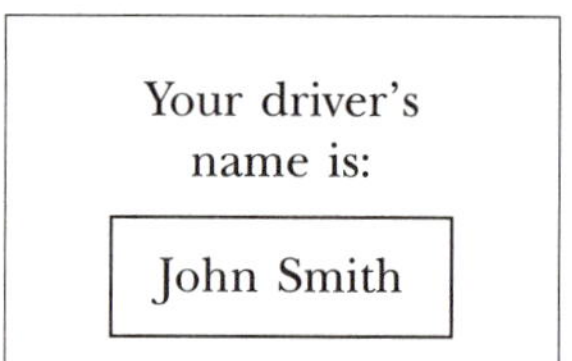

The phrase "your driver's name is" is like a label for this frame, and it corresponds to the *name* of a variable. Each bus driver has a metal or plastic plate that says "John Smith" or whoever it is. The driver inserts this plate, which corresponds to the *value* of the variable, into the frame. You can see why this is a closer metaphor than the mailbox. There is only one plate in the frame at a time. To find out who's driving the bus, you just have to look inside the frame; you don't have to remove the plate.

(To be strictly fair I should tell you that some Logoites don't like the whole idea of containers. They have a completely different metaphor, which involves sticking labels on things. But I think it would only confuse you if I explained that one right now.)

An Abbreviation

Examining the value of a variable is such a common thing to do in a Logo procedure that there is a special abbreviation for it. Instead of the expression

```
thing "person
```

you can simply say

```
:person
```

So in the `greet` procedure, we could have said

```
print sentence "hello :person
```

Please note that the colon is *not* just an abbreviation for the word `thing` but rather for the combination `thing`-quote.

When drawing plumbing diagrams, treat `:narf` as if it were spelled out as `thing "narf`.

More Procedures

It's time to invent more procedures. I'll give you a couple of examples and you should make up more on your own.

```
to primer :name
print (sentence first :name [is for] word :name ".)
print (sentence "Run, word :name ", "run.)
print (sentence "See :name "run.)
end
```

```
? primer "Paul
P is for Paul.
Run, Paul, run.
See Paul run.
```

`Primer` uses the extra-input kludge I mentioned near the end of Chapter 2. It also shows how the operations `word` and `sentence` can be used in combination to punctuate a sentence properly.

With all of these examples, incidentally, you should take the time to work through each instruction line to make sure you understand what is the input to what.

```
to soap.opera :him :her :it
print (sentence :him "loves word :her ".)
print (sentence "However, :her [doesn't care for] :him "particularly.)
print (sentence :her [is madly in love with] word :it ".)
print (sentence :him [doesn't like] :it [very much.])
end
```

```
? soap.opera "Bill "Sally "Fred
Bill loves Sally.
However, Sally doesn't care for Bill particularly.
Sally is madly in love with Fred.
Bill doesn't like Fred very much.
```

In this example you see that a procedure can have more than one input. `Soap.opera` has three inputs. You can also see why each input must have a name, so that the instructions inside the procedure have a way to refer to the particular input you want to use. You should also notice that `soap.opera` has a period in the middle of its name, not a space, because the name of a procedure must be a single Logo word.

For the next example I'll show how you can write an *interactive* procedure, which reads something you type on the keyboard. For this we need a new tool. `Readlist` is an operation with no inputs. Its output is always a list, containing whatever you type on a single line (up to a RETURN). `Readlist` waits for you to type a line, then outputs what you type.

```
to converse
print [Please type your full name.]
halves readlist
end

to halves :name
print sentence [Your first name is] first :name
print sentence [Your last name is] last :name
end
```

```
? converse
please type your full name.
Brian Harvey
Your first name is Brian
Your last name is Harvey
```

This program includes two procedures, `converse` and `halves`. (A *program* is a bunch of procedures that work together to achieve a common goal.) `Converse` is the *top-level procedure*. In other words, `converse` is the procedure that you invoke at the question-mark prompt to set the program in motion. `Halves` is a *subprocedure* of `converse`, which means that `halves` is invoked by an instruction inside `converse`. Similarly, `converse` is a *superprocedure* of `halves`.

There are two things you should notice about the terminology "subprocedure" and "superprocedure." The first thing is that these are *relative* terms. It doesn't mean anything to say "`Halves` is a subprocedure." Any procedure can be used as part of a larger program. `Converse`, for example, is a superprocedure of `halves`, but `converse` might at the same time be a subprocedure of some higher-level procedure we haven't written yet. The second point is that primitive procedures can also be considered as subprocedures. For example, `sentence` is a subprocedure of `halves`.

(Now that we're dealing with programs containing more than one defined procedure, it's a good time for me to remind you that the commands that act on procedures can accept a list as input as well as a single word. For example, you can say

```
po [converse halves]
```

and Logo will print out the definitions of both procedures.)

Why are two procedures necessary for this program? When the program reads your full name, it has to remember the name so that it can print two parts of it separately. It wouldn't work to say

```
to incorrect.converse
print [Please type your full name.]
print sentence [Your first name is] first readlist
print sentence [Your last name is] last readlist
end
```

because each invocation of `readlist` would read a separate line from the keyboard instead of using the same list for both first and last names. We solve this problem by using the output from `readlist` as the input to a subprocedure of `converse` and letting the subprocedure do the rest of the work.

One of the examples in Chapter 1 was this procedure:

```
to hi
print [Hi. What's your name?]
print sentence [How are you,] word first readlist "?
ignore readlist
print [That's nice.]
end
```

`Hi` uses a procedure called `ignore` that we haven't yet discussed. `Ignore` is predefined in Berkeley Logo but would be easy enough to define yourself:

```
to ignore :something
end
```

That's not a misprint; `ignore` really has no instructions in its definition. `Ignore` is a command that takes one input and has no effect at all! Its purpose is to ignore the input. In `hi`, the instruction

```
ignore readlist
```

waits for you to type a line on the keyboard, then just ignores whatever you type. (We couldn't just use `readlist` as an instruction all by itself because a complete instruction has to begin with a command, not an operation. That is, since `readlist` outputs a value, there must be a command to tell Logo what to do with that value. In this case, we want to `ignore` it.)

☞ Write a procedure to conjugate the present tense of a regular first-conjugation (-er) French verb. (Never mind if you don't know what any of that means! You're about to see.) That is, the letters `er` at the end of the verb should be replaced by a different ending for each pronoun:

```
? conj "jouer
je joue
tu joues
il joue
nous jouons
vous jouez
elles jouent
```

The verb `jouer` (to play) consists of the root `jou` combined with the infinitive ending `er`. Print six lines, as shown, in which the ending is changed to `e`, `es`, etc. Try your procedure on `monter` (to climb), `frapper` (to hit), and `garder` (to keep).

By the way, in a practical program we would have to deal with the fact that French contains many irregular verbs. In addition to wildly irregular ones like être (to be, irregular even in English) there are ones like manger, to eat, which are almost regular except that the first and second person plural forms keep the letter e: nous mangeons. Many issues in natural language programming (that is, getting computers to speak or understand human language) turn out like this—90% of the cases are trivial, but most of your effort goes into the other 10%.

An Aside on Variable Naming

In my metaphor about the frame containing the bus driver's name, the inscription on the frame tells you what to expect inside the frame. Variable names like `person` and `name` serve a similar purpose. (You might argue that the `it` in the group of names `him`, `her`, and `it` is a little misleading. But it serves to keep the story straight, probably better than an alternative like `him1` and `him2`.)

Another kind of frame is the one you sometimes see around a car's license plate:

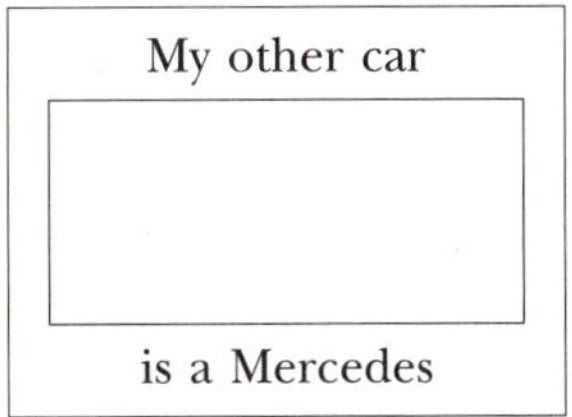

I know it's pedantic to pick apart a joke, but just the same I want to make the point that this one works only because the car itself provides enough clues that what belongs in the frame is indeed a license plate. If you were unfamiliar with the idea of license plates, that frame wouldn't help you.

The computer equivalent of this sort of joke is to give your variables names that don't reflect their purpose in the procedure. Some people like to name variables after their boyfriends or girlfriends or relatives. That's okay if you're writing simple programs, like the ones in this chapter, in which it's very easy to read the program and figure out what it does. But when you start writing more complicated programs, you'll need all the help you can get in remembering what each piece of the program does. I recommend starting early on the habit of using sensible variable names.

Don't Call It `x`

Another source of trouble in variable naming is lazy fingers. When I'm teaching programming classes, a big part of my job is reading program listings that students bring to me, saying, "I just can't find the bug in this program." I have an absolute rule that I refuse to read any program in which there is a variable named `x`.

My students always complain about this arbitrary rule at first. But more often than not, a student goes through a program renaming all the variables and then finds that the bug has disappeared! This magical result comes about because when you use variable names like `x`, you run the risk of using the same name for two different purposes at the same time. When you pick reasonable names, you'll pick two different names for the two purposes.

It is people who've programmed in BASIC who are most likely to make this mistake. For reasons that aren't very important any more, BASIC used to *require* single-letter variable names. Even now there are limits on longer names in most versions of BASIC that make it risky to use more than two or three letters in a name. So if you're a BASIC programmer, you've probably gotten into bad habits, which you should make a point of correcting.

Writing New Operations

So far all the procedures we've written have been commands. That is, our procedures have had an *effect* (like printing something) rather than an *output* to be used with other procedures. You can also write operations, once you know how to give your procedure an output. Here is an example:

```
to second :thing
output first butfirst :thing
end
```

```
? print second [the red computer]
red
```

`Second` is an operation with one input. Like the primitive operation `first`, it extracts a component of its input, either a character from a word or a member from a list. However, it outputs the second component instead of the first one.

What is new in this procedure definition is the use of the primitive command `output`. `Output` can be used only inside a procedure definition, not at top level. (In other words, not when you are typing in response to a question-mark prompt.) It takes one input, which can be any datum. The effect of `output` is to make the datum you supply as its input be the output from your procedure.

Some people find it confusing that `output` itself is a *command,* even though a procedure that uses `output` is an *operation.* But it makes sense for `output` to be the head of a complete instruction. The effect of the instruction is to inform Logo what output you want your procedure (the procedure named `second` in this case) to supply.

Another possible confusion is between `output` and `print`. The problem is that people talk about "computer output" while waving a stack of paper at you, so you think of "output" as meaning "stuff the computer printed." But in Logo, "output" is something one procedure hands to another procedure, not something that is printed.

I chose the name `thing` for the input to `second` to remind myself that the input can be anything, word or list. `Thing` is also, as you know, the name of a primitive procedure. This is perfectly okay. The same word can name both a procedure and a variable. Logo can tell which you mean by the context. A word that is used in an instruction without punctuation is a procedure name. A word that is used as an input to the procedure `thing` is a variable name. (This can happen because you put dots in front of the word as an abbreviation or because you explicitly typed `thing` and used the word as its input.) The expression `:thing` is an abbreviation for

```
thing "thing
```

in which the first `thing` names a procedure, and the second `thing` names a variable.

☞ Write an operation `query` that takes a sentence as input and that outputs a question formed by swapping the first two words and adding a question mark to the last word:

```
? print query [I should have known better]
should I have known better?
? print query [you are experienced]
are you experienced?
```

Scope of Variables

This is going to be a somewhat complicated section, and an important one, so slow down and read it carefully.

When one procedure with inputs invokes another procedure with inputs as a subprocedure, it's possible for them to share variables and it's also possible for them to have separate variables. The following example isn't meant to do anything particularly interesting, just to make explicit what the rules are.

```
to top :outer :inner
print [I'm in top.]
print sentence [:outer is] :outer
print sentence [:inner is] :inner
bottom "x
print [I'm in top again.]
print sentence [:outer is] :outer
print sentence [:inner is] :inner
end

to bottom :inner
print [I'm in bottom.]
print sentence [:outer is] :outer
print sentence [:inner is] :inner
end

? top "a "b
I'm in top.
:outer is a
:inner is b
I'm in bottom.
:outer is a
:inner is x
I'm in top again.
:outer is a
:inner is b
```

First, concentrate on the variable named `outer`. This name is used for the first input to `top`. `Bottom` doesn't have an input named `outer`. When `bottom` refers to `:outer`, since it doesn't have one of its own, the reference is to the variable `outer` that belongs to its superprocedure, `top`. That's why `a` is printed as the value of `outer` in both procedures.

If a procedure refers to a variable that does not belong to that procedure, Logo looks for a variable of that name in the superprocedure of that procedure.

Suppose procedure `a` invokes procedure `b`, and `b` invokes `c`. Suppose an instruction in procedure `c` refers to a variable `v`. First Logo tries to find a variable named `v` that belongs to `c`. If that fails, Logo looks for a variable named `v` that belongs to procedure

b. Finally, if neither c nor b has a variable named v, Logo looks for such a variable that belongs to procedure a.

Now look at inner. The important thing to understand is that *there are two variables named* inner, one belonging to each procedure. When top is invoked, its input named inner gets the word b as its value. When top invokes bottom, bottom's input (which is also named inner) gets the value x. But when bottom finishes, and top continues, the name inner once again refers to the variable named inner that belongs to top. The one that belongs to bottom has disappeared.

> **Variables that belong to a procedure are temporary. They exist only so long as that procedure is active. If one procedure has a variable with the same name as one belonging to its superprocedure, the latter is temporarily "hidden" while the subprocedure is running.**

Because each procedure has its own variable named inner, we refer to the procedure input variables as *local* to a particular procedure. Inputs are always local in Logo. There is also a name for the fact that a procedure can refer to variables belonging to its superprocedures. If you want to show off, you can explain to people that Logo has *dynamic scope,* which is what that rule is called.

The Little Person Metaphor

Earlier I told you my second favorite metaphor about variables. My very favorite is an old one, which Logo teachers have been using for years. It is a metaphor about procedures as well as variables, which is why I didn't present it earlier. Now that you're thinking about the issue of variable scope, you can see that to have a full understanding of variables, you have to be thinking about procedures at the same time.

The metaphor is that inside the computer there is a large community of little people. Each person is a specialist at a particular procedure. So there are print people and butfirst people and bottom people and greet people. I like to think of these people as elves, because I started teaching Logo on a computer called a PDP-11, and I like the pun of an elf inside an 11. But if you find elves too cute or childish, perhaps you should think of these people as doctors in white coats, specializing in dermatology or ophthalmology or whatever. Another terminology for the same idea, one which is becoming more and more widely used in advanced computer science circles, is to call the little people *actors* and to call their procedures *scripts.* Each actor has only one script, but several actors can have the same script.

In any case, what's important is that when a procedure is invoked, a little person who is an expert on that procedure goes to work. (It's important that the person is *an expert in* the procedure, and not the procedure *itself;* we'll see later that there can be two little people carrying out the same procedure at the same time. This is one of the more complicated ideas in Logo, so I think the expert metaphor will help you later.)

You may be wondering where the variables come in. Well, each elf is wearing a jerkin, a kind of vest, with a bunch of pockets. (If your people are doctors, the pockets are in those white lab coats.) A person has as many pockets as the procedure he or she knows has inputs. A `print` expert has one pocket; a `sentence` expert has two. Each pocket can contain a datum, the value of the variable. (The pockets are only big enough for a single datum.) Each pocket also has a name tag sewn on the inside, which contains the name of the variable.

The name tags are on the inside to make the point that other people don't need to know the names of an expert's variables. Other experts only need to know how many pockets someone has and what kind of thing to put in them.

When I typed

```
top "a "b
```

the Chief Elf (whose name is Evaluator) found an elf named Theresa, who is a `top` expert, and put an `a` in her first pocket and a `b` in her second pocket.

Theresa's first instruction is

```
print [I'm in top.]
```

To carry out that instruction, she handed the list `[I'm in top.]` to another elf named Peter, a `print` expert.

Theresa's second instruction is

```
print sentence [:outer is] :outer
```

To carry out this instruction, Theresa wanted to hire Peter again, but before she could give him his orders, she first had to deal with Sally, a `sentence` expert. (This is the old evaluation story from Chapter 2 again.) But Theresa didn't know what to put in Sally's second pocket until she got the information from Tom, a `thing` expert. (Remember that `:outer` is an abbreviation for `thing "outer`.)

What's important right now is how Tom does his job. Tom is a sort of pickpocket. He doesn't steal anything; he just sneaks looks in other people's pockets. There are lots of people inside the computer, but the only ones with things in their pockets are the ones who are actually employed at a given moment. Aside from Tom himself, the only person who was employed at the time was Theresa, so Tom could only look in her pockets for a name tag saying `outer`. (Theresa is *planning* to hire Sally and then Peter, to finish carrying out her instruction, but she can't hire them until she gets the information she needs from Tom.)

Later Theresa will hire Bonnie, a `bottom` specialist, to help with the instruction

```
bottom "x
```

Theresa will give Bonnie the word `x` to put in her pocket. Bonnie also has an instruction

```
print sentence [:outer is] :outer
```

As part of the process of carrying out this instruction, Bonnie will hire Tom to look for something named `outer`. In that case Tom first looks in the pockets of Bonnie, the person who hired him. Not finding a pocket named `outer`, Tom can *then* check the pockets of Theresa, the person who hired Bonnie. (If you're studying Logo in a class with other people, it can be both fun and instructive to act this out with actual people and pockets.)

Theresa Bonnie Tom

An appropriate aspect of this metaphor is that it's slightly rude to look in someone else's pockets, and you shouldn't do it unnecessarily. This corresponds to a widely accepted rule of Logo style: most of the time, you should write procedures so that they don't have to look at variables belonging to their superprocedures. Whatever information a procedure needs should be given to it explicitly, as an input. You'll find situations in which that rule seems very helpful, and other situations in which taking advantage of dynamic scope seems to make the program easier to understand.

☞ The `conj` procedure you wrote earlier deals only with the present tense of the verb. In French, many other tenses can be formed by a similar process of replacing the endings, but with different endings for different tenses. Also, second conjugation (-ir) and third conjugation (-re) verbs have different endings even in the present tense. You don't want to write dozens of almost-identical procedures for each of these cases. Instead, write a single procedure `superconj` that takes two inputs, a verb and a list of six endings, and performs the conjugation:

```
? superconj "jouer [ais ais ait ions iez aient]      ; imperfect tense
je jouais
tu jouais
il jouait
nous jouions
vous jouiez
elles jouaient
? superconj "finir [is is it issons issez issent]    ; 2nd conj present
je finis
tu finis
il finit
nous finissons
vous finissez
elles finissent
```

You can save some typing and take advantage of dynamic scope if you use a helper procedure. My `superconj` looks like this:

```
to superconj :verb :endings
sc1 "je 1
sc1 "tu 2
sc1 "il 3
sc1 "nous 4
sc1 "vous 5
sc1 "elles 6
end
```

Write the helper procedure `sc1` to finish this.

Changing the Value of a Variable

It is possible for a procedure to change the thing in a variable by using the make command. Make takes two inputs. The first input must be a word that is the name of a variable, just like the input to thing. Make's second input can be any datum. The effect of make is to make the variable named by its first input contain as its value the datum that is its second input, instead of whatever used to be its value. For example,

```
make "inner "y
```

would make the variable named inner have the word y as its value. (If there are two variables named inner, as is the case while bottom is running, it is the one in the lower-level procedure that is changed. This is the same as the rule for thing that we have already discussed.)

Suppose a procedure has variables named old and new and you want to copy the thing in old into new. You could say

```
make "new thing "old
```

or use the abbreviation

```
make "new :old
```

People who don't understand evaluation sometimes get very upset about the fact that a quotation mark is used to refer to new and a colon is used to refer to old. They think this is just mumbo-jumbo because they don't understand that a quotation mark is part of what the colon abbreviates! In both cases we are referring to the name of a variable. A variable name is a Logo word. To refer to a word in an instruction and have it evaluate to itself, not invoke a procedure named new or old, the word must be quoted. The difference is that the first input to make is the *name* of the variable we want to change (new), while the second input to make is, in this example, the *value* of a variable (old), which we get by invoking thing. Since you understand all this, you won't get upset. You also won't resort to magic formulas like "always use quote for the first variable and dots for the second" because you understand that the inputs to make can be computed with any expression you want! For example, we could copy old's value into new this way:

```
make first [new old] thing last [new old]
```

This instruction contains neither a quotation mark nor a colon, but the inputs to `make` are exactly the same as they were in the earlier version.

Earlier I mentioned that it is considered slightly rude for a procedure to read its superprocedures' variables. It is *extremely* rude for a procedure to change the values of other procedures' variables! Perhaps you can see why that's so. If you're trying to read the definition of a procedure, and part way through that procedure it invokes a subprocedure, there is no clue to the fact that the subprocedure changes a variable. If you break this rule, it makes your program very hard to read because you have to read all the procedures at once. If each procedure deals only with its own variables, you have written a *modular* program, in which each piece can be understood separately.

Global and Local Variables

What if the first input to `make` isn't the name of an input to an active procedure? In other words, what if you try to assign a value to a variable that doesn't exist? What happens is that a new variable is created that is *not* local to any procedure. The name for this kind of variable is a *global* variable. `Thing` looks at global variables if it can't find a local variable with the name you want.

A local variable disappears when the procedure it belongs to finishes. Global variables don't belong to any procedure, so they stay around forever. This can be convenient, when you have a permanent body of information that several procedures must use. But it can also lead to problems if you are careless about what's in which variable. Local variables come and go with the procedures they belong to, so it's easy to avoid clutter when you use them. Global variables are more like old socks under the bed.

If you are a BASIC programmer, you've become accustomed to a language in which all variables are global. I've learned over the years that it's impossible, at this point in your career, for you to appreciate the profound effect that's had on your style of programming. Only after you've used procedural languages like Logo for quite a while will you understand. Meanwhile there is only one hope for you: you are not allowed to use global variables *at all* for the next few months. Please take my word for it.

Sometimes it's convenient for a procedure to use a variable that is not an input, but which could just as well be local. To do this, you can use the `local` command. This command takes one input, a word. It creates a variable, local to the procedure that invoked `local`, with that word as its name. For example, we can use `local` to rewrite the earlier `converse` example without needing the `halves` subprocedure:

```
to new.converse
local "name
print [Please type your full name.]
make "name readlist
print sentence [Your first name is] first :name
print sentence [Your last name is] last :name
end
```

The instruction that invokes `local` can be anywhere in the procedure before the variable is given a value with `make`. It's traditional, though, to put `local` instructions at the beginning of a procedure.

The same procedure would work even without the `local`, but then it would create a global variable named `name`. It's much neater if you can avoid leaving unnecessary global variables around, so you should use `local` unless there is a reason why you really need a global variable.

Indirect Assignment

Earlier I showed you the example

```
make first [new old] thing last [new old]
```

in which the first input to `make` was the result of evaluating a complex expression rather than an explicit quoted word in the instruction. But the example was kind of silly, used only to make the point that such a thing is possible.

Here are a couple of examples in which the use of a computed first input to `make` really makes sense. These are tricky examples; it may take a couple of readings before you see what I'm doing here. The technique I'm using is an advanced part of Logo programming. First is the procedure `increment`:

```
to increment :variable
make :variable (thing :variable)+1
end
```

To *increment* a variable means to add something to it, usually (as in this procedure) to add one to it. The input to `increment` is the name of a variable. The procedure adds 1 to that variable:

```
? make "count 12
? print :count
12
? increment "count
? print :count
13
```

You may wonder what the point is. Why couldn't I just say

```
make "count :count+1
```

instead of the obscure `make` instruction I used? The answer is that if we have several variables in the program, each of which sometimes gets incremented, this technique allows a single procedure to be able to increment any variable. It's a kind of shorthand for something we might want to do repeatedly.

In the definition of `increment`, the first input to `make` is not `"variable` but rather `:variable`. Therefore, the word `variable` itself is not the name of the variable that is incremented. (To say that more simply, the variable named `variable` isn't incremented.) Instead the variable named `variable` contains as its value the name of *another* variable. (In the example the value of `variable` is the word `count`.) It is that second variable whose value is changed. (In the example `:count` was 12 and becomes 13.)

While reading `increment`, remember that in the second input to `make`,

```
thing :variable
```

is really an abbreviation for

```
thing thing "variable
```

In other words this expression asks for the value of the variable whose name is itself the value of `variable`.

As a second example suppose you're writing a program to play a game of Tic-Tac-Toe. The computer will play one side and a person can play the other side. The person gets to choose X or O (that is, going first or second). The choice might be made with procedures like these:

```
to computer.first
make "computer "X
make "person "O
end

to person.first
make "person "X
make "computer "O
end
```

Elsewhere in the program there will be a procedure that asks the person where he or she wants to move. Suppose the squares on the board are numbered 1 through 9, and suppose we have two variables, `Xsquares` and `Osquares`, which contain lists of numbers corresponding to the squares marked X and O. Look at this procedure:

```
to person.move :square
make word :person "squares sentence :square thing word :person "squares
end
```

The input to `person.move` is the number of the square into which the person has asked to move. The first input to `make` is the expression

```
word :person "squares
```

If the person has chosen to move first, then `:person` is the word `X`, and the value of this expression is the word `Xsquares`. If the person has chosen to move last, then `:person` is the word `O`, and the value of the expression is the word `Osquares`. Either way, the expression evaluates to the name of the appropriate variable, into which the newly chosen square is appended.

These are examples of *indirect assignment,* which means assigning a value to a variable whose name is computed by the program. This is an unusual, advanced technique. Most of the time you'll use an explicit quoted word as the first input to `make`. But the technique is a powerful one; many programming languages don't have this capability at all. In Logo it isn't something that had to be invented specially; it is a free consequence of the fact that the inputs to any procedure (including `make`) are evaluated before the procedure is invoked.

Functional Programming

But don't get carried away with the flexibility of `make`. *Another* advanced Logo technique avoids the whole idea of changing the value of a variable. Any procedure that uses `make` can be rewritten to use an input to a subprocedure instead; compare the two versions of the `converse` program in this chapter.

Why would you want to avoid `make`? One reason is that if the value of a variable changes partway through a procedure, then the sequence of steps within the procedure is very important. One hot area in computer science research is *parallel* computation: What if, instead of a computer that can only do one thing at a time, we build a computer that can do many things at once? It's hard to take advantage of that ability if each step of our program depends on the results of previous steps, and if later steps depend on the result of this one.

A procedure is *functional* if it always gives the same output when invoked with the same input(s). We need a few more Logo tools before we can write interesting functional programs, but we'll come back to this idea soon.

4 Predicates

By introducing variables in Chapter 3, we made it possible for a procedure to operate on different data each time you invoke it. But the *pattern* of what the procedure does with the data remains constant. We can get even more variety out of our procedures if we can vary the *instructions* that the procedure executes. We need a way to say, "Sometimes do this; other times do that."

True or False

One helpful metaphor is this: When you invoke a command, you're giving the computer an order. "Now hear this! `Print` such-and-such!" But when you invoke an operation, you're asking the computer a *question*. "What is the `first` member of such-and-such?"

In real life we single out as a special category *yes-or-no questions*. For example, these special questions form the basis of the game Twenty Questions. The corresponding category in Logo is the *predicate*. A predicate is an operation whose output is always either the word `true` or the word `false`.

For example, `listp` (pronounced "list-pea") is a predicate that takes one input. The input can be any datum. The output from `listp` is `true` if the input is a list, `false` if the input is a word.

`Wordp` is another predicate that takes one input. The input can be any datum. The output from `wordp` is `true` if the input is a word, `false` if the input is a list. (This is the opposite of the output from `listp`.)

`Emptyp` is also a predicate with one input. The input can be any datum. The output from `emptyp` is `true` if the input is either the empty word or the empty list; if the input is anything else, the output is `false`.

You'll have noticed by now that predicates tend to have names ending in the letter `p`. This is not quite a universal rule, but almost. It's a good idea to follow the same convention in naming your own predicates.*

As I'm describing primitive predicates, you might want to try them out on the computer. You can do experiments like this:

```
? print wordp "hello
true
? print wordp [hello]
false
? print emptyp []
true
? print emptyp 0
false
```

Of course, most of the time you won't actually want to print the output from a predicate. You'll see in a few moments how we can use a predicate to control the instructions carried out in a procedure.

But first here are a few more primitive predicates. `Numberp` takes one input, which can be any datum. The output from `numberp` is `true` if the input is a number, `false` otherwise.

`Equalp` takes two inputs, each of which can be any datum. The output from `equalp` is `true` if the two inputs are identical or if they're both numbers and they're numerically equal. That is, 3 and 3.0 are numerically equal even though they're not identical words. A list is never equal to a word.

```
? print equalp 3 3.0
true
? print equalp "hello [hello]
false
? print equalp "hello first [hello]
true
? print equalp " []
false
? print equalp [] butfirst [hello]
true
```

* Many versions of Logo use a question mark at the end of names of predicates, instead of a `p`. For example, you may see `list?` instead of `listp`. Berkeley Logo accepts either form, but I prefer the `p` version.

The equal sign (=) can be used as an *infix* equivalent of `equalp`:

```
? print "hello = first [hello]
true
? print 2 = 3
false
```

As I mentioned in Chapter 2, if you use infix operations you have to be careful about what is grouped with what. It varies between versions of Logo. Here is an example I tried in Berkeley Logo:

```
? print first [hello] = "hello
f
```

Among current commercial implementations, Object Logo and Microworlds give the same answer `f`. But here is the *same* example in Logowriter:

```
? print first [hello] = "hello
true
```

You can avoid confusion by using parentheses. The following instructions work reliably in any Logo:

```
? print (first [hello]) = "hello
true
? print first ([hello] = "hello)
f
```

`Memberp` is a predicate with two inputs. If the second input is a list, then the first can be any datum. If the second input is a word, then the first must be a one-character word. The output from `memberp` is true if the first input is a member of the second input.

```
? print memberp "rain [the rain in Spain]
true
? print memberp [the rain] [the rain in Spain]
false
? print memberp [the rain] [[the rain] in Spain]
true
? print memberp "e "please
true
? print memberp "e "plain
false
```

`Lessp` and `greaterp` are predicates that take two inputs. Both inputs must be numbers. The output from `lessp` is `true` if the first input is numerically less than the second; the output from `greaterp` is true if the first is greater than the second. Otherwise the output is `false`. (In particular, both `lessp` and `greaterp` output `false` if the two inputs are equal.) The infix forms for `lessp` (<) and `greaterp` (>) are also allowed.

Defining Your Own Predicates

Here are two examples of how you can create new predicates:

```
to vowelp :letter
output memberp :letter [a e i o u]
end

? print vowelp "e
true
? print vowelp "g
false

to oddp :number
output equalp (remainder :number 2) 1
end

? print oddp 5
true
? print oddp 8
false
```

Conditional Evaluation

The main use of predicates is to compute inputs to the primitive procedures `if` and `ifelse`. We'll get to `ifelse` in a while, but first we'll explore `if`.

`If` is a command with two inputs. The first input must be either the word `true` or the word `false`. The second input must be a list containing Logo instructions. If the first input is `true`, the effect of `if` is to evaluate the instructions in the second input. If the first input is `false`, `if` has no effect.

```
? if equalp 2 1+1 [print "Yup.]
Yup.
? if equalp 3 2 [print "Nope.]
?
```

Here is an example of how `if` can be used in a procedure. This is an extension of the `converse` example in Chapter 3:

```
to talk
local "name
print [Please type your full name.]
make "name readlist
print sentence [Your first name is] first :name
if (count :name) > 2 ~
   [print sentence [Your middle name is] first bf :name]
print sentence [Your last name is] last :name
end
```

```
? talk
Please type your full name.
George Washington
Your first name is George
Your last name is Washington
? talk
Please type your full name.
John Paul Jones
Your first name is John
Your middle name is Paul
Your last name is Jones
```

`Talk` asks you to type your name and reads what you type into a list, which is remembered in the variable named `name`. Your first and last names are printed as in the earlier version. If the list `:name` contains more than two members, however, `talk` also prints the second member as your middle name. If `:name` contains only two members, `talk` assumes that you don't have a middle name.

☞ Write a procedure of your own that asks a question and uses `if` to find out something about the response.

You can use `if` to help in writing more interesting predicates.

```
to about.computersp :sentence
if memberp "computer :sentence [output "true]
if memberp "computers :sentence [output "true]
if memberp "programming :sentence [output "true]
output "false
end
```

```
? print about.computersp [This book is about programming]
true
? print about.computersp [I like ice cream]
false
?
```

This procedure illustrates something I didn't explain before about `output`: An `output` command finishes the evaluation of the procedure in which it occurs. For example, in `about.computersp`, if the input sentence contains the word `computer`, the first `if` evaluates the `output` instruction that is its second input. The procedure immediately outputs the word `true`. The remaining instructions are not evaluated at all.

☞ Write `past.tensep`, which takes a word as input and outputs `true` if the word ends in `ed` or if it's one of a list of exceptions, like `saw` and `went`.

☞ Write `integerp`, which takes any Logo datum as input and outputs `true` if and only if the datum is an integer (a number without a fraction part). Hint: a number with a fraction part will contain a decimal point.

Choosing Between Alternatives

`If` gives the choice between carrying out some instructions and doing nothing at all. More generally, we may want to carry out either of *two* sets of instructions, depending on the output from a predicate. The primitive procedure `ifelse` meets this need.* `Ifelse` is an unusual primitive because it can be used either as a command or as an operation. We'll start with examples in which `ifelse` is used as a command.

`Ifelse` requires three inputs. The first input must be either the word `true` or the word `false`. The second and third inputs must be lists containing Logo instructions. If the first input is `true`, the effect of `if` is to evaluate the instructions in the second input. If the first input is `false`, the effect is to evaluate the instructions in the third input.

```
? ifelse 4 = 2+2 [print "Yup.] [print "Nope.]
Yup.
? ifelse 4 = 3+5 [print "Yup.] [print "Nope.]
Nope.
?
```

* In some versions of Logo, the name `if` is used both for the two-input command discussed earlier and for the three-input one presented here.

Here is an example of a procedure using `ifelse`:

```
to groupie
local "name
print [Hi, who are you?]
make "name readlist
ifelse :name = [Ray Davies] ~
     [print [May I have your autograph?]] ~
     [print sentence "Hi, first :name]
end
```

```
? groupie
Hi, who are you?
Frank Sinatra
Hi, Frank
? groupie
Hi, who are you?
Ray Davies
May I have your autograph?
```

☞ Write an operation `color` that takes as input a word representing a card, such as `10h` for the ten of hearts. Its output should be the word `red` if the card is a heart or a diamond, or `black` if it's a spade or a club.

☞ Write a conversational program that asks the user's name and figures out how to address him or her. For example:

```
? converse
Hi, what's your name?
Chris White
Pleased to meet you, Chris.

? converse
Hi, what's your name?
Ms. Grace Slick
Pleased to meet you, Ms. Slick.

? converse
Hi, what's your name?
J. Paul Getty
Pleased to meet you, Paul.

? converse
Hi, what's your name?
Sigmund Freud, M.D.
Pleased to meet you, Dr. Freud.
```

```
? converse
Hi, what's your name?
Mr. Lon Chaney, Jr.
Pleased to meet you, Mr. Chaney.
```

What should the program say if it meets Queen Elizabeth II?

Conditional Evaluation Another Way

The use of `ifelse` in the `groupie` example above makes for a rather long instruction line. If you wanted to do several instructions in each case, rather than just one `print`, the `if` line would become impossible to read. Logo provides another mechanism that is equivalent to the `ifelse` command but may be easier to read.

`Test` is a command that takes one input. The input must be either the word `true` or the word `false`. The effect of `test` is just to remember what its input was in a special place. You can think of this place as a variable without a name. This special variable is automatically local to the procedure from which `test` is invoked.

`Iftrue` (abbreviation `ift`) is a command with one input. The input must be a list of Logo instructions. The effect of `iftrue` is to evaluate the instructions in its input only if the unnamed variable set by the most recent `test` command in the same procedure is `true`. It is an error to use `iftrue` without first using `test`.

`Iffalse` (abbreviation `iff`) is a command with one input, which must be an instruction list. The effect of `iffalse` is to evaluate the instructions only if the remembered result of the most recent `test` command is `false`.

`Iftrue` and `iffalse` can be invoked as many times as you like after a `test`. This allows you to break up a long sequence of conditionally evaluated instructions into several instruction lines:

```
to better.groupie
local "name
print [Hi, who are you?]
make "name readlist
test equalp :name [Ray Davies]
iftrue [print [Wow, can I have your autograph?]]
iftrue [print [And can I borrow a thousand dollars?]]
iffalse [print sentence [Oh, hello,] first :name]
end
```

About Those Brackets

I hope that the problem I'm about to mention won't even have occurred to you because you are so familiar with the idea of evaluation that you understood right away. But you'll probably have to explain it to someone else, so I thought I'd bring it up here:

Some people get confused about why the second input to `if` (and the second and third inputs to `ifelse`) is surrounded by brackets but the first isn't. That is, they wonder, why don't we say

```
if [equalp 2 3] [print "really??]          ; (wrong!)
```

They have this problem because someone lazily told them to put brackets around the conditionally evaluated instructions without ever explaining about brackets and quotation.

I trust *you* aren't confused that way. You understand that, as usual, Logo evaluates the inputs to a procedure before invoking the procedure. The first input to `if` has to be either the word `true` or the word `false`. *Before* invoking `if`, Logo has to evaluate an expression like `equalp 2 3` to compute the input. (In this case, the result output by `equalp` will be `false`.) But if the `print` instruction weren't quoted, Logo would evaluate it, too, *before* invoking `if`. That's not what we want. We want the instruction list *itself* to be the second input, so that `if` can decide whether or not to carry out the instructions in the list. So, as usual, we use brackets to tell Logo to quote the list.

actual argument expression	→	actual argument value
`equalp 2 3`	→	`false`
`[print "really??]`	→	`[print "really??]`

Logical Connectives

Sometimes the condition under which you want to evaluate an instruction is complicated. You want to do it if *both* this *and* that are true, or if *either* this *or* that is true. Logo provides operations for this purpose.

`And` is a predicate with two inputs. Each input must be either the word `true` or the word `false`. The output from `and` is `true` if both inputs are `true`; the output is `false` if either input is `false`. (`And` can take more than two inputs if the entire expression is enclosed in parentheses. In that case the output from and will be true only if all of its inputs are true.)

Or is a predicate with two inputs. Each input must be either the word true or the word false. The output from or is true if either input is true (or both inputs are). The output is false if both inputs are false. (Extra-input or outputs true if any of its inputs are true, false if all inputs are false.)

Not is a predicate with one input. The input must be either the word true or the word false. The output from not is the opposite of its input: true if the input is false, or false if the input is true.

These three procedures are called *logical connectives* because they connect logical expressions together into bigger ones. (A *logical* expression is one whose value is true or false.) They can be useful in defining new predicates:

```
to fullp :datum
output not emptyp :datum
end

to realwordp :datum
output and wordp :datum not numberp :datum
end

to digitp :datum
output and numberp :datum equalp count :datum 1
end
```

Ifelse as an Operation

So far, we have applied the idea of conditional evaluation only to complete instructions. It is also possible to choose between two expressions to evaluate, by using ifelse as an operation.

When used as an operation, ifelse requires three inputs. The first input must be either the word true or the word false. The second and third inputs must be lists containing Logo expressions. The output from ifelse is the result of evaluating the second input, if the first input is true, or the result of evaluating the third input, if the first input is false.

```
? print sentence "It's ifelse 2=3 ["correct] ["incorrect]
It's incorrect
? print ifelse emptyp [] [sum 2 3] [product 6 7]
5
```

Here is one of the classic examples of a procedure in which `ifelse` is used as an operation. This procedure is an operation that takes a number as its input; it outputs the *absolute value* of the number:

```
to abs :number
output ifelse :number<0 [-:number] [:number]
end
```

Expression Lists and Plumbing Diagrams

`If` and `ifelse` require *instruction lists* or *expression lists* as inputs. This requirement is part of their semantics, not part of the syntax of an instruction. Just as the arithmetic operators require numbers as inputs (semantics), but those numeric values can be provided either as explicit numbers in the instruction or as the result of an arbitrarily complicated subexpression (syntax), the procedures that require instruction or expression lists as input don't interpret those inputs until after Logo has set up the plumbing for the instructions that invoke them.

What does that mean? Consider the instruction

```
ifelse "false ["stupid "list] [print 23]
```

Even though the second input to `ifelse`—that is, the first of the two literal lists—makes no sense as an instruction list, this instruction will work correctly without printing an error message. The Logo interpreter knows that `ifelse` accepts three inputs, and it sees that the three input expressions provided are a literal (quoted) word and two literal lists. It sets up the plumbing without paying any attention to the semantics of `ifelse`; in particular, Logo doesn't care whether the given inputs are meaningful for use with `ifelse`. Then, once `ifelse` starts running, it examines its first input value. Since that input is the word `false`, the `ifelse` procedure ignores its second input completely and executes the instruction in its third input.

The use of quotation marks and square brackets to indicate literal inputs is part of the plumbing syntax, not part of the procedure semantics. Don't say, "`Ifelse` requires one predicate input and two inputs in square brackets." The instruction

```
ifelse last [true false] list ""stupid ""list list bf "sprint 23
```

has a very different plumbing diagram (syntax) from that of the earlier example, but provides exactly the same input values to `ifelse`.

Consider these two instructions:

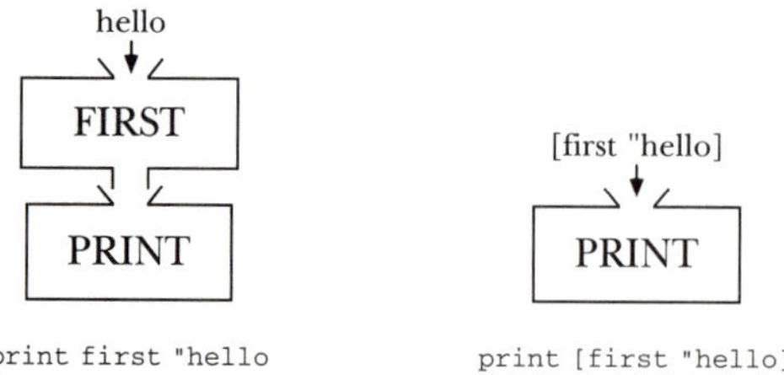

Since the effect of `print` is easy to observe, it's not hard to see the relationship among the instructions, the plumbing diagrams, and the effects when these instructions are run. Why are brackets used around the `first` expression in one case but not in the other? Because in one case the expression is how we tell Logo to set up the plumbing diagram, while in the second case we are giving `print` as input a literal list that just happens to look like an expression. When the context is something like `ifelse` instead of `print`, the syntactic situation is really quite similar, but may be harder to see. Consider this instruction:

```
print ifelse emptyp :a [emptyp :b] [emptyp :c]
```

Why do we put brackets around two `emptyp` expressions but not around another similar-looking one? ☞ Draw a plumbing diagram for this instruction, paying no attention to your mental model of the meaning of the `ifelse` procedure, treating it as if it were the nonsense procedure `zot3`. You will see that the first input to `ifelse` is an expression whose value will be the word `true` or the word `false`, because Logo will carry out that first `emptyp` computation before invoking `ifelse`. The remaining two inputs, however, are literal lists that happen to contain the word `emptyp` but do not involve an invocation of `emptyp` in the plumbing diagram. Once `ifelse` is actually invoked, precisely one of those two list inputs will be interpreted as a Logo expression, for which a *new* plumbing diagram is (in effect) drawn by Logo. The other input list is ignored.

Stopping a Procedure

I'd like to examine more closely one of the examples from the first chapter:

```
to music.quiz
print [Who is the greatest musician of all time?]
if equalp readlist [John Lennon] [print [That's right!] stop]
print [No, silly, it's John Lennon.]
end
```

You now know about almost all of the primitive procedures used in this example. The only one we haven't discussed is the `stop` command in the second instruction line.

`Stop` is a command that takes no inputs. It is only allowed inside a procedure; you can't type `stop` to a top-level prompt. The effect of `stop` is to finish the evaluation of the procedure in which it is used. Later instructions in the same procedure are skipped.

Notice that `stop` does not stop *all* active procedures. If procedure A invokes procedure B, and there is a `stop` command in procedure B, then procedure A continues after the point where it invoked B.

Recall that the `output` command also stops the procedure that invokes it. The difference is that if you're writing an operation, which should have an output, you use `output`; if you're writing a command, which doesn't have an output, you use `stop`.

In `music.quiz`, the effect of the `stop` is that if you get the right answer, the final `print` instruction isn't evaluated. The same effect could have been written this way:

```
ifelse equalp readlist [John Lennon] ~
    [print [That's right!]] ~
    [print [No, silly, it's John Lennon.]]
```

The alternative form uses the three-input `ifelse` command. One advantage of using `stop` is precisely that it allows the use of shorter lines. But in this example, where there is only one instruction after the `if`, it doesn't matter much. `Stop` is really useful when you want to stop only in an unusual situation and otherwise you have a lot of work still to do:

```
to quadratic :a :b :c
local "discriminant
make "discriminant (:b * :b)-(4 * :a * :c)
if :discriminant < 0 [print [No solution.] stop]
make "discriminant sqrt :discriminant
local "x1
local "x2
make "x1 (-:b + :discriminant)/(2 * :a)
make "x2 (-:b - :discriminant)/(2 * :a)
print (sentence [x =] :x1 [or] :x2)
end
```

This procedure applies the quadratic formula to solve the equation

$$ax^2 + bx + c = 0$$

The only interesting thing about this example for our present purpose is the fact that sometimes there is no solution. In that case the procedure stops as soon as it finds out.

Don't forget that you need stop only if you want to stop a procedure before its last instruction line. A common mistake made by beginners who've just learned about stop is to use it in every procedure. If you look back at the examples so far you'll see that many procedures get along fine without invoking stop.

Improving the Quiz Program

When I first introduced the music.quiz example in Chapter 1, we hadn't discussed things like user procedures with inputs. We are now in a position to generalize the quiz program:

```
to qa :question :answer
print :question
if equalp readlist :answer [print [That's right!] stop]
print sentence [Sorry, it's] :answer
end

to quiz
qa [Who is the best musician of all time?] [John Lennon]
qa [Who wrote "Compulsory Miseducation"?] [Paul Goodman]
qa [What color was George Washington's white horse?] [white]
qa [how much is 2+2?] [5]
end
```

Procedure qa is our old friend music.quiz, with variable inputs instead of a fixed question and answer. Quiz uses qa several times to ask different questions.

☞ Here are a couple of suggestions for further improvements you should be able to make to quiz and qa:

1. Qa is very fussy about getting one particular answer to a question. If you answer Lennon instead of John Lennon, it'll tell you you're wrong. There are a couple of ways you might fix this. One is to look for a single-word answer *anywhere within* what the user types. So if :answer is the word Lennon, the program will accept "Lennon," "John Lennon," or "the Lennon Sisters." The second approach would be for qa to take a *list* of possible answers as its second input:

```
qa [Who is the best musician of all time?] ~
   [[John Lennon] [Lennon] [the Beatles]]
```

Qa then has to use a different predicate, to see if what the user types is any of the answers in the list.

2. By giving quiz a local variable named score, you could have quiz and qa cooperate to keep track of how many questions the user gets right. At the end the score could be printed. (This is an opportunity to think about the stylistic virtues and vices of letting a subprocedure modify a variable that belongs to its superprocedure. If you say

```
make "score :score+1
```

inside qa, doesn't that make quiz somewhat mysterious to read? For an alternative, read the next section.)

Reporting Success to a Superprocedure

Suppose we want the quiz program to give the user three tries before revealing the right answer. There are several ways this could be programmed. Here is a way that uses the tools you already know about.

The general idea is that the procedure that asks the question is written as an *operation,* not as a command. To be exact, it's a predicate; it outputs true if the user gets the right answer. This asking procedure, ask.once, is invoked as a subprocedure of ask.thrice, which is in charge of allowing three tries. ask.thrice invokes ask.once up to three times, but stops if ask.once reports success.

```
to ask.thrice :question :answer
repeat 3 [if ask.once :question :answer [stop]]
print sentence [The answer is] :answer
end

to ask.once :question :answer
print :question
if equalp readlist :answer [print [Right!] output "true]
print [Sorry, that's wrong.]
output "false
end
```

You've seen repeat in the first chapter, but you haven't been formally introduced. Repeat is a command with two inputs. The first input must be a non-negative whole number. The second input must be a list of Logo instructions. The effect of repeat is to evaluate its second input, the instruction list, the number of times given as the first input.

The programming style used in this example is a little controversial. In general, it's considered a good idea not to mix effect and output in one procedure. But in this example, `ask.once` has an effect (it prints the question, reads an answer, and comments on its correctness) and also an output (`true` or `false`).

I think the general rule I've just cited is a good rule, but there are exceptions to it. Using an output of `true` or `false` to report the success or failure of some process is one of the situations that I consider acceptable style. The real point of the rule, I think, is to separate *calculating* something from *printing* it. For example, it's a mistake to write procedures like this one:

```
to prsecond :datum
print first butfirst :datum
end
```

A more powerful technique is to write the `second` operation from Chapter 2; instead of

```
prsecond [something or other]
```

you can then say

```
print second [something or other]
```

It may not be obvious from this example why I call `second` more powerful than `prsecond`. But remember that an operation can be combined with other operations, as in the plumbing diagrams we used earlier. For example, the operation `second` can extract the word `or` from the list as shown here. But you can *also* use it as part of a more complex instruction to extract the letter `o`:

```
print first second [something or other]
```

If you'd written the command `prsecond` to solve the first problem, you'd have to start all over again to solve this new one. (Of course, both of these examples must seem pretty silly; why bother extracting a word or a letter from this list? But I'm trying to use examples that are simple enough not to obscure this issue with the kinds of complications we'll see in more interesting programs.)

☞ If you made the improvements to `quiz` and `qa` that I suggested earlier, you might like to see if they can fit easily with a new version of `quiz` using `ask.thrice`.

5 Functions of Functions

We now have many of the tools we need to write computer programs. We have the primitive operations for arithmetic computation, the primitive operations to manipulate words and sentences, and a way to choose between alternative computations. One thing that we still lack is a way to deal systematically with data *aggregates*—collections of data. We want to be able to say "carry out this computation for each member of that aggregate." Processing large amounts of data uniformly is one of the abilities that distinguish computers from mere pocket calculators.

The Problem: `Initials`

To make this concrete, we'll look at a very simple example. I'd like to write a procedure that can figure out a person's initials, like this:

```
? show initials [George Harrison]
[G H]
```

One obvious approach is to find the initials of the first name and the last name:

```
to initials :name
output sentence (first first :name) (first last :name)
end
```

The trouble is that this approach doesn't work for people with middle names. We'd like our `initials` procedure to be able to handle any length name. But it doesn't:

```
? show initials [John Alec Entwistle]
[J E]
? show initials [Peter Blair Denis Bernard Noone]
[P N]
```

What we want is this:

```
? show initials.in.our.dreams [John Alec Entwistle]
[J A E]
? show initials.in.our.dreams [Peter Blair Denis Bernard Noone]
[P B D B N]
```

If we knew that the input would have exactly five names, we could extract the first letter of each of them explicitly. But you never know when some smart alec will ask you to

```
show initials [Princess Angelina Contessa Louisa Francesca ~
              Banana Fana Bo Besca the Third]
```

One Solution: Numeric Iteration

If you've programmed before in other languages, then one solution will immediately occur to you. You create a variable `n` whose value is the number of words in the input, then you have a variable `i` that takes on all possible values from 1 to `n`, and you select the `i`th word from the input and pull out its first letter. Most languages have a special notation for this sort of computation:

```
for i = 1 to n : ... : next i              (BASIC)
for 1 := 1 to n do begin ... end           (Pascal)
for (i=1; i<=n; i++) { ... }               (C)
```

All of these have the same meaning: Carry out some instructions (the part shown as `...` above) repeatedly, first with the variable named `i` having the value `1`, then with `i` equal to `2`, and so on, up to `i` equal to `n`. This technique is called *numeric iteration.* "Iteration" means repetition, and it's "numeric" iteration because the repetition is controlled by a variable that takes on a sequence of numeric values.

We can do the same thing in Logo, although, as we'll soon learn, it's not the usual approach that Logo programmers take to this problem.

```
to initials :name
local "result
make "result []
for [i 1 [count :name]] ~
    [make "result sentence :result first (item :i :name)]
output :result
end
```

(The reason I declare `result` as local, but not `i`, is that Logo's `for` automatically makes its index variable local to the `for` itself. There is no variable `i` outside of the `for` instruction.)

The command `for` takes two inputs. The second input is an instruction list that will be carried out repeatedly. The first input controls the repetition; it is a list of either three or four members: a variable name, a starting value, a limit value, and an optional increment. (The variable named by the first member of the list is called the *index variable.* For example:

```
? for [number 4 7] [print :number]
4
5
6
7
? for [value 4 11 3] [print :value]
4
7
10
```

In the first example, `number` takes on all integer values between 4 and 7. In the second, `value`'s starting value is 4, and on each repetition its new value is 3 more than last time. `Value` never actually has its limiting value of 11; the next value after 10 would have been 13, but that's bigger than the limit.

`For` can count downward instead of upward:

```
? for [i 7 5] [print :i]
7
6
5
? for [n 15 2 -6] [print :n]
15
9
3
? for [x 15 2 6] [print :x]
?
```

The last example has no effect. Why? The increment of 6 implies that this invocation of `for` should count upward, which means that the `for` continues until the value of `x` is greater than the limit, 2. But the starting value, 15, is *already* greater than 2.

If no increment is given in the first input to `for`, then `for` will use either `1` or `-1` as the increment, whichever is compatible with the starting and limit values.

Although I've been using constant numbers as the starting value, limit value, and increment in these examples, `for` can handle any Logo expression, represented as a list, for each of these:

```
to spread :ends
for [digit [first :ends] [last :ends]] [type :digit]
print []
end

? spread 19
123456789
? spread 83
876543
```

More formally, the effect of `for` is as follows. First it creates the local index variable and assigns it the starting value. Then `for` carries out three steps repeatedly: testing, action, and incrementing. The testing step is to compare the current value of the index variable with the limit value. If the index variable has passed the limit, then the `for` is finished. ("Passed" means that the index variable is greater than the limit, if the increment is positive, or that the index variable is less than the limit, if the increment is negative.) The action step is to evaluate the instructions in the second input to `for`. The incrementing step is to assign a new value to the index variable by adding the increment to the old value. Then comes another round of testing, action, and incrementing.

So, for example, if we give Logo the instruction

```
show initials [Raymond Douglas Davies]
```

then the `for` instruction within `initials` is equivalent to this sequence of instructions:

```
local "i                                   ; initialize index variable
make "i 1

if (:i > 3) [stop]                         ; testing
make "result (se :result first "Raymond)   ; action  (result is [R])
make "i :i+1                               ; incrementing  (i is 2)

if (:i > 3) [stop]                         ; testing
make "result (se :result first "Douglas)   ; action  (result is [R D])
make "i :i+1                               ; incrementing  (i is 3)
```

```
if (:i > 3) [stop]                       ; testing
make "result (se :result first "Davies)  ; action   (result is [R D D])
make "i :i+1                             ; incrementing  (i is 4)

if (:i > 3) [stop]                       ; testing
```

except that the `stop` instruction in the testing step stops only the `for` instruction, not the `initials` procedure.

Critique of Numeric Iteration

Computers were originally built to deal with numbers. Numeric iteration matches closely the behind-the-scenes sequence of steps by which computers actually work. That's why just about every programming language supports this style of programming.

Nevertheless, a `for` instruction isn't anything like the way you, a human being, would solve the `initials` problem without a computer. First of all, you wouldn't begin by counting the number of words in the name; you really don't have to know that. You'd just say, for example, "First of Raymond is R; first of Douglas is D; first of Davies is D." When you ran out of names, you'd stop.

The manipulation of the `result` variable to collect the results also seems unnatural. You wouldn't think, "I'm going to start with an empty result; then, whatever value `result` has, I'll throw in an R; then, whatever value `result` now has, I'll throw in a D" and so on.

In fact, if you had to explain to someone else how to solve this problem, you probably wouldn't talk about a sequence of steps at all. Rather, you'd draw a picture like this one:

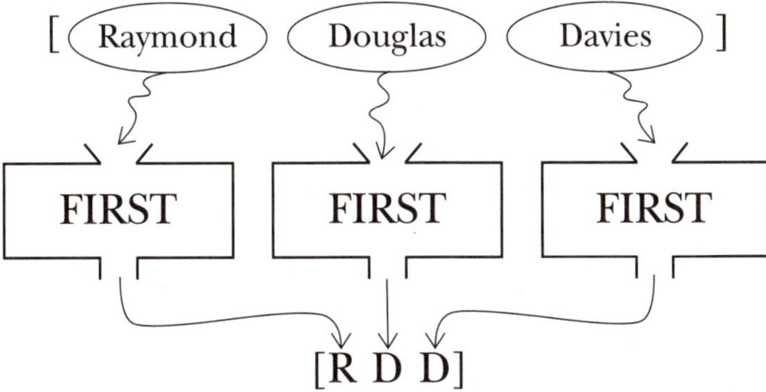

To explain the picture, you'd say something like "Just take the `first` of each word." You wouldn't even mention the need to put the results together into a sentence; you'd take that for granted.

In Logo we can write an `initials` procedure using the same way of thinking that you'd use in English:

```
to initials :name
output map "first :name
end
```

The `map` procedure means "collect the results of doing *this* for each of *those*."

As this example illustrates, `map` is easy to use. But it's a little hard to talk about, because it's a function of a function. So first we'll take a detour to talk more precisely about functions in general.

What's a Function?

A *function* is a rule for turning one value (called the *argument*) into another. If you've studied algebra you'll remember numeric function rules such as

$$f(x) = 3x - 6$$

but not all functions are numeric, and not all rules need be expressed as algebraic formulas. For example, here is the Instrument function, which takes a Beatle as its argument and returns his instrument:

argument	**result**
John	rhythm guitar
Paul	bass guitar
George	lead guitar
Ringo	drums

This particular function has only four possible arguments. Other functions, like $f(x)$ above, may have infinitely many possible arguments. The set of possible arguments is called the *domain* of the function. Similarly, the set of possible result values is called the *range* of the function.*

* It's a little awkward to talk about the domain of a function that takes two arguments. That is, it's easy to say that the domain of the function represented by the `first` operation is words or lists, but how do we describe `item`? We could loosely say "its domain is numbers and words or lists," but that sounds as if either argument could be any of those. The most precise way to say it is this: "The

Functions can be represented in many ways. (We've seen two in this section: formulas and tables.) One way to represent a function is with a Logo operation. Here are Logo representations of the two functions we've discussed:

```
to f :x
output 3*:x - 6
end

to instrument :beatle
if :beatle = "John [output [rhythm guitar]]
if :beatle = "Paul [output [bass guitar]]
if :beatle = "George [output [lead guitar]]
if :beatle = "Ringo [output [drums]]
end
```

(What if we give `instrument` an input that's not in the domain of the function? In that case, it won't output any value, and a Logo error message will result. Some people would argue that the procedure should provide its own, more specific error message.)

I've been careful to say that the Logo operation *represents* the function, not that it *is* the function. In particular, two Logo procedures can compute the same function—the same relationship between input and output values—by different methods. For example, consider these Logo operations:

```
to f :x
output 3*:x - 6
end
```

```
to g :x
output 3 * (:x-2)
end
```

The Logo operations `f` and `g` carry out two different computations, but they represent the same function. For example, to compute `f 10` we say $3 \times 10 = 30$, $30 - 6 = 24$; to compute `g 10` we say $10 - 2 = 8$, $3 \times 8 = 24$. Different computations, but the same answer. Functional programming means, in part, focusing our attention on the inputs and outputs of programs rather than on the sequence of computational steps.

Just as a Logo operation represents a function, the procedure's inputs similarly *represent* the arguments to the corresponding function. For example, that instrument function I presented earlier has Beatles (that is to say, people) as its domain and has

---

domain of `item` is pairs of values, in which the first member of the pair is a positive integer and the second member is a word or list of length greater than or equal to the first member of the pair." But for ordinary purposes we just rephrase the sentence to avoid the word "domain" altogether: "`Item` takes two inputs; the first must be a positive integer and the second must be a word or list..."

musical instruments as its range. But Logo doesn't have people or instruments as data types, and so the procedure `instrument` takes as its input *the name of* a Beatle (that is, a word) and returns as its output *the name of* an instrument (a sentence). Instrument is a function from Beatles to instruments, but `instrument` is an operation from words to sentences.

We're about to see a similar situation when we explore `map`. The map function—that is, the function that `map` represents—is a *function of functions.* One of the arguments to the map function is itself a function. The corresponding input to Logo's `map` procedure should be a procedure. But it turns out that Logo doesn't quite allow a procedure to be an input to another procedure; instead, we must use the *name* of the procedure as the input, just as we use the name of a Beatle as the input to `instrument`.

I know this sounds like lawyer talk, and we haven't written any programs for a while. But here's why this is important: In order to understand the *purpose* of `map`, you have to think about the map function, whose domain is functions (and other stuff, as we'll see in a moment). But in order to understand the *notation* that you use with `map` in Logo, you have to think in terms of the Logo operation, whose input is words (names of procedures). You have to be clear about this representation business in order to be able to shift mentally between these viewpoints.

Functions of Functions: `Map`

`Map` takes two inputs. The first is a word, which must be the name of a one-input Logo operation. The second can be any datum. The output from `map` is either a word or a list, whichever is the type of the second input. The members of the output are the results of applying the named operation to the members of the second input.

```
? show map "first [Rod Argent]
[R A]
```

In this example, the output is a list of two members, just as the second input is a list of two members. Each member of the output is the result of applying `first` to one of the members of `map`'s second input.

Many people, when they first meet `map`, are confused by the quoting of its first input. After all, I made a fuss back in Chapter 2 about the difference between these two examples:

```
? print Hello
I don't know how  to Hello
? print "Hello
Hello
```

You learned that a quoted word means the word itself, while an unquoted word asks Logo to invoke a procedure. But now, when I want to use the `first` procedure as input to `map`, I'm quoting its name. Why?

All that effort about the domains of functions should help you understand the notation used here. Start by ignoring the Logo notation and think about the domain of the map function. We want the map function to have *another function,* the function "first" in this case, as one of its arguments:

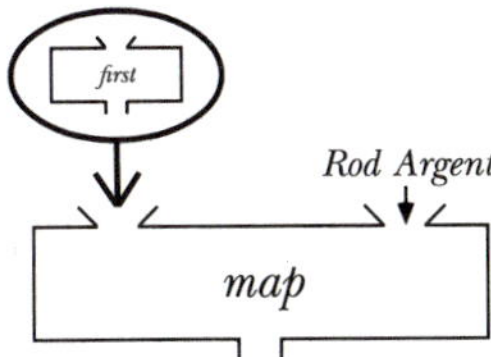

It's tempting to say that in Logo, a function is represented by a procedure, so `map` represents map, and `first` represents first. If this were algebra notation, I'd say *map*(*first*, *Rod Argent*), so in Logo I'll say

```
show map first [Rod Argent]                ;; wrong!
```

But when a Logo instruction has two unquoted procedure names in a row, that doesn't mean that the second function is used as argument to the first! Instead, it means that *the output from invoking* the second function is used as the argument to the first. In this case, we'd be *composing* `map` and `first`:

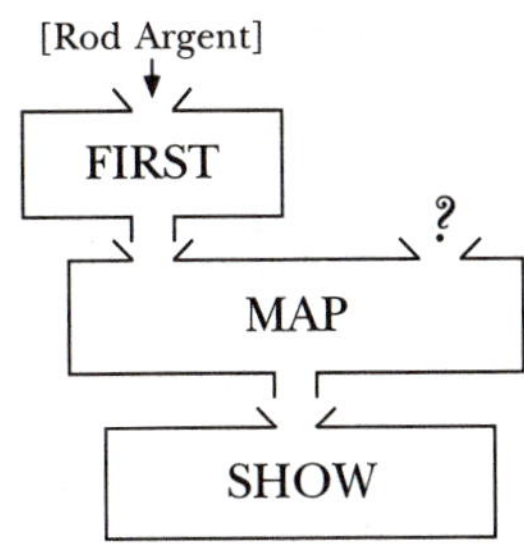

As the plumbing diagram shows, the list that we intended as the second input to `map` actually ends up as the input to `first`, and Logo will complain because `map` isn't given enough inputs.

Instead, as I said earlier, we must use *the name of* the `first` procedure to represent it. That gives this diagram:

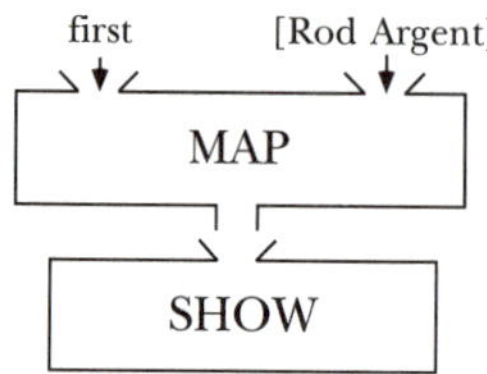

Here's another simple example. Logo has a primitive operation `uppercase` that takes a word as input, and outputs the same word but in all capital letters:

```
? print uppercase "young
YOUNG
```

What if we want to translate an entire sentence to capital letters? The `uppercase` primitive doesn't accept a sentence as its input:

```
? show uppercase [neil young]
uppercase doesn't like [neil young] as input.
```

But we can use `map` to translate each word separately and combine the results:

```
? show map "uppercase [neil young]
[NEIL YOUNG]
```

Ordinarily `map` works with one-argument functions. But we can give `map` extra arguments (by enclosing the invocation of `map` in parentheses, as usual) so that it can work with functions of more than one argument.

```
? show (map "item [2 1 2 3] [john paul george ringo])
[o p e n]
? show (map "sum [1 2 3] [40 50 60] [700 800 900])
[741 852 963]
```

Each input after the first provides values for one input to the mapped function. For example, [2 1 2 3] provides four values for the first input to item. The input lists must all have the same length (two lists of length four in the item example, three lists of length three in the sum example).

In the examples so far, the input data have been lists. Here's an example in which we use map with words. Let's say we're writing a program to play Hangman, the word game in which one player guesses letters in a secret word chosen by the other player. At first the guesser sees only a row of dashes indicating the number of letters in the word; for each guess, more letters are revealed. We aren't going to write the entire program yet, but we're ready to write the operation that takes the secret word, and a list of the letters that have been guessed so far, and outputs a row of letters and dashes as appropriate.

```
to hangword :secret :guessed
output map "hangletter :secret
end

to hangletter :letter
output ifelse memberp :letter :guessed [:letter] ["_]
end

? print hangword "potsticker [e t a o i n]
_ot_ti__er
? print hangword "gelato [e t a o i n]
_e_ato
```

Notice that hangletter depends on Logo's dynamic scope to have access to hangword's local variable named guessed.

☞ Write an operation exaggerate that takes a sentence as input and outputs an exaggerated version:

```
? print exaggerate [I ate 3 potstickers]
I ate 6 potstickers
? print exaggerate [The chow fun is good here]
The chow fun is great here
```

It should double all the numbers in the sentence, and replace "good" with "great," "bad" with "terrible," and so on.

A function whose domain or range includes functions is called a *higher order function.* The function represented by map is a higher order function. (We may speak loosely and say that map is a higher order function, as long as you remember that Logo procedures aren't really functions!) It's tempting to say that the `map` procedure itself is a "higher order procedure," but in Logo that isn't true. Procedures aren't data in Logo; the only data types are words and lists. That's why the input to `map` is a word, the name of a procedure, and not the procedure itself. Some languages do treat procedures themselves as data. In particular, the language Scheme is a close relative of Logo that can handle procedures as data. If this way of thinking appeals to you, consider learning Scheme next!

Higher Order Selection: `Filter`

The purpose of `map` is to *transform* each member of an aggregate (a list or a word) by applying some function to it. Another higher order function, `filter`, is used to *select* some members of an aggregate, but not others, based on a criterion expressed as a predicate function. For example:

```
? show filter "numberp [76 trombones, 4 calling birds, and 8 days]
[76 4 8]

to vowelp :letter
output memberp :letter "aeiou
end

? show filter "vowelp "spaghetti
aei

to beatlep :person
output memberp :person [John Paul George Ringo]
end

? show filter "beatlep [Bob George Jeff Roy Tom]
[George]
```

What happens if we use the `initials` procedure that we wrote with people's names in mind for other kinds of names, such as organizations or book titles? Some of them work well:

```
? show initials [Computer Science Logo Style]
[C S L S]
? show initials [American Civil Liberties Union]
[A C L U]
```

but others don't give quite the results we'd like:

```
? show initials [Association for Computing Machinery]
[A f C M]
? show initials [People's Republic of China]
[P R o C]
```

We'd like to eliminate words like "for" and "of" before taking the first letters of the remaining words. This is a job for `filter`:

```
to importantp :word
output not memberp :word [the an a of for by with in to and or]
end

to initials :name
output map "first (filter "importantp :name)
end

? show initials [Association for Computing Machinery]
[A C M]
? show initials [People's Republic of China]
[P R C]
```

Many to One: Reduce

Of course, what we'd *really* like is to have those initials in the form of a single word: ACLU, CSLS, ACM, and so on. For this purpose we need yet another higher order function, one that invokes a combining function to join the members of an aggregate.

```
? show reduce "word [C S L S]
CSLS
? show reduce "sum [3 4 5 6]
18
? show reduce "sentence "UNICEF
[U N I C E F]
```

`Reduce` takes two inputs. The first must be the name of a two-input operation; the second can be any *nonempty* word or list.

```
to acronym :name
output reduce "word initials :name
end
```

In practice, the first input to `reduce` won't be any old operation; it'll be a *constructor.* It'll be something that doesn't care about the grouping of operands; for example, `sum` is a good choice but `difference` is problematic because we don't know whether

```
reduce "difference [5 6 7]
```

means 5 – (6 – 7) or (5 – 6) – 7, and the grouping affects the answer. Almost all the time, the constructor will be `word`, `sentence`, `sum`, or `product`. But here's an example of another one:

```
to bigger :a :b
output ifelse :a > :b [:a] [:b]
end

to biggest :nums
output reduce "bigger :nums
end

? show biggest [5 7 781 42 8]
781
```

Choosing the Right Tool

So far you've seen three higher order functions: `map`, `filter`, and `reduce`. How do you decide which one to use for a particular problem?

`Map` transforms each member of a word or list individually. The result contains as many members as the input.

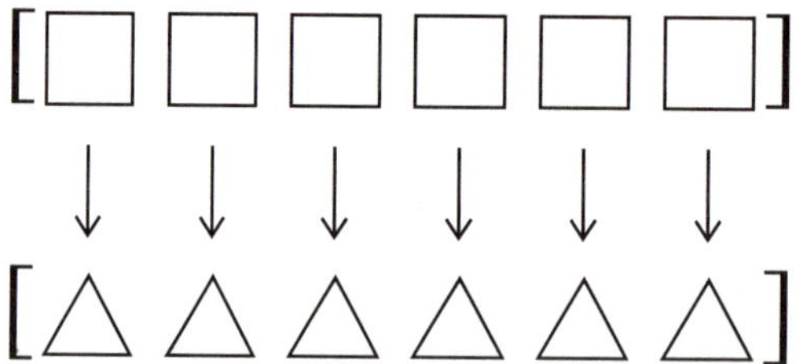

`Filter` selects certain members of a word or list and discards the others. The members of the result are members of the input, without transformation, but the result may be smaller than the original.

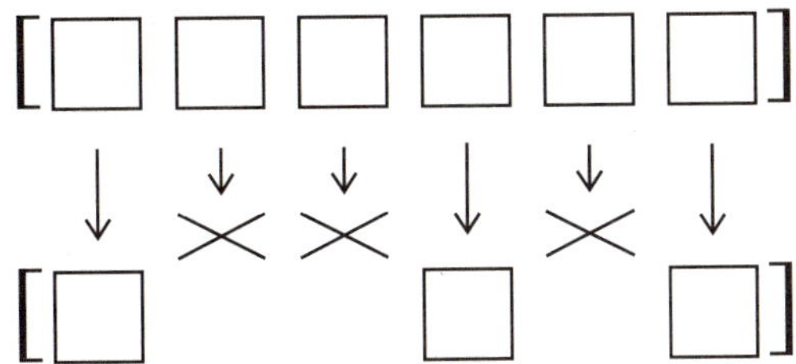

`Reduce` transforms the entire word or list into a single result by combining all of the members in some way.

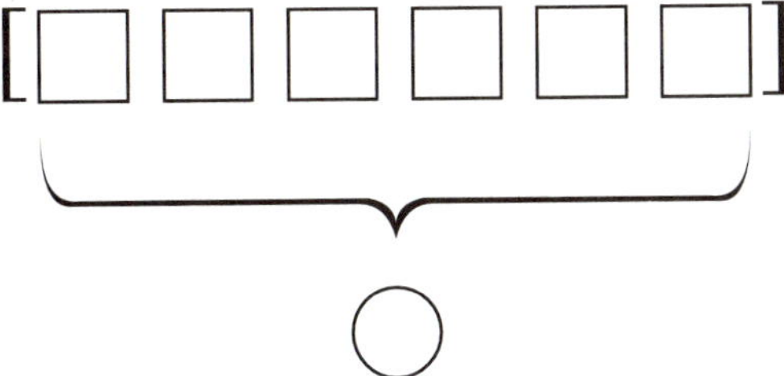

Anonymous Functions

In several of the examples in this chapter, I've had to write "helper" procedures such as `hangletter`, `importantp`, and `bigger` that will never be used independently, but are needed only to provide the function argument to a higher order function. It would be simpler if we could avoid writing these as separate procedures.

Does that sound confusing? This is one of those ideas for which an example is worth 1000 words:

```
to hangword :secret :guessed
output map [ifelse memberp ? :guessed [?] ["-]] :secret
end
```

Until now, the first input to map has always been a word, used to represent the function with that word as its name. In this example we see how a nameless function can be represented: as a list containing a Logo expression, but with question marks where the function's argument belongs. Such a list is called a *template.*

```
? show filter [memberp ? [John Paul George Ringo]] ~
              [Bob George Jeff Roy Tom]
[George]
```

Anonymous functions of more than one argument are a little uglier. Instead of ? for the argument, you must use ?1 for the first, ?2 for the second, and so on.

```
to biggest :nums
output reduce [ifelse ?1 > ?2 [?1] [?2]] :nums
end
```

Notice that the templates don't say output, as the named procedures did. That's because procedures are made of *instructions,* whereas these are *expression* templates. When input values are "plugged in" for the question marks, the template becomes a Logo expression, which means that when evaluated it has a value. If the template said output, it would be saying to use that value as the output *from the procedure containing it!* (I'm just repeating the point made earlier that output immediately stops the procedure it's in, even if there are more instructions below it.)

Higher Order Miscellany

Map combines the partial results into a list, if the second argument is a list, or into a word, if it's a word. Sometimes this behavior isn't quite what you want. An alternative is map.se (map to sentence), which makes a sentence of the results. Here are some examples.

```
? make "numbers [zero one two three four five six seven eight nine]
? show map [item ?+1 :numbers] 5789
fiveseveneightnine
? show map.se [item ?+1 :numbers] 5789
[five seven eight nine]

? show map [sentence (word "With ?) "You] [in out]
[[Within You] [Without You]]
? show map.se [sentence (word "With ?) "You] [in out]
[Within You Without You]
```

```
? show map.se [sentence ? "Warner] [Yakko Wakko Dot]
[Yakko Warner Wakko Warner Dot Warner]
? show map [sentence ? "Warner] [Yakko Wakko Dot]
[[Yakko Warner] [Wakko Warner] [Dot Warner]]
```

As these examples show, sometimes `map` does what you want, but sometimes `map.se` does, depending on the "shape" you want your result to have. Do you want a word, a sentence, or a structured list?

Suppose we have two sets of things, and we want all the pairings of one of these with one of those. An example will make clear what's desired:

```
? show crossproduct [red blue green] [shirt pants]
[[red shirt] [blue shirt] [green shirt] [red pants] [blue pants]
 [green pants]]
```

This is a tricky example because there are two different mistakes we could make. We don't want to "flatten" the result into a sentence:

```
[red shirt blue shirt green shirt red pants blue pants green pants]
```

but we also don't want all the shirts in one list and all the pants in another:

```
[[[red shirt] [blue shirt] [green shirt]]
 [[red pants] [blue pants] [green pants]]]
```

Here's the solution:

```
to crossproduct :these :those
output map.se [prepend.each :these ?] :those
end

to prepend.each :these :that
output map [sentence ? :that] :these
end
```

☞ Notice that this solution uses both `map` and `map.se`. Try to predict what would happen if you used `map` both times, or `map.se` both times, or interchanged the two. Then try it on the computer and be sure you understand what happens and why!

By the way, this is a case in which we still need a named helper function despite the use of templates, because otherwise we'd have one template inside the other, and Logo couldn't figure out which `?` to replace with what:

```
to crossproduct :these :those
output map.se [map [sentence ? ?] :these] :those     ; (wrong!)
end
```

Just as `map.se` is a variant of `map`, `find` is a variant of `filter`, for the situations in which you only want to find *one* member that meets the criterion, rather than all the members. (Perhaps you know in advance that there will only be one, or perhaps if there are more than one, you don't care which you get.)

```
to spellout :card
output (sentence (butlast :card) "of
                 (find [equalp last :card first ?]
                       [hearts spades diamonds clubs]))
end
```

```
? print spellout "5d
5 of diamonds
? print spellout "10h
10 of hearts
```

Sometimes what you want isn't a function at all. You want to take some *action* for each member of an aggregate. The most common one is to print each member on a separate line, in situations where you've computed a long list of things. You can use `foreach` with an *instruction* template, rather than an expression template as used with the others. The template is the last argument, rather than the first, to follow the way in which the phrase "for each" is used in English: For each of these things, do that.

```
? foreach (crossproduct [[ultra chocolate] pumpkin [root beer swirl]
      ginger] [cone cup]) "print
ultra chocolate cone
pumpkin cone
root beer swirl cone
ginger cone
ultra chocolate cup
pumpkin cup
root beer swirl cup
ginger cup
```

If you look closely at the letters on your computer screen you'll see that they are made up of little dots. One simple pattern represents each letter in a rectangle of dots five wide and seven high, like this:

```
  *    *****  *****  ****   *****
 * *   *   *  *      *   *  *
*   *  *   *  *      *   *  *
*****  ****   *      *   *  ***
*   *  *   *  *      *   *  *
*   *  *   *  *      *   *  *
*   *  *****  *****  ****   *****
```

The following program allows you to spell words on the screen in big letters like these. Each letter's shape is kept as the value of a global variable with the letter as its name. (I haven't actually listed all 26 letters.) The value is a list of seven words, each of which contains five characters, some combination of spaces and asterisks.

```
to say :word
for [row 1 7] [foreach :word [sayrow :row ?] print []]
print []
end

to sayrow :row :letter
type item :row thing :letter
type "|  |
end

make "b [|*****| |*   *| |*   *| |**** | |*   *| |*   *| |*****|]
make "r [|*****| |*   *| |*   *| |*****| |* *  | |*  * | |*   *|]
make "i [|*****| |  *  | |  *  | |  *  | |  *  | |  *  | |*****|]
make "a [|  *  | | * * | |*   *| |*****| |*   *| |*   *| |*   *|]
make "n [|*   *| |**  *| |**  *| |* * *| |*  **| |*  **| |*   *|]
```

```
? say "brian
*****  *****  *****    *    *   *
*   *  *   *    *     * *   **  *
*   *  *   *    *    *   *  **  *
****   *****    *    *****  * * *
*   *  * *      *    *   *  *  **
*   *  *  *     *    *   *  *  **
*****  *   *  *****  *   *  *   *
```

☞ Modify the program so that `say` takes another input, a number representing the size in which you want to print the letters. If the number is 1, then the program should work as before. If the number is 2, each dot should be printed as a two-by-two square of spaces or asterisks; if the number is 3, a three-by-three square, and so on.

Repeated Invocation: Cascade

Finally, sometimes you want to compose a function with itself several times:

```
? print first bf bf bf bf [The Continuing Story of Bungalow Bill]
Bungalow
? print first (cascade 4 "bf [The Continuing Story of Bungalow Bill])
Bungalow
```

`Cascade` takes three inputs. The first is a number, indicating how many times to invoke the function represented by the second argument. The third argument is the starting value.

```
to power :base :exponent
output cascade :exponent [? * :base] 1
end

? print power 2 8
256

to range :from :to
output cascade :to-:from [sentence ? (1+last ?)] (sentence :from)
end

? show range 3 8
[3 4 5 6 7 8]
```

Like `map`, `cascade` can be used with extra inputs to deal with more than one thing at a time. One example in which multi-input `cascade` is useful is the Fibonacci sequence. Each number in the sequence is the sum of the two previous numbers; the first two numbers are 1. So the sequence starts

$$1, 1, 2, 3, 5, 8, 13, \ldots$$

A formal definition of the sequence looks like this:

$$\begin{aligned} F_0 &= 1, \\ F_1 &= 1, \\ F_n &= F_{n-1} + F_{n-2}, \qquad n \geq 2. \end{aligned}$$

In order to compute, say, F_{23}, we must know both F_{22} and F_{21}. As we work our way up, we must always remember the two most recent values, like this:

	Most recent value	Next most recent value
start	1	0
step 1	1	1
step 2	2	1
step 3	3	2
step 4	5	3
...	...	...
step 22	F_{22}	F_{21}
step 23	$F_{22} + F_{21}$	F_{22}

To express this using `cascade`, we can use `?1` to mean the most recent value and `?2` to mean the next most recent. Then at each step, we need a function to compute the new `?1` by adding the two known values, and a function to copy the old `?1` as the new `?2`:

```
to fib :n
output (cascade :n [?1+?2] 1 [?1] 0)
end

? fib 5
8
? fib 23
46368
```

Another situation in which multi-input `cascade` can be useful is to process every member of a list, using `?1` to remember the already-processed ones and `?2` to remember the still-waiting ones. The simplest example is reversing the words in a sentence:

```
to reverse :sent
output (cascade (count :sent)
                [sentence (first ?2) ?1] []
                [butfirst ?2] :sent)
end

? print reverse [how now brown cow]
cow brown now how
```

	`?1`	`?2`
start	`[]`	`[how now brown cow]`
step 1	`[how]`	`[now brown cow]`
step 2	`[now how]`	`[brown cow]`
step 3	`[brown now how]`	`[cow]`
step 4	`[cow brown now how]`	`[]`

Here is the general notation for multi-input `cascade`:

```
(cascade howmany function1 start1 function2 start2 ...)
```

There must be as many *`function`* inputs as *`start`* inputs. Suppose there are n pairs of inputs; then each of the *`function`*s must accept n inputs. The *`start`*s provide the initial values for `?1`, `?2`, and so on; each function provides the next value for one of those. `Cascade` returns the final value of `?1`.

A Mini-project: Mastermind

It's time to put these programming tools to work in a more substantial project. You're ready to write a computer program that plays a family of games like Mastermind^{TM}. The computer picks a secret list of colors; the human player makes guesses. (The number of possible colors can be changed to tune the difficulty of the game.) At each turn, the program should tell the player how many colors in the guess are in the correct positions in the secret list and also how many are in the list, but not at the same positions. For example, suppose the program's secret colors are

```
red green blue violet
```

and the player guesses

```
red orange yellow green
```

There is one correct-position match (red, because it's the first color in both lists) and one incorrect-position match (green, because it's second in the computer's list but fourth in the player's list).

In the program, to reduce the amount of typing needed to play the game, represent each color as a single letter and each list of colors as a word. In the example above, the computer's secret list is represented as `rgbv` and the player's guess as `royg`.

There are two possible variations in the rules, depending on whether or not color lists with duplications (such as `rgrb`, in which red appears twice) are allowed. The program will accept a true-or-false input to determine whether or not duplicates are allowed.

Here's an example of what an interaction with the program should look like:

```
? master "roygbiv 4 "false

What's your guess?
royg
You have 1 correct-position matches
and 2 incorrect-position matches.

What's your guess?
rogy
You have 1 correct-position matches
and 2 incorrect-position matches.

What's your guess?
orygbv
You must guess exactly 4 colors.

What's your guess?
oryx
The available colors are: roygbiv

What's your guess?
oryr
No fair guessing the same color twice!

What's your guess?
oryg
You have 0 correct-position matches
and 3 incorrect-position matches.

What's your guess?
rbyg
You have 1 correct-position matches
and 2 incorrect-position matches.

What's your guess?
boyg
You have 0 correct-position matches
and 3 incorrect-position matches.

What's your guess?
roby
You have 1 correct-position matches
and 3 incorrect-position matches.
```

```
What's your guess?
rybo
You have 2 correct-position matches
and 2 incorrect-position matches.

What's your guess?
ryob
You win in 8 guesses!
?
```

If you prefer, just jump in and start writing the program. But I have a particular design in mind, and you may find it easier to follow my plan. The core of my program is written sequentially, in the form of a `for` instruction that carries out a sequence of steps once for each guess the user makes. But most of the "smarts" of the program are in a collection of subprocedures that use functional programming style. That is, these procedures are operations, not commands; they merely compute and output a value without taking any actions. Pay attention to how these two styles fit together. In writing the operations, don't use `make` or `print`; each operation will consist of a single `output` instruction.

☞ The first task is for the computer to make a random selection from the available colors. Write two versions: `choose.dup` that allows the same color to be chosen more than once, and `choose.nodup` that does not allow duplication. Each of these operations should take two inputs: a number, indicating how many colors to choose, and a word of all the available colors. For example, to choose four colors from the rainbow without duplication, you'd say

```
? print choose.nodup 4 "roygbiv
briy
```

You'll find the Logo primitive `pick` helpful. It takes a word or list as its input, and returns a randomly chosen member:

```
? print pick [Pete John Roger Keith]
John
? print pick [Pete John Roger Keith]
Keith
? print pick "roygbiv
b
```

Writing choose.dup is a straightforward combination of pick and cascade.

Choose.nodup is a little harder. Since we want to eliminate any color we choose from further consideration, it's plausible to use a multi-input cascade sort of like this:

```
(cascade :number-wanted
         [add one color] "
         [remove that color] :colors)
```

If we always wanted to choose the first available color, this would be just like the reverse example earlier. But we want to choose a color randomly each time. One solution is to *rotate* the available colors by some random amount, then choose what is now the first color. To use that idea you'll need a rotate operation that rotates a word some random number of times, like this:

```
? rotate "roygbiv
ygbivro
? rotate "roygbiv
vroygbi
? rotate "roygbiv
bivroyg
```

You can write rotate using cascade along with the Logo primitive operation random. Random takes a positive integer as its input, and outputs a nonnegative integer less than its input. For example, random 3 will output 0, 1, or 2.

☞ The second task is to evaluate the player's guess. You'll need an operation called exact that takes two words as inputs (you may assume they are the same length) and outputs the number of correct-position matches, and another operation called inexact that computes the number of wrong-position matches. (You may find it easier to write a helper procedure anymatch that takes two words as inputs, but outputs the total number of matches, regardless of position.) Be sure to write these so that they work even with the duplicates-allowed rule in effect. For example, if the secret word is rgrb and the user guesses yrrr, then you must report one exact and one inexact match, not one exact and two inexact.

```
? print exact "rgrb "yrrr
1
? print inexact "rgrb "yrrr
1
? print inexact "royg "rgbo
2
```

Exact is a straightforward application of multi-input map, since you want to look at each letter of the secret word along with the same-position letter of the user's guess. My solution to anymatch was to use map to consider each of the available colors. For each color, the number of matches is the smaller of the number of times it appears in the secret word and the number of times it appears in the guess. (You'll need a helper procedure howmany that takes two inputs, a letter and a word, and outputs the number of times that letter occurs in that word.)

☞ Up to this point, we've assumed that the player is making legitimate guesses. A valid guess has the right number of colors, chosen from the set of available colors, and (perhaps, depending on the chosen rules) with no color duplicated. Write a predicate valid.guessp that takes a guess as its input and returns true if the guess is valid, false otherwise. In this procedure, for the first time in this project, it's a good idea to violate functional programming style by printing an appropriate error message when the output will be false.

☞ We now have all the tools needed to write the top-level game procedure master. This procedure will take three inputs: a word of the available colors, the number of colors in the secret word, and a true or false to indicate whether or not duplicate colors are allowed. After using either choose.dup or choose.nodup to pick the secret word, I used a for loop to carry out the necessary instructions for each guess.

6 Example: Tic-Tac-Toe

Program file for this chapter: `ttt`

This chapter is the first application of the ideas we've explored to a sizable project. The primary purpose of the chapter is to introduce the techniques of *planning* a project, especially the choice of how to organize the information needed by the program. This organization is called the *data structure* of the program. Along the way, we'll also see a new data type, the array, and a few other details of Logo programming.

The Project

Tic-tac-toe is not a very challenging game for human beings. If you're an enthusiast, you've probably moved from the basic game to some variant like three-dimensional tic-tac-toe on a larger grid.

If you sit down right now to play ordinary three-by-three tic-tac-toe with a friend, what will probably happen is that every game will come out a tie. Both you and your friend can probably play perfectly, never making a mistake that would allow your opponent to win.

But can you *describe* how you know where to move each turn? Most of the time, you probably aren't even aware of alternative possibilities; you just look at the board and instantly know where you want to move. That kind of instant knowledge is great for human beings, because it makes you a fast player. But it isn't much help in writing a computer program. For that, you have to know very explicitly what your strategy is.

By the way, although the example of tic-tac-toe strategy is a relatively trivial one, this issue of instant knowledge versus explicit rules is a hot one in modern psychology. Some cognitive scientists, who think that human intelligence works through mechanisms similar to computer programs, maintain that when you know how to do something without knowing *how* you know, you have an explicit set of rules deep down inside. It's just that the rules have become a habit, so you don't think about them deliberately.

They're "compiled," in the jargon of cognitive psychology. On the other hand, some people think that your implicit how-to knowledge is very different from the sort of lists of rules that can be captured in a computer program. They think that human thought is profoundly different from the way computers work, and that a computer cannot be programmed to simulate the full power of human problem-solving. These people would say, for example, that when you look at a tic-tac-toe board you immediately grasp the strategic situation as a whole, and your eye is drawn to the best move without any need to examine alternatives according to a set of rules. (You might like to try to be aware of your own mental processes as you play a game of tic-tac-toe, to try to decide which of these points of view more closely resembles your own experience—but on the other hand, the psychological validity of such introspective evidence is *another* hotly contested issue in psychology!)

☞ Before you read further, try to write down a set of strategy rules that, if followed consistently, will never lose a game. Play a few games using your rules. Make sure they work even if the other player does something bizarre.

I'm going to number the squares in the tic-tac-toe board this way:

1	2	3
4	5	6
7	8	9

Squares 1, 3, 7, and 9 are *corner squares.* I'll call 2, 4, 6, and 8 *edge squares.* And of course number 5 is the *center square.* I'll use the word *position* to mean a specific partly-filled-in board with X and O in certain squares, and other squares empty.

One way you might meet my challenge of describing your strategy explicitly is to list all the possible sequences of moves up to a certain point in the game, then say what move you'd make next in each situation. How big would the list have to be? There are nine possibilities for the first move. For each first move, there are eight possibilities for the second move. If you continue this line of reasoning, you'll see that there are nine factorial, or 362880, possible sequences of moves. Your computer may not have enough memory to list them all, and you certainly don't have enough patience!

Fortunately, not all these sequences are interesting. Suppose you are describing the rules a computer should use against a human player, and suppose the human being moves first. Then there are, indeed, nine possible first moves. But for each of these, there is only *one* possible computer move! After all, we're programming the computer. We get to decide which move it will choose. Then there are seven possible responses by the opponent, and so on. The number of sequences when the human being plays first is 9 times 7 times 5 times 3, or 945. If the computer plays first, it will presumably always make the single best choice. Then there are eight possible responses, and so on. In this case the number of possible game sequences is 8 times 6 times 4 times 2, or 384. Altogether we have 1329 cases to worry about, which is much better than 300,000 but still not an enjoyable way to write a computer program.

In fact, though, this number is still too big. Not all games go for a full nine moves before someone wins. Also, many moves force the opponent to a single possible response, even though there are other vacant squares on the board. Another reduction can be achieved by taking advantage of *symmetry.* For example, if X starts in square 5, any game sequence in which O responds in square 1 is equivalent to a sequence in which O responds in square 3, with the board rotated 90 degrees. In fact there are only two truly different responses to a center-square opening: any corner square, or any edge square.

With all of these factors reducing the number of distinct positions, it would probably be possible to list all of them and write a strategy program that way. I'm not sure, though, because I didn't want to use that technique. I was looking for rules expressed in more general terms, like "all else being equal, pick a corner rather than an edge."

Why should I prefer a corner? Each corner square is part of three winning combinations. For example, square 1 is part of `123`, `147`, and `159`. (By expressing these winning combinations as three-digit numbers, I've jumped ahead a bit in the story with a preview of how the program I wrote represents this information.) An edge square, on the other hand, is only part of two winning combinations. For example, square 2 is part of `123` and `258`. Taking a corner square makes three winning combinations available to me and unavailable to my opponent.

Since I've brought up the subject of winning combinations, how many of *them* are there? Not very many: three horizontal, three vertical, and two diagonal. Eight altogether. That *is* a reasonable amount of information to include in a program, and in fact there is a list of the eight winning combinations in this project.

You might, at this point, enjoy playing a few games with the program, to see if you can figure out the rules it uses in its strategy. If you accepted my earlier challenge to write down your own set of strategy rules, you can compare mine to yours. Are they the same? If not, are they equally good?

The top-level procedure in this project is called `ttt`. It takes no inputs. When you invoke this procedure, it will ask you if you'd like to play first (X) or second (O). Then you enter moves by typing a digit 1–9 for the square you select. The program draws the game board on the Logo graphics screen.

I'm about to start explaining my strategy rules, so stop reading if you want to work out your own and haven't done it yet.

Strategy

The highest-priority and the lowest-priority rules seemed obvious to me right away. The highest-priority are these:

1. If I can win on this move, do it.

2. If the other player can win on the next move, block that winning square.

Here are the lowest-priority rules, used only if there is nothing suggested more strongly by the board position:

$n-2$. Take the center square if it's free.

$n-1$. Take a corner square if one is free.

n. Take whatever is available.

The highest priority rules are the ones dealing with the most urgent situations: either I or my opponent can win on the next move. The lowest priority ones deal with the least urgent situations, in which there is nothing special about the moves already made to guide me.

What was harder was to find the rules in between. I knew that the goal of my own tic-tac-toe strategy was to set up a *fork*, a board position in which I have two winning moves, so my opponent can only block one of them. Here is an example:

```
 x | o |
---+---+---
   | x |
---+---+---
 x |   | o
```

X can win by playing in square 3 or square 4. It's O's turn, but poor O can only block one of those squares at a time. Whichever O picks, X will then win by picking the other one.

Given this concept of forking, I decided to use it as the next highest priority rule:

3. If I can make a move that will set up a fork for myself, do it.

That was the end of the easy part. My first attempt at writing the program used only these six rules. Unfortunately, it lost in many different situations. I needed to add something, but I had trouble finding a good rule to add.

My first idea was that rule 4 should be the defensive equivalent of rule 3, just as rule 2 is the defensive equivalent of rule 1:

4a. If, on the next move, my opponent can set up a fork, block that possibility by moving into the square that is common to his two winning combinations.

In other words, apply the same search technique to the opponent's position that I applied to my own.

This strategy works well in many cases, but not all. For example, here is a sequence of moves under this strategy, with the human player moving first:

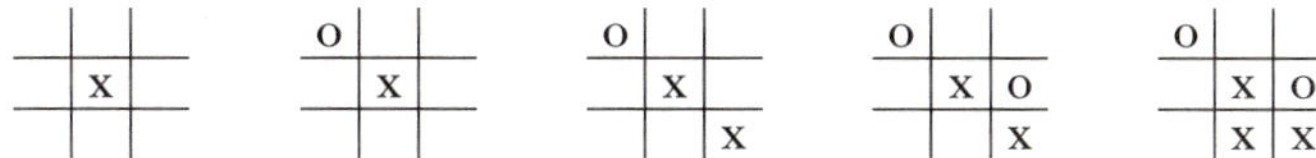

In the fourth grid, the computer (playing O) has discovered that X can set up a fork by moving in square 6, between the winning combinations `456` and `369`. The computer moves to block this fork. Unfortunately, X can also set up a fork by moving in squares 3, 7, or 8. The computer's move in square 6 has blocked one combination of the square-3 fork, but X can still set up the other two. In the fifth grid, X has moved in square 8. This sets up the winning combinations `258` and `789`. The computer can only block one of these, and X will win on the next move.

Since X has so many forks available, does this mean that the game was already hopeless before O moved in square 6? No. Here is something O could have done:

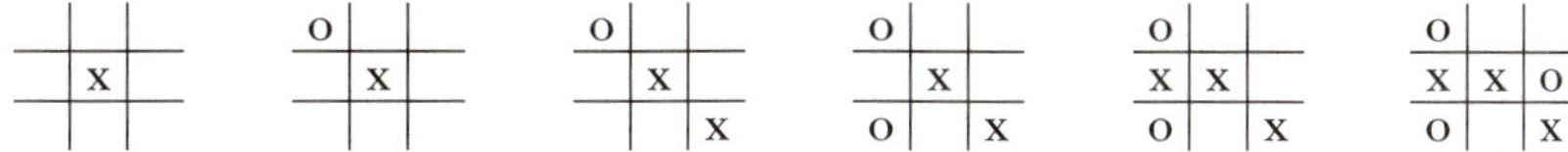

In this sequence, the computer's second move is in square 7. This move also blocks a fork, but it wasn't chosen for that reason. Instead, it was chosen *to force X's next move.* In the fifth grid, X has had to move in square 4, to prevent an immediate win by O. The advantage of this situation for O is that square 4 was *not* one of the ones with which X could set up a fork. O's next move, in the sixth grid, is also forced. But by then the board is too crowded for either player to force a win; the game ends in a tie, as usual.

This analysis suggests a different choice for an intermediate-level strategy rule, taking the offensive:

4b. If I can make a move that will set up a winning combination for myself, do it.

Compared to my earlier try, this rule has the benefit of simplicity. It's much easier for the program to look for a single winning combination than for a fork, which is two such combinations with a common square.

Unfortunately, this simple rule isn't quite good enough. In the example just above, the computer found the winning combination `147` in which it already had square 1, and the other two were free. But why should it choose to move in square 7 rather than square 4? If the program did choose square 4, then X's move would still be forced, into square 7.

We would then have forced X into creating a fork, which would defeat the program on the next move.

It seems that there is no choice but to combine the ideas from rules 4a and 4b:

4. If I can make a move that will set up a winning combination for myself, do it. But ensure that this move does not force the opponent into establishing a fork.

What this means is that we are looking for a winning combination in which the computer already owns one square and the other two are empty. Having found such a combination, we can move in either of its empty squares. Whichever we choose, the opponent will be forced to choose the other one on the next move. If one of the two empty squares would create a fork for the opponent, then the computer must choose that square and leave the other for the opponent.

What if *both* of the empty squares in the combination we find would make forks for the opponent? In that case, we've chosen a bad winning combination. It turns out that there is only one situation in which this can happen:

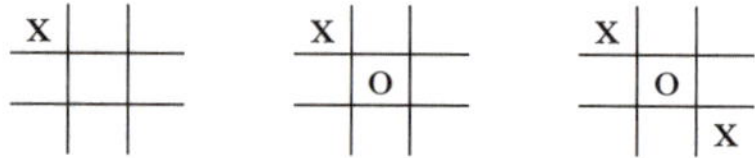

Again, the computer is playing O. After the third grid, it is looking for a possible winning combination for itself. There are three possibilities: `258`, `357`, and `456`. So far we have not given the computer any reason to prefer one over another. But here is what happens if the program happens to choose `357`:

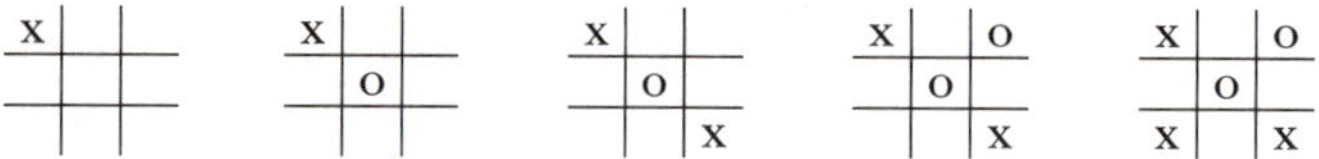

By this choice, the computer has forced its opponent into a fork that will win the game for the opponent. If the computer chooses either of the other two possible winning combinations, the game ends in a tie. (All moves after this choice turn out to be forced.)

This particular game sequence was very troublesome for me because it goes against most of the rules I had chosen earlier. For one thing, the correct choice for the program is any edge square, while the corner squares must be avoided. This is the opposite of the usual priority.

Another point is that this situation contradicts rule 4a (prevent forks for the other player) even more sharply than the example we considered earlier. In that example, rule 4a wasn't enough guidance to ensure a correct choice, but the correct choice was at least *consistent* with the rule. That is, just blocking a fork isn't enough, but threatening a win and *also* blocking a fork is better than just threatening a win alone. This is the meaning of rule 4. But in this new situation, the corner square (the move we have to avoid) *does* block a fork, while the edge square (the correct move) *doesn't* block a fork!

When I discovered this anomalous case, I was ready to give up on the idea of beautiful, general rules. I almost decided to build into the program a special check for this precise board configuration. That would have been pretty ugly, I think. But a shift in viewpoint makes this case easier to understand: What the program must do is force the other player's move, and force it in a way that helps the computer win. If one possible winning combination doesn't allow us to meet these conditions, the program should try another combination. My mistake was to think either about forcing alone (rule 4b) or about the opponent's forks alone (rule 4a).

As it turns out, the board situation we've been considering is the only one in which a possible winning combination could include two possible forks for the opponent. What's more, in this board situation, it's a diagonal combination that gets us in trouble, while a horizontal or vertical combination is always okay. Therefore, I was able to implement rule 4 in a way that only considers one possible winning combination by setting up the program's data structures so that diagonal combinations are the last to be chosen. This trick makes the program's design less than obvious from reading the actual program, but it does save the program some effort.

Program Structure and Modularity

Most game programs—in fact, most interactive programs of any kind—consist of an initialization section followed by a sequence of steps carried out repeatedly. In the case of the tic-tac-toe game, the overall program structure will be something like this:

```
to ttt
initialize
forever [
   if game.is.over [stop]
   record.human.move get.human.move
   if game.is.over [stop]
   record.program.move compute.program.move
]
end
```

The parts of this structure shown in `italics` are just vague ideas. At this point in the planning, I don't know what inputs these procedures might need, for example. In fact, there may not be procedures exactly like this in the final program. One example is that the test that I've called *game.is.over* here will actually turn out to be two separate tests `already.wonp` and `tiedp` (using a final letter `p` to indicate a predicate, following the convention established by the Logo primitive predicates).

This half-written procedure introduces a Logo primitive we haven't used before: `forever`. It takes a list of Logo instructions as its input, and carries out those instructions repeatedly, much as `repeat`, `for`, and `foreach` do. But the number of repetitions is unlimited; the repetition stops only if, as in this example, the primitive `stop` or `output` is invoked within the repeated instructions. `Forever` is useful when the ending condition can't be predicted in advance, as in a game situation in which a player might win at any time.

It may not be obvious why I've planned for one procedure to figure out the next move and a separate procedure to record it. (There are two such pairs of procedures, one for the program's moves and the other for the human opponent's moves.) For one thing, I expect that the recording of moves will be much the same whether it's the program or the person moving, while the decision about where to move will be quite different in the two cases. For the program's move we must apply strategy rules; for the human player's moves we simply ask the player. Also, I anticipate that the selection of the program's moves, which will be the hardest part of the program, can be written in functional style. The strategy procedure is a function that takes the current board position as its input, always returning the same chosen square for any given input position.

This project contains 28 procedures. These procedures can be divided into related groups like this:

7 overall orchestration
6 initialization
2 get opponent's moves
9 compute program's moves
4 draw moves on screen

As you might expect, figuring out the computer's strategy is the most complex part of the program's job. But this strategic task is still only about a third of the complete program.

The five groups are quite cleanly distinguishable in this project. There are relatively few procedure invocations between groups, compared to the number within a group. It's easy to read the procedures within a group and understand how they work without having to think about other parts of the program at the same time.

The following diagram shows the subprocedure/superprocedure relationships within the program, and indicates which procedures are in each of the five groups listed above.

Some people find diagrams like this one very helpful in understanding the structure of a program. Other people don't like these diagrams at all. If you find it helpful, you may want to draw such diagrams for your own projects.

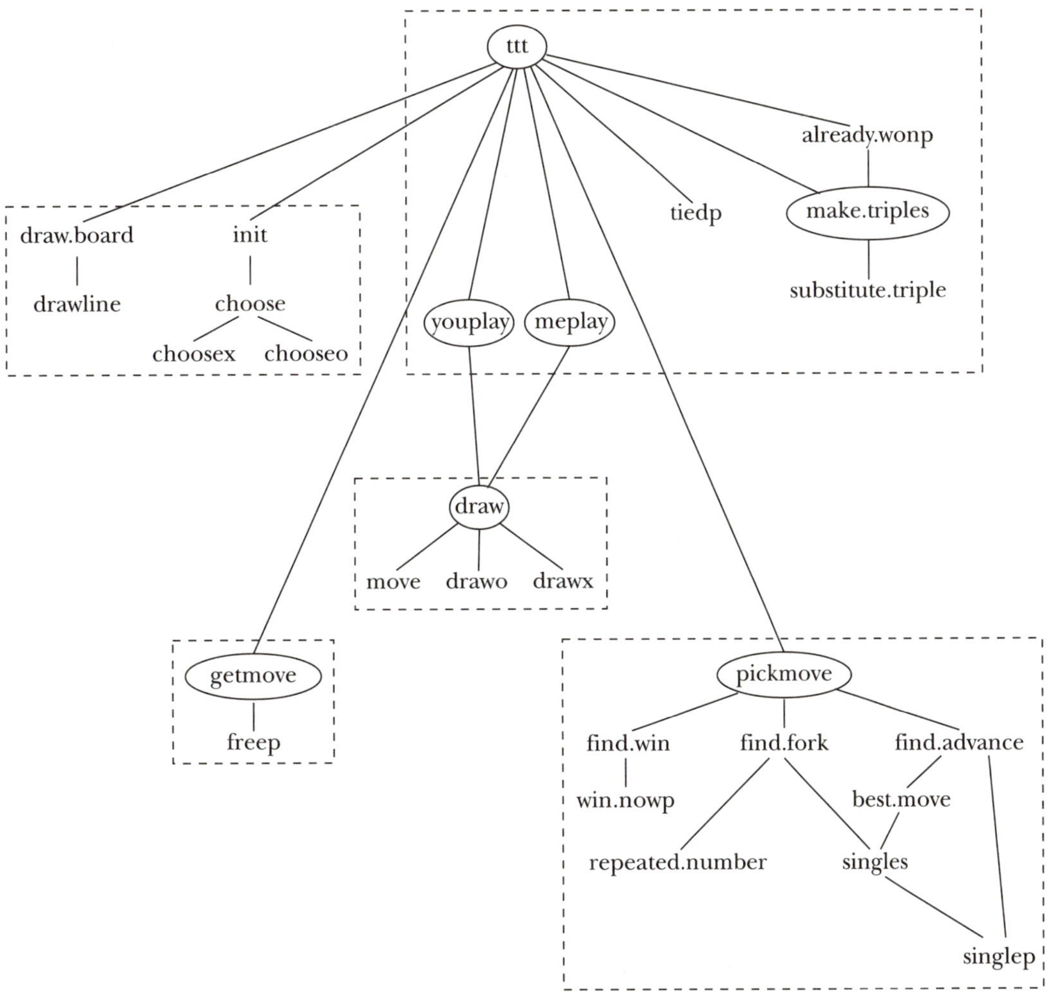

In the diagram, I've circled the names of seven procedures. If you understand the purpose of each of these, then you will understand the general structure of the entire program. (Don't turn to the end and read the actual procedures just now. Instead, see if you can understand the following paragraphs just from the diagram.)

`Ttt` is the top-level procedure for which I gave a rough outline earlier. It calls initialization procedures (`draw.board` and `init`) to set up the game, then repeatedly alternates between the human opponent's moves and the program's moves. It calls `getmove` to find out the next move by the opponent, `youplay` to record that move, then `pickmove` to compute the program's next move and `meplay` to record it.

`Make.triples` translates from one representation of the board position to another. The representation used within `ttt` is best suited for display and for user interaction, while the representation output by `make.triples` is best for computing the program's strategy. We'll look into data representation more closely later.

`Getmove` invites the opponent to type in a move. It ensures that the selected move is legal before accepting it. The output from `getmove` is a number from 1 to 9 representing the chosen square.

`Pickmove` figures out the program's next move. It is the "smartest" procedure in the program, embodying the strategy rules I listed earlier. It, too, outputs a number from 1 to 9.

`Youplay` and `meplay` are simple procedures that actually carry out the moves chosen by the human player and by the program, respectively. Each contains only two instructions. The first invokes `draw` to draw the move on the screen. The second modifies the `position` array to remember that the move has been made.

`Draw` moves the turtle to the chosen square on the tic-tac-toe board. Then it draws either an X or an O. (We haven't really talked about Logo's turtle graphics yet. If you're not familiar with turtle graphics from earlier Logo experience, you can just take this part of the program on faith; there's nothing very interesting about it.)

Notice, in the diagram, that the lines representing procedure calls come into a box only at the top. This is one sign of a well-organized program: The dashed boxes in the diagram truly do represent distinct parts of the program that don't interact very much.

Data Representation

I've written several tic-tac-toe programs, in different programming languages. This experience has really taught me about the importance of picking a good data representation. For my first tic-tac-toe program, several years ago, I decided without much prior thought that a board position should be represented as three lists of numbers, one with X's squares, one with O's squares, and one with the free squares. So this board position

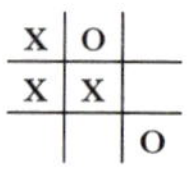

```
 x | o |
---+---+---
 x | x |
---+---+---
   |   | o
```

could be represented like this:

```
make "xsquares [1 4 5]
make "osquares [2 9]
make "free [3 6 7 8]
```

These three variables would change in value as squares moved from `:free` to one of the others. This representation was easy to understand, but not very helpful for writing the program!

What questions does a tic-tac-toe program have to answer about the board position? If, for example, the program wants to print a display of the position, it must answer questions of the form "Who's in square 4?" With the representation shown here, that's not as easy a question as we might wish:

```
to occupant :square                              ;; old program
if memberp :square :xsquares [output "x]
if memberp :square :osquares [output "o]
output "free
end
```

On the other hand, this representation isn't so bad when we're accepting a move from the human player and want to make sure it's a legal move:

```
to freep :square                                 ;; old program
output memberp :square :free
end
```

Along with this representation of the board, my first program used a constant list of winning combinations:

```
make "wins [[1 2 3] [4 5 6] [7 8 9] [1 4 7] [2 5 8]
            [3 6 9] [1 5 9] [3 5 7]]
```

It also had a list of all possible forks. I won't bother trying to reproduce this very long list for you, since it's not used in the current program, but the fork set up by X in the board position just above was represented this way:

```
[4 [1 7] [5 6]]
```

This indicates that square 4 is the pivot of a fork between the winning combinations `[1 4 7]` and `[4 5 6]`. Each member of the complete list of forks was a list like this sample.

The list of forks was fairly long. Each edge square is the pivot of a fork. Each corner square is the pivot of three forks. The center square is the pivot of six forks. This adds up to 22 forks altogether.

Each time the program wanted to choose a move, it would first check all eight possible winning combinations to see if two of the squares were occupied by the program and the third one free. Since any of the three squares might be the free one, this is a fairly tricky program in itself:

```
to checkwin :candidate :mysquares :free      ;; old program
if memberp first :candidate :free ~
   [output check1 butfirst :candidate :mysquares]
if memberp last :candidate :free ~
   [output check1 butlast :candidate :mysquares]
if memberp first butfirst :candidate :free ~
   [output check1 list first :candidate last :candidate :mysquares]
output "false
end

to check1 :sublist :mysquares                ;; old program
output and (memberp first :sublist :mysquares) ~
           (memberp last :sublist :mysquares)
end
```

This procedure was fairly slow, especially when invoked eight times, once for each possible win. But the procedure to check each of the possible forks was even worse!

In the program that I wrote for the first edition of *Computer Science Logo Style,* a very different approach is used. This approach is based on the realization that, at any moment, a particular winning combination may be free for anyone (all three squares free), available only to one player, or not available to anyone. It's silly for the program to go on checking a combination that can't possibly be available. Instead of a single list of wins, the new program has three lists:

`mywins`	wins available to the computer
`yourwins`	wins available to the opponent
`freewins`	wins available to anyone

Once I decided to organize the winning combinations in this form, another advantage became apparent: for each possible winning combination, the program need only remember the squares that are free, not the ones that are occupied. For example, the board position shown above would contain these winning combinations, supposing the computer is playing X:

```
make "mywins [[7] [6] [3 7]]
make "yourwins [[3 6] [7 8]]
make "freewins []
```

The sublist [7] of :mywins indicates that the computer can win simply by filling square 7. This list represents the winning combination that was originally represented as [1 4 7], but since the computer already occupies squares 1 and 4 there is no need to remember those numbers.

The process of checking for an immediate win is streamlined with this representation for two reasons, compared with the checkwin procedure above. First, only those combinations in :mywins must be checked, instead of all eight every time. Second, an immediate win can be recognized very simply, because it is just a list with one member, like [7] and [6] in the example above. The procedure single looks for such a list:

```
to single :list                                ;; old program
output find [equalp (count ?) 1] :list
end
```

The input to single is either :mywins, to find a winning move for the computer (rule 1), or :yourwins, to find and block a winning move for the opponent (rule 2).

Although this representation streamlines the strategy computation (the pickmove part of the program), it makes the recording of a move quite difficult, because combinations must be moved from one list to another. That part of the program was quite intricate and hard to understand.

Arrays

This new program uses *two* representations, one for the interactive part of the program and one for the strategy computation. The first of these is simply a collection of nine words, one per square, each of which is the letter X, the letter O, or the number of the square. With this representation, recording a move means changing one of the nine words. It would be possible to keep the nine words in a list, and compute a new list (only slightly different) after each move. But Logo provides another data type, the *array,* which allows for changing one member while keeping the rest unchanged.

If arrays allow for easy modification and lists don't, why not always use arrays? Why did I begin the book with lists? The answer is that each data type has advantages and disadvantages. The main disadvantage of an array is that you must decide in advance how big it will be; there aren't any constructors like sentence to lengthen an array.

In this case, the fixed length of an array is no problem, because a tic-tac-toe board has nine squares. The `init` procedure creates the position array with the instruction

```
make "position {1 2 3 4 5 6 7 8 9}
```

The braces `{}` indicate an array in the same way that brackets indicate a list.

If player X moves in square 7, we can record that information by saying

```
setitem 7 :position "x
```

(Of course, the actual instruction in procedures `meplay` and `youplay` uses variables instead of the specific values 7 and X.) `Setitem` is a command with three inputs: a number indicating which member of the array to change, the array itself, and the new value for the specified member.

To find out who owns a particular square, we could write this procedure:

```
to occupant :square
output item :square :position
end
```

(The `item` operation can select a member of an array just as it can select a member of a list or of a word.) In fact, though, it turns out that I don't have an `occupant` procedure in this program. But the parts of the program that examine the board position do use `item` in a similar way, as in this example:

```
to freep :square
output numberp item :square :position
end
```

To create an array without explicitly listing all of its members, use the operation `array`. It takes a number as argument, indicating how many members the array should have. It returns an array of the chosen size, in which each member is the empty list. Your program can then use `setitem` to assign different values to the members.

The only primitive operation to select a member of an array is `item`. Word-and-list operations such as `butfirst` can't be used with arrays. There are operations `arraytolist` and `listtoarray` to convert a collection of information from one data type to the other.

Triples

The position array works well as a long-term representation for the board position, because it's easy to update; it also works well for interaction with the human player, because it's easy to find out the status of a particular square. But for computing the program's moves, we need a representation that makes it easy to ask questions such as "Is there a winning combination for my opponent on the next move?" That's why, in the first edition of these books, I used the representation with three lists of possible winning combinations.

When Matthew Wright and I wrote the book *Simply Scheme,* we decided that the general idea of combinations was a good one, but the three lists made the program more complicated than necessary. Since there are only eight possible winning combinations in the first place, it's not so slow to keep one list of all of them, and use that list as the basis for all the questions we ask in working out the program's strategy. If the current board position is

x	o	
x	x	
		o

we represent the three horizontal winning combinations with the words `xo3`, `xx6`, and `78o`. Each combination is represented as a three-"letter" word containing an `x` or an `o` for an occupied square, or the square's number for a free square. By using words instead of lists for the combinations, we make the entire set of combinations more compact and easier to read. Each of these words is called a *triple.* The job of procedure `make.triples` is to combine the information in the position array with a list of the eight winning combinations:

```
? show make.triples
[xo3 xx6 78o xx7 ox8 36o xxo 3x7]
```

`Make.triples` takes no inputs because the list of possible winning combinations is built into it, and the position array is in `ttt`'s local variable `position`:

```
to make.triples
output map "substitute.triple [123 456 789 147 258 369 159 357]
end

to substitute.triple :combination
output map [item ? :position] :combination
end
```

This short subprogram will repay careful attention. It uses `map` twice, once in `make.triples` to compute a function of each possible winning combination, and once in `substitute.triple` to compute a function of each square in a given combination. (That latter function is the one that looks up the square in the array `:position`.)

Once the program can make the list of triples, we can use that to answer many questions about the status of the game. For example, in the top-level `ttt` procedure we must check on each move whether or not a certain player has already won the game. Here's how:

```
to already.wonp :player
output memberp (word :player :player :player) (make.triples)
end
```

If we had only the `position` array to work with, it would be complicated to check all the possible winning combinations. But once we've made the list of triples, we can just ask whether the word `xxx` or the word `ooo` appears in that list.

Here is the actual top-level procedure definition:

```
to ttt
local [me you position]
draw.board
init
if equalp :me "x [meplay 5]
forever [
  if already.wonp :me [print [I win!] stop]
  if tiedp [print [Tie game!] stop]
  youplay getmove                         ;; ask person for move
  if already.wonp :you [print [You win!] stop]
  if tiedp [print [Tie game!] stop]
  meplay pickmove make.triples            ;; compute program's move
]
end
```

Notice that `position` is declared as a local variable. Because of Logo's dynamic scope, all of the subprocedures in this project can use `position` as if it were a global variable, but Logo will "clean up" after the game is over.

Two more such quasi-global variables are used to remember whether the computer or the human opponent plays first. The value of `me` will be either the word `x` or the word `o`, whichever letter the program itself is playing. Similarly, the value of `you` will be `x` or `o` to indicate the letter used by the opponent. All of these variables are given their values by the initialization procedure `init`.

This information could have been kept in the form of a single *flag variable,* called something like `mefirst`, that would contain the word `true` if the computer is X, or `false` if the computer is O. (A flag variable is one whose value is always `true` or `false`, just as a predicate is a procedure whose output is `true` or `false`.) It would be used something like this:

```
if :mefirst [draw "x :square] [draw "o :square]
```

But it turned out to be simpler to use two variables and just say

```
draw :me :square
```

One detail in the final program that wasn't in my first rough draft is the instruction

```
if equalp :me "x [meplay 5]
```

just before the `forever` loop. It was easier to write the loop so that it always gets the human opponent's move first, and then computes a move for the program, rather than having two different loops depending on which player goes first. If the program moves first, its strategy rules would tell it to choose the center square, because there is nothing better to do when the board is empty. By checking for that case before the loop, we are ready to begin the loop with the opponent as the next to move.

Variables in the Workspace

There are nine global variables that are part of the workspace, entered directly with top-level `make` instructions rather than set up by `init`, because their values are never changed. Their names are `box1` through `box9`, and their values are the coordinates on the graphics screen of the center of each square. For example, `:box1` is `[-40 50]`. These variables are used by `move`, a subprocedure of `draw`, to know where to position the turtle before drawing an X or an O.

The use of variables loaded with a workspace file, rather than given values by an initialization procedure, is a practice that Logo encourages in some ways and discourages in others. Loading variables in a workspace file makes the program start up faster, because it decreases the amount of initialization required. On the other hand, variables are sort of second-class citizens in workspace files. In many versions of Logo the `load` command lists the names of the procedures in the workspace file, but not the names of the variables. Similarly, `save` often reports the number of procedures saved, but not the number of variables. It's easy to create global variables and forget that they're there.

Certainly preloading variables makes sense only if the variables are really constants; in other words, a variable whose value may change during the running of a program should be initialized explicitly when the program starts. Otherwise, the program will probably give incorrect results if you run it a second time. (One of the good ideas in the programming language Pascal is that there is a sort of thing in the language called a *constant*; it has a name and a value, like a variable, but you can't give it a new value in mid-program. In Logo, you use a global variable to hold a constant, and simply refrain from changing its value. But being able to *say* that something is a constant makes the program easier to understand.)

One reason the use of preloaded variables is sometimes questioned as a point of style is that when people are sloppy in their use of global variables, it's hard to know which are really meant to be preloaded and which are just left over from running the program. That is, if you write a program, test it by running it, and then save it on a diskette, any global variables that were created during the program execution will still be in the workspace when you load that diskette file later. If there are five intentionally-loaded variables along with 20 leftovers, it's particularly hard for someone to understand which are which. This is one more reason not to use global variables when what you really want are variables local to the top-level procedure.

The User Interface

The only part of the program that really interacts with the human user is `getmove`, the procedure that asks the user where to move.

```
to getmove
local "square
forever [
  type [Your move:]
  make "square readchar
  print :square
  if numberp :square
     [if and (:square > 0) (:square < 10)
         [if freep :square [output :square]]]
  print [not a valid move.]
]
end
```

There are two noteworthy things about this part of the program. One is that I've chosen to use `readchar` to read what the player types. This primitive operation, with no inputs, waits for the user to type any single character on the keyboard, and outputs whatever character the user types. This "character at a time" interaction is in contrast with the more usual "line at a time" typing, in which you can type characters, erase some if you make a mistake, and finally use the RETURN or ENTER key to indicate that the entire line you've typed should be made available to your program. (In Chapter 1 you met Logo's `readlist` primitive for line at a time typing.) Notice that if tic-tac-toe had ten or more squares in its board I wouldn't have been able to make this choice, because the program would have to allow the entry of two-digit numbers.

`Readchar` was meant for fast-action programs such as video games. It therefore does not display (or *echo*) the character that you type on the computer screen. That's why `getmove` includes a `print` instruction to let the user see what she or he has typed!

The second point to note in `getmove` is how careful it is to allow for the possibility of a user error. Ordinarily, when one procedure uses a value that was computed by another procedure, the programmer can assume that the value is a legitimate one for the intended purpose. For example, when you invoke a procedure that computes a number, you assume that you can add the output to another number; you don't first use the `number?` predicate to double-check that the result was indeed a number. But in `getmove` we are dealing with a value that was typed by a human being, and human beings are notoriously error-prone! The user is *supposed* to type a number between 1 and 9. But perhaps someone's finger might slip and type a zero instead of a nine, or even some character that isn't a number at all. Therefore, `getmove` first checks that what the user typed is a number. If so, it then checks that the number is in the allowed range. (We'd get a Logo error message if `getmove` used the < operation with a non-numeric input.) Only if these conditions are met do we use the user's number as the square-selecting input to `freep`.

Implementing the Strategy Rules

To determine the program's next move, `ttt` invokes `pickmove`; since many of the strategy rules will involve an examination of possible winning combinations, `pickmove` is given the output from `make.triples` as its input.

The strategy I worked out for the program consists of several rules, in order of importance. So the structure of `pickmove` should be something like this:

```
to pickmove :triples
if first.rule.works [output first.rule's.square]
if second.rule.works [output second.rule's.square]
...
end
```

This structure would work, but it would be very inefficient, because the procedure to determine whether a rule is applicable does essentially the same work as the procedure to choose a square by following the rule. For example, here's a procedure to decide whether or not the program can win on this move:

```
to can.i.win.now
output not emptyp find "win.nowp :triples
end

to win.nowp :triple
output equalp (filter [not numberp ?] :triple) (word :me :me)
end
```

The subprocedure `win.nowp` decides whether or not a particular triple is winnable on this move, by looking for a triple containing one number and two letters equal to whichever of X or O the program is playing. For example, `3xx` is a winnable triple if the program is playing X.

The procedure to pick a move if there is a winnable triple also must apply `win.nowp` to the triples:

```
to find.winning.square
output filter "numberp find "win.nowp :triples
end
```

If there is a winnable triple `3xx`, then the program should move in square 3. We find that out by looking for the number within the first winnable triple we can find.

It seems inelegant to find a winnable triple just to see if there are any, then find the same triple again to extract a number from it. Instead, we take advantage of the fact that the procedure I've called `find.winning.square` will return a distinguishable value—namely, an empty list—if there is no winnable triple. We say

```
to pickmove :triples
local "try
make "try find.winning.square
if not emptyp :try [output :try]
...
end
```

In fact, instead of the procedure `find.winning.square` the actual program uses a similar `find.win` procedure that takes the letter X or O as an input; this allows the same procedure to check both rule 1 (can the computer win on this move) and rule 2 (can the opponent win on the following move).

`Pickmove` checks each of the strategy rules with a similar pair of instructions:

```
make "try something
if not emptyp :try [output :try]
```

Here is the complete procedure:

```
to pickmove :triples
local "try
make "try find.win :me                    ; rule 1: can computer win?
if not emptyp :try [output :try]
make "try find.win :you                   ; rule 2: can opponent win?
if not emptyp :try [output :try]
make "try find.fork                       ; rule 3: can computer fork?
if not emptyp :try [output :try]
make "try find.advance                    ; rule 4: can computer force?
if not emptyp :try [output :try]
output find [memberp ? :position] [5 1 3 7 9 2 4 6 8]   ; rules 5-7
end
```

The procedures that check for each rule have a common flavor: They all use `filter` and `find` to select interesting triples and then to select an available square from the chosen triple. I won't go through them in complete detail, but there's one that uses a Logo feature I haven't described before. Here is `find.fork`:

```
to find.fork
local "singles
make "singles singles :me                      ; find triples like 14x, x23
if emptyp :singles [output []]
output repeated.number reduce "word :singles ; find square in two triples
end
```

Suppose the computer is playing X and the board looks like this:

x	o	
	x	
		o

`Find.fork` calls `singles` (a straightforward procedure that you can read in the complete listing at the end of this chapter) to find all the triples containing one X and two vacant squares. It outputs

```
[4x6 x47 3x7]
```

indicating that the middle row, the left column, and one of the diagonals meet these conditions. To find a fork, we must find a vacant square that is included in two of these triples. The expression

```
reduce "word :singles
```

strings these triples together into the word `4x6x473x7`. The job of `repeated.number` is to find a digit that occurs more than once in this word. Here is the procedure:

```
to repeated.number :squares
output find [memberp ? ?rest] filter "numberp :squares
end
```

The expression

```
filter "numberp :squares
```

gives us the word `464737`, which is the input word with the letters removed. We use `find` to find a repeated digit in this number. The new feature is the use of `?rest` in the predicate template

```
[memberp ? ?rest]
```

`?rest` represents the part of the input to `find` (or any of the other higher-order functions that understand templates) to the right of the value being used as `?`. So in this example, `find` first computes the value of the expression

```
memberp 4 64737
```

This happens to be `true`, so `find` returns the value 4 without looking at the remaining digits. But if necessary, `find` would have gone on to compute

```
memberp 6 4737
memberp 4 737
memberp 7 37
memberp 3 7
memberp 7 "
```

(using the empty word as `?rest` in the last line) until one of these turned out to be true.

Further Explorations

The obvious first place to look for improvements to this project is in the strategy.

At the beginning of the discussion about strategy, I suggested that one possibility would be to make a complete list of all possible move sequences, with explicit next-move choices recorded for each. How many such sequences are there? If you write the program in a way that considers rotations of the board as equivalent, perhaps not very many. For example, if the computer moves first (in the center, of course) there are really only two responses the opponent can make: a corner or an edge. Any corner is equivalent to any other. From that point on, the entire sequence of the game can be forced by the computer, to a tie if the opponent played a corner, or to a win if the opponent played an edge. If the opponent moves first, there are three cases, center, corner, or edge. And so on.

An intermediate possibility between the complete list of cases and the more general rules I used would be to keep a complete list of cases for, say, the first two moves. After that, general rules could be used for the "endgame." This is rather like the way people, and some computer programs, play chess: they have the openings memorized, and don't really have to start thinking until several moves have passed. This book-opening approach is particularly appealing to me because it would solve the problem of the anomalous sequence that made such trouble for me in rule 4.

A completely different approach would be to have no rules at all, but instead to write a *learning* program. The program might recognize an immediate win (rule 1) and the threat of an immediate loss (rule 2), but otherwise it would move randomly and record the results. If the computer loses a game, it would remember the last unforced choice it made in that game, and keep a record to try something else in the same situation next time. The result, after many games, would be a complete list of all possible sequences, as I suggested first, but the difference is that you wouldn't have to do the figuring out of each sequence. Such learning programs are frequently used in the field of artificial intelligence.

It is possible to combine different approaches. A famous checkers-playing program written by Arthur Samuel had several general rules programmed in, like the ones in this tic-tac-toe program. But instead of having the rules arranged in a particular priority sequence, the program was able to learn how much weight to give each rule, by seeing which rules tended to win the game and which tended to lose.

If you're tired of tic-tac-toe, another possibility would be to write a program that plays some other game according to a strategy. Don't start with checkers or chess! Many people have written programs in which the computer acts as dealer for a game of Blackjack; you could reverse the roles so that you deal the cards, and the computer tries to bet with a winning strategy. Another source of ideas is Martin Gardner, author of many books of mathematical games.

Program Listing

```
;; Overall orchestration

to ttt
local [me you position]
draw.board
init
if equalp :me "x [meplay 5]
forever [
  if already.wonp :me [print [I win!] stop]
  if tiedp [print [Tie game!] stop]
  youplay getmove                          ;; ask person for move
  if already.wonp :you [print [You win!] stop]
  if tiedp [print [Tie game!] stop]
  meplay pickmove make.triples             ;; compute program's move
]
end

to make.triples
output map "substitute.triple [123 456 789 147 258 369 159 357]
end

to substitute.triple :combination
output map [item ? :position] :combination
end
```

```
to already.wonp :player
output memberp (word :player :player :player) (make.triples)
end

to tiedp
output not reduce "or map.se "numberp arraytolist :position
end

to youplay :square
draw :you :square
setitem :square :position :you
end

to meplay :square
draw :me :square
setitem :square :position :me
end

;; Initialization

to draw.board
splitscreen clearscreen hideturtle
drawline [-20 -50] 0 120
drawline [20 -50] 0 120
drawline [-60 -10] 90 120
drawline [-60 30] 90 120
end

to drawline :pos :head :len
penup
setpos :pos
setheading :head
pendown
forward :len
end

to init
make "position {1 2 3 4 5 6 7 8 9}
print [Do you want to play first (X)]
type [or second (O)? Type X or O:]
choose
print [For each move, type a digit 1-9.]
end
```

```
to choose
local "side
forever [
  make "side readchar
  pr :side
  if equalp :side "x [choosex stop]
  if equalp :side "o [chooseo stop]
  type [Huh? Type X or O:]
]
end

to chooseo
make "me "x
make "you "o
end

to choosex
make "me "o
make "you "x
end

;; Get opponent's moves

to getmove
local "square
forever [
  type [Your move:]
  make "square readchar
  print :square
  if numberp :square [
     [if and (:square > 0) (:square < 10)
         [if freep :square [output :square]]]
  print [not a valid move.]
]
end

to freep :square
output numberp item :square :position
end
```

```
;; Compute program's moves

to pickmove :triples
local "try
make "try find.win :me
if not emptyp :try [output :try]
make "try find.win :you
if not emptyp :try [output :try]
make "try find.fork
if not emptyp :try [output :try]
make "try find.advance
if not emptyp :try [output :try]
output find [memberp ? :position] [5 1 3 7 9 2 4 6 8]
end

to find.win :who
output filter "numberp find "win.nowp :triples
end

to win.nowp :triple
output equalp (filter [not numberp ?] :triple) (word :who :who)
end

to find.fork
local "singles
make "singles singles :me
if emptyp :singles [output []]
output repeated.number reduce "word :singles
end

to singles :who
output filter [singlep ? :who] :triples
end

to singlep :triple :who
output equalp (filter [not numberp ?] :triple) :who
end

to repeated.number :squares
output find [memberp ? ?rest] filter "numberp :squares
end

to find.advance
output best.move filter "numberp find [singlep ? :me] :triples
end
```

```
to best.move :my.single
local "your.singles
if emptyp :my.single [output []]
make "your.singles singles :you
if emptyp :your.singles [output first :my.single]
ifelse (count filter [? = first :my.single]
                     reduce "word :your.singles) > 1 ~
       [output first :my.single] ~
       [output last :my.single]
end

;; Drawing moves on screen

to draw :who :square
move :square
ifelse :who = "x [drawx] [drawo]
end

to move :square
penup
setpos thing word "box :square
end

to drawo
pendown
arc 360 18
end

to drawx
setheading 45
pendown
repeat 4 [forward 25.5 back 25.5 right 90]
end

make "box1 [-40 50]
make "box2 [0 50]
make "box3 [40 50]
make "box4 [-40 10]
make "box5 [0 10]
make "box6 [40 10]
make "box7 [-40 -30]
make "box8 [0 -30]
make "box9 [40 -30]
```

We could keep this up for longer and longer input words, but each procedure gets more and more complicated. Here's downup3:

```
to downup3 :word
print :word
print butlast :word
print butlast butlast :word
print butlast :word
print :word
end
```

☞ How many print instructions would I need to write downup4 this way? How many would I need for downup20?

Luckily there's an easier way. Look at the result of invoking downup3:

```
? downup3 "dot
dot
do
d
do
dot
```

The trick is to recognize that the boxed lines are what we'd get by invoking downup2 with the word do as input. So we can find the instructions in downup3 that print those three lines and replace them with one instruction that calls downup2:

```
to downup3 :word
print :word
downup2 butlast :word
print :word
end
```

You might have to think a moment to work out where the butlast came from, but consider that we're given the word dot and we want the word do.

Once we've had this idea, it's easy to extend it to longer words:

```
to downup4 :word
print :word
downup3 butlast :word
print :word
end
```

```
to downup5 :word
print :word
downup4 butlast :word
print :word
end
```

☞ Can you rewrite downup2 so that it looks like these others?

☞ Before going on, make sure you really understand these procedures by answering these questions: What happens if you use one of these numbered versions of downup with an input that is too long? What if the input is too short?

Generalizing the Pattern

We're now in good shape as long as we want to downup short words. We can pick the right version of downup for the length of the word we have in mind:

```
? downup5 "hello
hello
hell
hel
he
h
he
hel
hell
hello
? downup7 "goodbye
goodbye
goodby
goodb
good
goo
go
g
go
goo
good
goodb
goodby
goodbye
```

Having to count the number of characters in the word is a little unaesthetic, but we could even have the computer do that for us:

```
to downup :word
if equalp count :word 1 [downup1 :word]
if equalp count :word 2 [downup2 :word]
if equalp count :word 3 [downup3 :word]
if equalp count :word 4 [downup4 :word]
if equalp count :word 5 [downup5 :word]
if equalp count :word 6 [downup6 :word]
if equalp count :word 7 [downup7 :word]
end
```

There's only one problem. What if we want to be able to say

```
downup "antidisestablishmentarianism
```

You wouldn't want to have to type in separate versions of `downup` all the way up to `downup28`!

What I hope you're tempted to do is to take advantage of the similarity of all the numbered `downup` procedures by combining them into a single procedure that looks like this:

```
to downup :word
print :word
downup butlast :word
print :word
end
```

(Remember that Logo's `to` command won't let you redefine `downup` if you've already typed in my earlier version with all the `if` instruction lines. Before you can type in the new version, you have to `erase` the old one.)

Compare this version of `downup` with one of the numbered procedures like `downup5`. Do you see that this combined version should work just as well, if all the numbered `downup` procedures are identical except for the numbers in the procedure names? Convince yourself that that makes sense.

☞ Okay, now try it.

What Went Wrong?

You probably saw something like this:

```
? downup "hello
hello
hell
hel
he
h

butlast doesn't like  as input in downup
```

There's nothing wrong with the reasoning I used in the last section. If all the numbered downup procedures are identical except for the numbers, it should work to replace them all with a single procedure following the same pattern.

The trouble is that the numbered downup procedures *aren't* quite all identical. The exception is downup1. If it were like the others, it would look like this:

```
to downup1 :word
print :word
downup0 butlast :word
print :word
end
```

Review the way the numbered downups work to make sure you understand why downup1 is different. Here's what happens when you invoke one of the numbered versions:

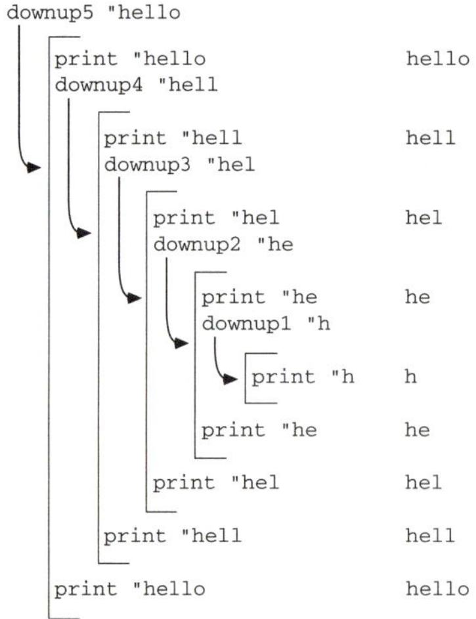

In this chart, instructions within a particular procedure are indented the same amount. For example, the lines `print "hello` and `downup4 "hell` are part of `downup5`, as is the line `print "hello` at the very end of the chart. The lines in between are indented more because they're part of `downup4` and its subprocedures.

(By the way, the lines in the chart don't show actual instructions in the procedure definitions. Otherwise all the `print` lines would say `print :word` instead of showing actual words. In the chart I've already evaluated the inputs to the commands.)

The point of the chart is that `downup1` has to be special because it marks the end of the "down" part of the problem and the beginning of the "up" part. `downup1` doesn't invoke a lower-numbered `downup` subprocedure because there's no smaller piece of the word to print.

☞ Okay, Logo knows when to stop the "down" part of the program because `downup1` is different from the other procedures. Question: How does Logo know when to stop the "up" part of the program? Why doesn't `downup5`, in this example, have to be written differently from the others?

The Stop Rule

Our attempt to write a completely general `downup` procedure has run into trouble because we have to distinguish two cases: the special case in which the input word contains only one character and the general case for longer input words. We can use `ifelse` to distinguish the two cases:

```
to downup :word
ifelse equalp count :word 1 [downup.one :word] [downup.many :word]
end

to downup.one :word
print :word
end

to downup.many :word
print :word
downup butlast :word
print :word
end
```

You'll find that this version of the downup program actually works correctly. Subprocedure downup.one is exactly like the old downup1, while downup.many is like the version of downup that didn't work.

It's possible to use the same general idea, however—distinguishing the special case of a one-letter word—without having to set up this three-procedure structure. Instead we can take advantage of the fact that downup.one's single instruction is the same as the first instruction of downup.many; we can use a single procedure that stops early if appropriate.

```
to downup :word
print :word
if equalp count :word 1 [stop]
downup butlast :word
print :word
end
```

The if instruction in this final version of downup is called a *stop rule.*

Downup illustrates the usual pattern of a recursive procedure. There are three kinds of instructions within its definition: (1) There are the ordinary instructions that carry out the work of the procedure for a particular value of the input, in this case the print instructions. (2) There is at least one *recursive call,* an instruction that invokes the same procedure with a smaller input. (3) There is a stop rule, which prevents the recursive invocation when the input is too small.

It's important to understand that the stop rule always comes *before* the recursive call or calls. One of the common mistakes made by programmers who are just learning about recursion is to think this way: "The stop rule *ends* the program, so it belongs at the *end* of the procedure." The right way to think about it is that the purpose of the stop rule is to stop the innermost invocation of the procedure *before* it has a chance to invoke itself recursively, so the stop rule must come *before* the recursive call.

Local Variables

When you're thinking about a recursive procedure, it's especially important to remember that each invocation of a procedure has its own local variables. It's possible to get confused about this because, of course, if a procedure invokes itself as a subprocedure, each invocation uses the same *names* for local variables. For example, each invocation of downup has a local variable (its input) named word. But each invocation has a *separate* input variable.

It's hard to talk about different invocations in the abstract. So let's look back at the version of the program in which each invocation had a different procedure name: downup1, downup2, and so on.

If you type the instruction

```
downup5 "hello
```

the procedure downup5 is invoked, with the word hello as its input. Downup5 has a local variable named word, which contains hello as its value. The first instruction in downup5 is

```
print :word
```

Since :word is hello, this instruction prints hello. The next instruction is

```
downup4 butlast :word
```

This instruction invokes procedure downup4 with the word hell (the butlast of hello) as input. downup4 has a local variable that is also named word. The value of *that* variable is the word hell.

At this point there are two separate variables, both named word. Downup5's word contains hello; downup4's word contains hell. I won't go through all the details of how downup4 invokes downup3 and so on. But eventually downup4 finishes its task, and downup5 continues with its final instruction, which is

```
print :word
```

Even though different values have been assigned to variables named word in the interim, *this* variable named word (the one that is local to downup5) still has its original value, hello. So that's what's printed.

In the recursive version of the program exactly the same thing happens about local variables. It's a little harder to describe, because all the procedure invocations are invocations of the same procedure, downup. So I can't say things like "the variable word that belongs to downup4"; instead, you have to think about "the variable named word that belongs to the second invocation of downup." But even though there is only one *procedure* involved, there are still five procedure *invocations,* each with its own local variable named word.

More Examples

☞ Before I go on to show you another example of a recursive procedure, you might try to write down and up, which should work like this:

```
? down "hello
hello
hell
hel
he
h
? up "hello
h
he
hel
hell
hello
```

As a start, notice that there are two print instructions in downup and that one of them does the "down" half and the other does the "up" half. But you'll find that just eliminating one of the prints for down and the other for up doesn't *quite* work.

After you've finished down and up, come back here for a discussion of a similar project, which I call inout:

```
? inout "hello
hello
 ello
  llo
   lo
    o
   lo
  llo
 ello
hello
```

At first glance inout looks just like downup, except that it uses the butfirst of its input instead of the butlast. Inout is somewhat more complicated than downup, however, because it has to print spaces before some of the words in order to line up the rightmost letters. Downup lined up the leftmost letters, which is easy.

Suppose we start, as we did for downup, with a version that only works for single-letter words:

```
to inout1 :word
print :word
end
```

But we can't quite use `inout1` as a subprocedure of `inout2`, as we did in the `downup` problem. Instead we need a different version of `inout1`, which types a space before its input:

```
to inout2 :word
print :word
inout2.1 butfirst :word
print :word
end

to inout2.1 :word
type "| |                    ; a word containing a space
print :word
end
```

`Type` is a command, which requires one input. The input can be any datum. `Type` prints its input, like `print`, but does not move the cursor to a new line afterward. The cursor remains right after the printed datum, so the next `print` or `type` command will continue on the same line.

We need another specific case or two before a general pattern will become apparent. Here is the version for three-letter words:

```
to inout3 :word
print :word
inout3.2 butfirst :word
print :word
end

to inout3.2 :word
type "| |
print :word
inout3.1 butfirst :word
type "| |
print :word
end
```

```
to inout3.1 :word
repeat 2 [type "| |]
print :word
end
```

Convince yourself that each of these procedures types the right number of spaces before its input word.

Here is one final example, the version for four-letter words:

```
to inout4 :word
print :word
inout4.3 butfirst :word
print :word
end

to inout4.3 :word
type "| |
print :word
inout4.2 butfirst :word
type "| |
print :word
end

to inout4.2 :word
repeat 2 [type "| |]
print :word
inout4.1 butfirst :word
repeat 2 [type "| |]
print :word
end

to inout4.1 :word
repeat 3 [type "| |]
print :word
end
```

☞ Try this out and try writing `inout5` along the same lines.

How can we find a common pattern that will combine the elements of all these procedures? It will have to look something like this:

```
to inout :word
repeat something [type "| |]
print :word
if something [stop]
inout butfirst :word
repeat something [type "| |]
print :word
end
```

This is not a finished procedure because we haven't figured out how to fill the blanks. First I should remark that the stop rule is where it is, after the first `print`, because that's how far the innermost procedures (`inout2.1`, `inout3.1`, and `inout4.1`) get. They type some spaces, print the input word, and that's all.

Another thing to remark is that the first input to the `repeat` commands in this general procedure will sometimes be zero, because the outermost procedures (`inout2`, `inout3`, and `inout4`) don't type any spaces at all. Each subprocedure types one more space than its superprocedure. For example, `inout4` types no spaces. Its subprocedure `inout4.3` types one space. `inout4.3`'s subprocedure `inout4.2` types two spaces. Finally, `inout4.2`'s subprocedure `inout4.1` types three spaces.

In order to vary the number of spaces in this way, the solution is to use another input that will have this number as its value. We can call it `spaces`. The procedure will then look like this:

```
to inout :word :spaces
repeat :spaces [type "| |]
print :word
if equalp count :word 1 [stop]
inout (butfirst :word) (:spaces+1)
repeat :spaces [type "| |]
print :word
end
```

```
? inout "hello 0
hello
 ello
  llo
   lo
    o
   lo
  llo
 ello
hello
```

Notice that, when we use `inout`, we have to give it a zero as its second input. We could eliminate this annoyance by writing a new `inout` that invokes this one as a subprocedure:

```
to inout :word
inout.sub :word 0
end

to inout.sub :word :spaces
repeat :spaces [type "| |]
print :word
if equalp count :word 1 [stop]
inout.sub (butfirst :word) (:spaces+1)
repeat :spaces [type "| |]
print :word
end
```

(The easiest way to make this change is to edit `inout` with the Logo editor and change its title line and its recursive call so that its name is `inout.sub`. Then, still in the editor, type in the new superprocedure `inout`. When you leave the editor, both procedures will get their new definitions.)

This program structure, with a short superprocedure and a recursive subprocedure, is very common. The superprocedure's only job is to provide the initial values for some of the subprocedure's inputs, so it's sometimes called an *initialization procedure.* In this program `inout` is an initialization procedure for `inout.sub`.

By the way, the parentheses in the recursive call aren't really needed; I just used them to make it more obvious which input is which.

Other Stop Rules

The examples I've shown so far use this stop rule:

```
if equalp count :word 1 [stop]
```

Perhaps you wrote your `down` procedure the same way:

```
to down :word
print :word
if equalp count :word 1 [stop]
down butlast :word
end
```

Here is another way to write `down`, which has the same effect. But this is a more commonly used style:

```
to down :word
if emptyp :word [stop]
print :word
down butlast :word
end
```

This version of `down` has the stop rule as its first instruction. After that comes the instructions that carry out the specific work of the procedure, in this case the `print` instruction. The recursive call comes as the last instruction.

A procedure in which the recursive call is the last instruction is called *tail recursive.* We'll have more to say later about the meaning of tail recursion. (Actually, to be precise, I should have said that a *command* in which the recursive call is the last instruction is tail recursive. What constitutes a tail recursive operation is a little tricker, and so far we haven't talked about recursive operations at all.)

Here's another example:

```
to countdown :number
if equalp :number 0 [print "Blastoff! stop]
print :number
countdown :number-1
end

? countdown 10
10
9
8
7
6
5
4
3
2
1
Blastoff!
```

In this case, instead of a word that gets smaller by `butfirsting` or `butlasting` it, the input is a number from which 1 is subtracted for each recursive invocation. This example also shows how some special action (the `print "Blastoff!` instruction) can be taken in the innermost invocation of the procedure.

☞ Here are some ideas for recursive programs you can write. In each case I'll show an example or two of what the program should do. Start with `one.per.line`, a command with one input. If the input is a word, the procedure should print each letter of the word on a separate line. If the input is a list, the procedure should print each member of the list on a separate line:

```
? one.per.line "hello
h
e
l
l
o
? one.per.line [the rain in spain]
the
rain
in
spain
```

(You already know how to do this without recursion, using `foreach` instead. Many, although not all, recursive problems can also be solved using higher order functions. You might enjoy this non-obvious example:

```
to down :word
ignore cascade (count :word) [print ? butlast ?] :word
end
```

While you're learning about recursion, though, don't use higher order functions. Once you're comfortable with both techniques you can choose which to use in a particular situation.)

☞ As an example in which an initialization procedure will be helpful, try `triangle`, a command that takes a word as its single input. It prints the word repeatedly on the same line, as many times as its length. Then it prints a second line with one fewer repetition, and so on until it prints the word just once:

```
? triangle "frog
frog frog frog frog
frog frog frog
frog frog
frog
```

☞ A more ambitious project is `diamond`, which takes as its input a word with an odd number of letters. It displays the word in a diamond pattern, like this:

```
? diamond "program
   g
  ogr
 rogra
program
 rogra
  ogr
   g
```

(Hint: Write two procedures `diamond.top` and `diamond.bottom` for the growing and shrinking halves of the display. As in `inout`, you'll need an input to count the number of spaces by which to indent each line.) Can you write `diamond` so that it does something sensible for an input word with an even number of letters?

8 Practical Recursion: the Leap of Faith

When people first meet the idea of recursive procedures, they almost always think there is some sort of magic involved. "How can that possibly work? That procedure uses itself as a subprocedure! That's not fair." To overcome that sense of unfairness, the combining method works up to a recursive procedure by starting small, so that each step is completely working before the next step, to solve a larger problem, relies on it. There is no mystery about allowing `downup5` to rely on `downup4`.

The trouble with the combining method is that it's too much effort to be practical. Once you believe in recursion, you don't want to have to write a special procedure for a size-one problem, then another special procedure for a size-two problem, and so on; you want to write the general recursive solution right away. I'm calling this the "leap of faith" method because you write a procedure while taking on faith that you can invoke the same procedure to handle a smaller subproblem.

Recursive Patterns

Let's look, once more, at the problem we were trying to solve when writing the `downup` procedure. We wanted the program to behave like this:

```
? downup "hello
hello
hell
hel
he
h
he
hel
hell
hello
```

The secret of recursive programming is the same as a secret of problem solving in general: see if you can reduce a big problem to a smaller problem. In this case we can look at the printout from downup this way:

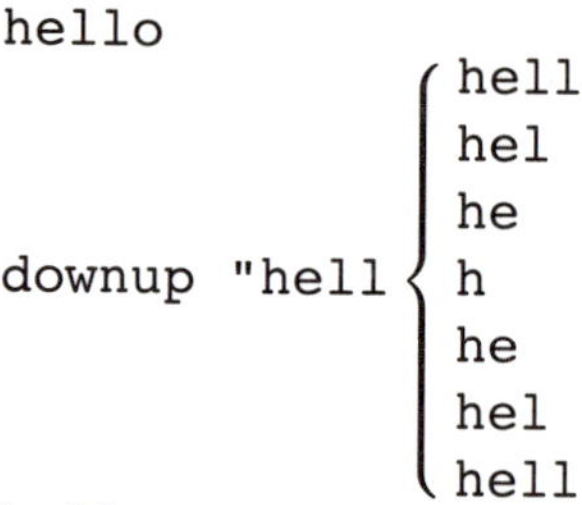
hello
hell
hel
he
downup "hell
h
he
hel
hell
hello

What I've done here is to notice that the printout from applying downup to a five-letter word, `hello`, includes within itself the printout that would result from applying downup to a smaller word, `hell`.

This is where the leap of faith comes in. I'm going to pretend that downup *already works* for the case of four-letter words. We haven't begun to write the procedure yet, but never mind that. So it seems that in order to evaluate the instruction

```
downup "hello
```

we must carry out these three instructions:

```
print "hello
downup "hell
print "hello
```

(The two `print` instructions print the first and last lines of the desired result, the ones that aren't part of the smaller downup printout.)

To turn these instructions into a general procedure, we must use a variable in place of the specific word `hello`. We also have to figure out the general relationship that is exemplified by the transformation from `hello` into `hell`. This relationship is, of course, simply `butlast`. Here is the procedure that results from this process of generalization:

```
to downup :word
print :word
downup butlast :word
print :word
end
```

As you already know, this procedure won't quite work. It lacks a stop rule. But once we have come this far, it's a relatively simple matter to add the stop rule. All we have to do is ask ourselves, "What's the smallest case we want the program to handle?" The answer is that for a single-letter word the downup should just print the word once. In other words, for a single-letter word, downup should carry out its first instruction and then stop. So the stop rule goes after that first instruction, and it stops if the input has only one letter:

```
to downup :word
print :word
if equalp count :word 1 [stop]
downup butlast :word
print :word
end
```

Voilà!

The trick is *not* to think about the stop rule at first. Just accept, on faith, that the procedure will somehow manage to work for inputs that are smaller than the one you're interested in. Most people find it hard to do that. Since you haven't written the program yet, after all, the faith I'm asking you to show is really unjustified. Nevertheless you have to pretend that someone has already written a version of the desired procedure that works for smaller inputs.

Let's take another example from Chapter 7.

```
? one.per.line "hello
h
e
l
l
o
```

There are two different ways in which we can find a smaller pattern within this one. First we might notice this one:

```
h   (first of hello)
                 ⎧ e
one.per.line     ⎨ l
    "ello        ⎪ l
                 ⎩ o
```

This pattern would lead to the following procedure, for which I haven't yet invented a stop rule.

```
to one.per.line :word
print first :word
one.per.line butfirst :word
end
```

Alternatively we might notice this pattern:

```
                  ⎧ h
one.per.line      ⎨ e
    "hell         ⎪ l
                  ⎩ l
o    (last of hello)
```

In that case we'd have a different version of the procedure. This one, also, doesn't yet have a stop rule.

```
to one.per.line :word
one.per.line butlast :word
print last :word
end
```

Either of these procedures can be made to work by adding the appropriate stop rule:

```
if emptyp :word [stop]
```

This instruction should be the first in either procedure. Since both versions work, is there any reason to choose one over the other? Well, there's no theoretical reason but there is a practical one. It turns out that `first` and `butfirst` work faster than `last` and `butlast`. It also turns out that procedures that are tail recursive (that is, with the recursion step at the end) can survive more levels of invocation, without running out of memory, than those that are recursive in other ways. For both of these reasons the first version of `one.per.line` is a better choice than the second. (Try timing both versions with a very long list as input.)

☞ Rewrite the `say` procedure from page 95 recursively.

The Leap of Faith

If we think of

```
to one.per.line :word
print first :word
one.per.line butfirst :word
end
```

merely as a statement of a true fact about the "shape" of the result printed by one.per.line, it's not very remarkable. The amazing part is that this fragment is *runnable!** It doesn't *look* runnable because it invokes itself as a helper procedure, and—if you haven't already been through the combining method—that looks as if it can't work. "How can you use one.per.line when you haven't written it yet?"

The leap of faith method is the assumption that the procedure we're in the middle of writing already works. That is, if we're thinking about writing a one.per.line procedure that can compute one.per.line "hello, we assume that one.per.line "ello will work.

Of course it's not *really* a leap of faith, in the sense of something accepted as miraculous but not understood. The assumption is justified by our understanding of the combining method. For example, we understand that the five-letter one.per.line is relying on the four-letter version of the problem, not really on itself, so there's no circular reasoning involved. And we know that if we had to, we could write one.per.line1 through one.per.line4 "by hand."

The reason that the technique in this chapter may seem more mysterious than the combining method is that this time we are thinking about the problem top-down. In the combining method, we had already written whatever4 before we even raised the question of whatever5. Now we start by thinking about the larger problem and assume that we can rely on the smaller one. Again, we're entitled to that assumption because we've gone through the process from smaller to larger so many times already.

The leap of faith method, once you understand it, is faster than the combining method for writing new recursive procedures, because you can write the recursive solution immediately, without bothering with many individual cases. The reason I showed you the combining method first is that the leap of faith method seems too much like magic, or like "cheating," until you've seen several believable recursive programs. The combining method is the way to learn about recursion; the leap of faith method is the way to write recursive procedures once you've learned.

The Tower of Hanoi

One of the most famous recursive problems is a puzzle called the Tower of Hanoi. You can find this puzzle in toy stores; look for a set of three posts and five or six disks. You

* Well, almost. It needs a base case.

start out with the puzzle arranged like this:

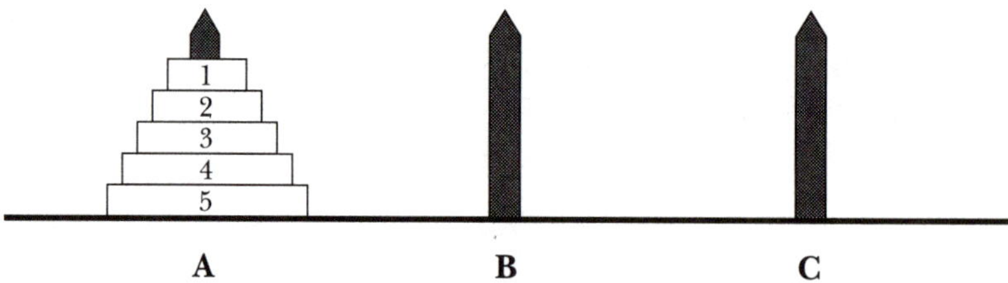

The object of the puzzle is to move all of the disks to the second post, like this:

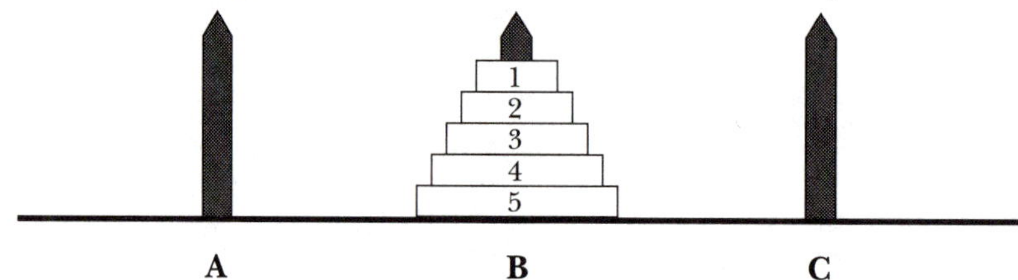

This looks easy, but there are rules you must follow. You can only move one disk at a time, and you can't put a disk on top of a smaller disk. You might start trying to solve the puzzle this way:

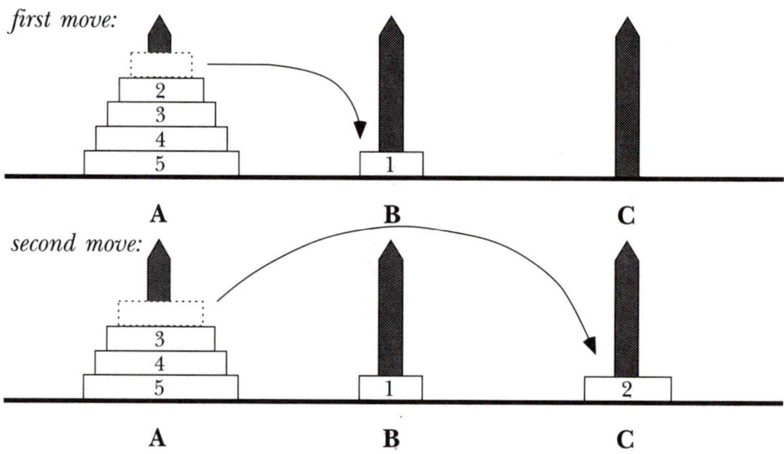

After that, you could move disk number 1 either onto post A, on top of disk 3, or onto post C, on top of disk 2.

I'm about to describe a solution to the puzzle, so if you want to work on it yourself first, stop reading now.

In the examples of `downup` and `one.per.line`, we identified each problem as one for which a recursive program was appropriate because within the pattern of the overall solution we found a smaller, similar pattern. The same principle will apply in this case. We want to end up with all five disks on post B. To do that, at some point we have to move disk 5 from post A to post B. To do *that,* we first have to get the other four disks out of the way. Specifically, "out of the way" must mean onto post C. So the solution to the problem can be represented graphically this way, in three parts:

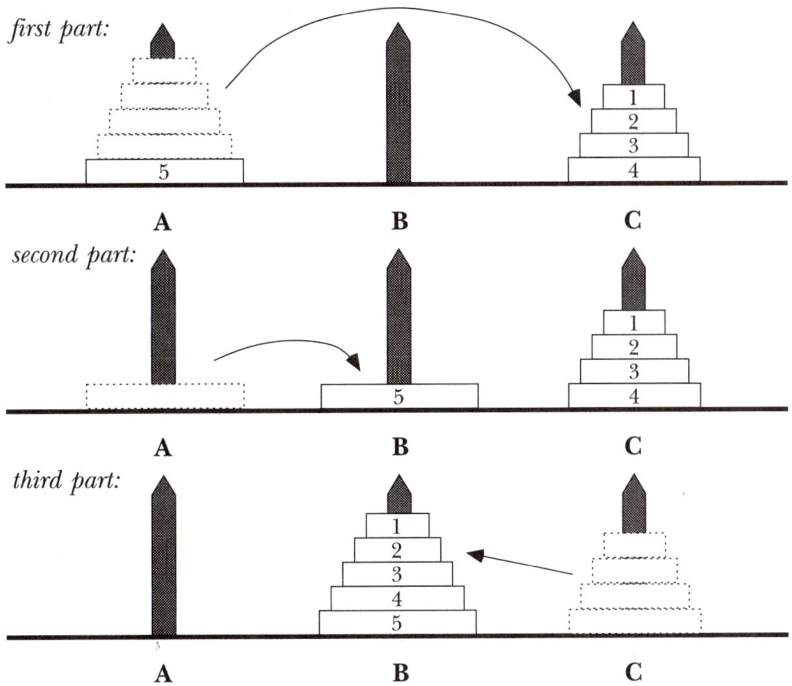

The first part of the solution is to move disks 1 through 4 from post A to post C. The second part is a single step, moving disk 5 from post A to post B. The third part, like the first, involves several steps, to move disks 1 through 4 from post C to post B.

If you've developed the proper recursive spirit, you'll now say, "Aha! The first part and the third part are just like the entire puzzle, only with four disks instead of five!" I hope that after this example you'll develop a sort of instinct that will let you notice patterns like that instantly. You should then be ready to make a rough draft of a procedure to solve the puzzle:

```
to hanoi :number
hanoi :number-1
movedisk :number
hanoi :number-1
end
```

Of course, this isn't at all a finished program. For one thing, it lacks a stop rule. (As usual, we leave that part for last.) For another, we have to write the subprocedure `movedisk` that moves a single disk. But a more important point is that we've only provided for changing the disk number we're moving, not for selecting which posts to move from and to. You might want to supply `hanoi` with two more inputs, named `from` and `to`, which would be the names of the posts. So to solve the puzzle we'd say

```
hanoi 5 "A "B
```

But that's not quite adequate. `Hanoi` also needs to know the name of the *third* post. Why? Because in the recursive calls, that third post becomes one of the two "active" ones. For example, here are the three steps in solving the five-disk puzzle:

```
hanoi 4 "A "C
movedisk 5 "A "B
hanoi 4 "C "B
```

You can see that both of the recursive invocations need to use the name of the third post. Therefore, we'll give `hanoi` a fourth input, called `other`, that will contain that name. Here is another not-quite-finished version:

```
to hanoi :number :from :to :other
hanoi :number-1 :from :other :to
movedisk :number :from :to
hanoi :number-1 :other :to :from
end
```

This version still lacks a stop rule, and we still have to write `movedisk`. But we're much closer. Notice that `movedisk` does *not* need the name of the third post as an input. Its job is to take a single step, moving a single disk. The unused post really has nothing to do with it. Here's a simple version of `movedisk`:

```
to movedisk :number :from :to
print (sentence [Move disk] :number "from :from "to :to)
end
```

What about the stop rule in `hanoi`? The first thing that will come to your mind, probably, is that the case of moving disk number 1 is special because there are no preconditions. (No other disk can ever be on top of number 1, which is the smallest.) So you might want to use this stop rule:

```
if equalp :number 1 [movedisk 1 :from :to stop]
```

Indeed, that will work. (Where would you put it in the procedure?) But it turns out that a slightly more elegant solution is possible. You can let the procedure for disk 1 go ahead and invoke itself recursively for disk number 0. Since there is no such disk, the procedure then has nothing to do. By this reasoning the stop rule should be this:

```
if equalp :number 0 [stop]
```

You may have to trace out the procedure to convince yourself that this really works. Convincing yourself is worth the effort, though; it turns out that very often you can get away with allowing an "extra" level of recursive invocation that does nothing. When that's possible, it makes for a very clean-looking procedure. (Once again, I've left you on your own in deciding where to insert this stop rule in `hanoi`.)

If your procedure is working correctly, you should get results like this for a small version of the puzzle:

```
? hanoi 3 "A "B "C
Move disk 1 from A to B
Move disk 2 from A to C
Move disk 1 from B to C
Move disk 3 from A to B
Move disk 1 from C to A
Move disk 2 from C to B
Move disk 1 from A to B
```

If you like graphics programming and have been impatient to see a turtle in this book, you might want to write a graphic version of `movedisk` that would actually display the moves on the screen.

More Complicated Patterns

Suppose that, instead of `downup`, we wanted to write `updown`, which works like this:

```
? updown "hello
h
he
hel
hell
hello
hell
hel
he
h
```

It's harder to find a smaller subproblem within this pattern. With downup, removing the first and last lines of the printout left a downup pattern for a shorter word. But the middle lines of this updown pattern aren't an updown. The middle lines don't start with a single letter, like the h in the full pattern. Also, the middle lines are clearly made out of the word hello, not some shortened version of it. ☞ You might want to try to find a solution yourself before reading further.

There are several approaches to writing updown. One thing we could do is to divide the pattern into two parts:

```
h     ⎫
he    ⎪
hel   ⎬ up "hello
hell  ⎪
hello ⎭

hell  ⎫
hel   ⎬ down "hell
he    ⎪
h     ⎭
```

It is relatively easy to invent the procedures up and down to create the two parts of the pattern.

```
to up :word
if emptyp :word [stop]
up butlast :word
print :word
end

to down :word
if emptyp :word [stop]
print :word
down butlast :word
end
```

Then we can use these as subprocedures of the complete updown:

```
to updown :word
up :word
down butlast :word
end
```

Another approach would be to use numbers to keep track of things, as in the `inout` example of Chapter 7. In this case we can consider the middle lines as a smaller version of the problem.

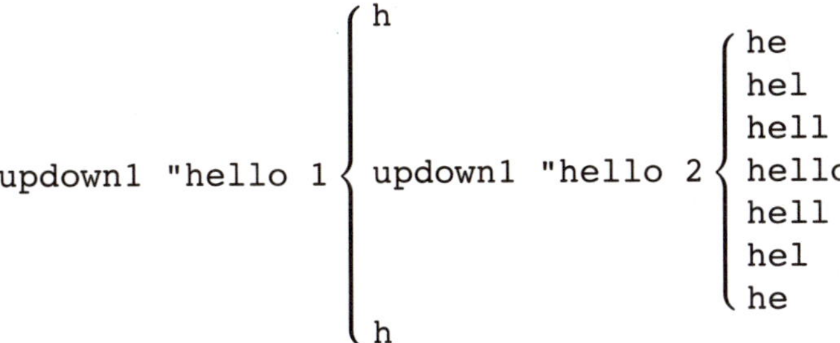

In this point of view all the inner, smaller `updown` patterns are made from the same word, `hello`. But each invocation of `updown1` (which is what I'll call this version of `updown`) will use a second input, a number that tells it how many letters to print in the first and last lines:

```
? updown1 "hello 3
hel
hell
hello
hell
hel
? updown1 "hello 5
hello
```

We need a subprocedure, `truncate`, that prints the beginning of a word, up to a certain number of letters.

```
to truncate :word :size
if equalp count :word :size [print :word stop]
truncate butlast :word :size
end

to updown1 :word :size
truncate :word :size
if equalp count :word :size [stop]
updown1 :word :size+1
truncate :word :size
end
```

(The helper procedure `truncate` is the sort of thing that should really be an operation, for the same reason that `second` was better than `prsecond` on page 76. We'll come back to the writing of recursive operations in Chapter 11.)

Finally, we can write a new superprocedure called `updown` that uses `updown1` with the correct inputs. (If you try all these approaches on the computer, remember that you can have only one procedure named `updown` in your workspace at a time.)

```
to updown :word
updown1 :word 1
end
```

A third approach, which illustrates a very powerful technique, also uses an initialization procedure `updown` and a subprocedure `updown1` with two inputs. In this version, though, both inputs to the subprocedure are words: the partial word that we're printing right now and the partial word that is not yet to be printed.

```
                     ⎧ h
                     ⎪                     ⎧ he
                     ⎪                     ⎪ hel
                     ⎪                     ⎪ hell
updown1 "h "ello ⎨ updown1 "he "llo ⎨ hello
                     ⎪                     ⎪ hell
                     ⎪                     ⎪ hel
                     ⎪                     ⎩ he
                     ⎩ h
```

In this example, to print an `updown` pattern for the word `hello`, the two subprocedure inputs would be `h` (what's printed on the first line) and `ello` (what isn't printed there). For the inner pattern with the first and last lines removed, the two inputs would be `he` and `llo`. Here is the program:

```
to updown1 :now :later
print :now
if emptyp :later [stop]
updown1 (word :now first :later) butfirst :later
print :now
end

to updown :word
updown1 first :word butfirst :word
end
```

This program may be a little tricky to understand. The important part is `updown1`. Read it first without paying attention to the stop rule; see if you can understand how it corresponds to the `updown` pattern. A trace of its recursive invocations might help:

```
updown "hello
  updown1 "h "ello
    updown1 "he "llo
      updown1 "hel "lo
        updown1 "hell "o
          updown1 "hello "
```

The innermost level of recursion has been reached when the second input is the empty word. Notice how `first`, `butfirst`, and `word` are used in combination to calculate the inputs.

☞ Write a recursive procedure `slant` that takes a word as input and prints it on a diagonal, one letter per line, like this:

```
? slant "salami
s
 a
  l
   a
    m
     i
```

A Mini-project: Scrambled Sentences

Just as Logo programs can be iterative or recursive, so can English sentences. People are pretty good at understanding even rather long iterative sentences: "This is the farmer who kept the cock that waked the priest that married the man that kissed the maiden that milked the cow that tossed the dog that worried the cat that killed the rat that ate the malt that lay in the house that Jack built." But even a short recursive (nested) sentence is confusing: "This is the rat the cat the dog worried killed."

☞ Write a procedure that takes as its first input a list of noun-verb pairs representing actor and action, and as its second input a word representing the object of the last action in the list. Your procedure will print two sentences describing the events, an iterative one and a nested one, following this pattern:

```
? scramble [[girl saw] [boy owned] [dog chased] [cat bit]] "rat
This is
the girl that saw
the boy that owned
the dog that chased
the cat that bit
the rat

This is
the rat
the cat
the dog
the boy
the girl
saw
owned
chased
bit
```

You don't have to worry about special cases like "that Jack built"; your sentences will follow this pattern exactly.

Ordinarily the most natural way to program this problem would be as an operation that outputs the desired sentence, but right now we are concentrating on recursive commands, so you'll write a procedure that `prints` each line as shown above.

Procedure Patterns

Certain patterns come up over and over in programming problems. It's worth your while to learn to recognize some of them. For example, let's look again at `one.per.line`:

```
to one.per.line :word
if emptyp :word [stop]
print first :word
one.per.line butfirst :word
end
```

This is an example of a very common pattern:

```
to procedure :input
if emptyp :input [stop]
do.something.to first :input
procedure butfirst :input
end
```

A procedure pattern is different from the *result* patterns we examined earlier in this chapter. Before we were looking at what we wanted a not-yet-written procedure to accomplish; now we are looking at already-written procedures to find patterns in their instructions. A particular procedure might look like this pattern with the blanks filled in. Here's an example:

```
to praise :flavors
if emptyp :flavors [stop]
print sentence [I love] first :flavors
praise butfirst :flavors
end
```

```
? praise [[ultra chocolate] [chocolate cinnamon raisin] ginger]
I love ultra chocolate
I love chocolate cinnamon raisin
I love ginger
```

Do you see how `praise` fits the pattern?

☞ Continuing our investigation of literary forms, write a procedure to compose love poems, like this:

```
? lovepoem "Mary
M is for marvelous, that's what you are.
A is for awesome, the best by far.
R is for rosy, just like your cheek.
Y is for youthful, with zest at its peak.
Put them together, they spell Mary,
The greatest girl in the world.
```

The core of this project is a database of deathless lines, in the form of a list of lists:

```
make "lines [[A is for albatross, around my neck.]
             [B is for baloney, your opinions are dreck.]
             [C is for corpulent, ...] ...]
```

and a recursive procedure `select` that takes a letter and a list of lines as inputs and finds the appropriate line to print by comparing the letter to the beginning of each line in the list.

Another common pattern is a recursive procedure that counts something numerically, like `countdown`:

```
to countdown :number
if equalp :number 0 [stop]
print :number
countdown :number-1
end
```

And here is the pattern:

```
to procedure :number
if equalp :number 0 [stop]
do.something
procedure :number-1
end
```

A procedure built on this pattern is likely to have additional inputs so that it can do something other than just manipulate the number itself. For example:

```
to manyprint :number :text
if equalp :number 0 [stop]
print :text
manyprint :number-1 :text
end
```

```
? manyprint 4 [Lots of echo in this cavern.]
Lots of echo in this cavern.
Lots of echo in this cavern.
Lots of echo in this cavern.
Lots of echo in this cavern.
```

```
to multiply :letters :number
if equalp :number 0 [stop]
print :letters
multiply (word :letters first :letters) :number-1
end
```

```
? multiply "f 5
f
ff
fff
ffff
fffff
```

One way to become a skillful programmer is to study other people's programs carefully. As you read the programs in this book and others, keep an eye open for examples of patterns that you think might come in handy later on.

Tricky Stop Rules

Suppose that instead of `one.per.line` we'd like a procedure to print the members of a list *two* per line. (This is plausible if we have a list of many short items, for example. We'd probably want to control the spacing on each line so that the items would form two columns, but let's not worry about that yet.)

The recursive part of this program is fairly straightforward:

```
to two.per.line :stuff
print list (first :stuff) (first butfirst :stuff)
two.per.line butfirst butfirst :stuff
end
```

The only thing out of the ordinary is that the recursive step uses a subproblem that's smaller by two members, instead of the usual one.

But it's easy to fall into a trap about the stop rule. It's not good enough to say

```
if emptyp :stuff [stop]
```

because in this procedure it matters whether the length of the input is odd or even. These two possibilities give rise to *two* stop rules. For an even-length list, we stop if the input is empty. But for an odd-length list, we must treat the case of a one-member list specially also.

```
to two.per.line :stuff
if emptyp :stuff [stop]
if emptyp butfirst :stuff [show first :stuff stop]
print list (first :stuff) (first butfirst :stuff)
two.per.line butfirst butfirst :stuff
end
```

It's important to get the two stop rules in the right order; we must be sure the input isn't empty before we try to take its `butfirst`.

☞ Why does this procedure include one `show` instruction and one `print` instruction? Why aren't they either both `show` or both `print`?

9 How Recursion Works

The last two chapters were about how to write recursive procedures. This chapter is about how to *believe in* recursive procedures, and about understanding the process by which Logo carries them out.

Little People and Recursion

In Chapter 3, I introduced you to the metaphor of a computer full of little elves. Each elf is an expert on a particular procedure. I promised that this metaphor would be helpful later, when we'd have to think about two little people carrying out the same procedure at the same time. Well, "later" is now.

I want to use the elf metaphor to think about the `downup` example of the previous chapter:

```
to downup :word
print :word
if equalp count :word 1 [stop]
downup butlast :word
print :word
end
```

Recall that we are imagining the computer to be full of elves, each of whom is a specialist in carrying out some procedure. There are `print` elves, `count` elves, `stop` elves, and so on. Each elf has some number of pockets, used to hold the inputs for a particular invocation of a procedure. So a `print` elf will have one pocket, while an `equalp` elf needs two pockets.

We're going to be most interested in the downup elves and the contents of their pockets. To help you keep straight which elf is which, I'm going to name the downup elves alphabetically: the first one will be Ann, then Bill, then Cathy, then David, and so on. Since we aren't so interested in the other elves, I won't bother naming them.

☞ If you're reading this with a group of other people, you may find it helpful for each of you to take on the role of one of the downup elves and actually stick words in your pockets. If you have enough people, some of you should also serve as elves for the primitive procedures used, like print and if.

What happens when you type the instruction

```
downup "hello
```

to Logo? The Chief Elf reads this instruction and sees that it calls for the use of the procedure named downup. She therefore recruits Ann, an elf who specializes in that procedure. Since downup has one input, the Chief Elf has to give Ann something to put in her one pocket. Fortunately, the input you provided is a quoted word, which evaluates to itself. No other elves are needed to compute the input. Ann gets the word hello in her pocket.

Ann's task is to carry out the instructions that make up the definition of downup. The first instruction is

```
print :word
```

This, you'll remember, is an abbreviation for

```
print thing "word
```

Ann must hire two more elves, a print specialist and a thing specialist. The print elf can't begin his work until he's given something to put in his pocket. Ann asks the thing elf to figure out what that input should be. The thing elf also gets an input, namely the word word. As we saw in Chapter 3, word is what's written on the name tag in Ann's pocket, since word is the name of downup's input. So the thing elf looks in that pocket, where it finds the word hello. That word is then given to the print elf, who prints it on your computer screen.

Ann is now ready to evaluate the second instruction:

```
if equalp count :word 1 [stop]
```

Ann must hire several other elves to help her: an `if` elf, a `count` elf, and a `thing` elf. I won't go through all the steps in computing the inputs to `if`; since the `count` of the word `hello` is not 1, the first input to `if` turns out to be the word `false`. The second input to `if` is, of course, the list `[stop]`. (Notice that Ann does *not* hire a `stop` specialist. A list inside square brackets evaluates to itself, just like a quoted word, without invoking any procedures. If the first input to `if` had turned out to be `true`, it would have been the `if` elf who would have hired a `stop` elf to carry out the instruction inside the list.) Since its first input is `false`, the `if` elf ends up doing nothing.

Ann's third instruction is

```
downup butlast :word
```

Here's where things start to get interesting. Ann must hire *another* `downup` specialist, named Bill. (Ann can't carry out this new `downup` instruction herself because she's already in the middle of a job of her own.) Ann must give Bill an input to put in his pocket; to compute this input, she hires a `butlast` elf and a `thing` elf. They eventually come up with the word `hell` (the `butlast` of `hello`), and that's what Ann puts in Bill's pocket.

We now have two active `downup` elves, Ann and Bill. Each has a pocket. Both pockets are named `word`, but they have different contents: Ann's `word` pocket contains `hello`, while Bill's `word` pocket contains `hell`.

Ann Bill

Here is what this metaphor represents, in more technical language: Although there is only one *procedure* named `downup`, there can be more than one *invocation* of that procedure in progress at a particular moment. (An invocation of a procedure is also sometimes called an *instantiation* of the procedure.) Each invocation has its own local variables; at this moment there are *two* variables named `word`. It is perfectly possible for two variables to have the same name as long as they are associated with (local to) different procedure invocations.

If you had trouble figuring out how downup works in Chapter 7, it's almost certainly because of a misunderstanding about this business of local variables. That's what makes the elf metaphor so helpful. For example, if you're accustomed to programming in BASIC, then you're familiar with *global* variables as the only possibility in the language. If all variables were global in Logo, then there could only be one variable in the entire computer named word. Instead of representing variables as pockets in the elves' clothes, we'd have to represent them as safe deposit boxes kept in some central bank and shared by all the elves.

But even if you're familiar with Logo's use of local variables, you may have been thinking of the variables as being local to a *procedure,* instead of understanding that they are local to an *invocation* of a procedure. In that case you may have felt perfectly comfortable with the procedures named downup1, downup2, and so on, each of them using a separate variable named word. But you may still have gotten confused when the *same* variable word, the one belonging to the single procedure downup, seemed to have several values at once.

If you were confused in that way, here's how to use the elf metaphor to help yourself get unconfused: Suppose the procedure definitions are written on scrolls, which are kept in a library. There is only one copy of each scroll. (That is, there is only one definition for a given procedure.) All the elves who specialize in a particular procedure, like downup, have to share the same scroll. Well, if variables were local to a procedure, they'd be pockets in the *scroll,* rather than pockets in the *elves' jackets.* By directing your attention to the elves (the invocations) instead of the scrolls (the procedure definitions), you can see that there can be two variables with the same name (word), associated with the same procedure (downup), but belonging to different invocations (represented by the elves Ann and Bill).

We still have several more elves to meet, so I'm going to pass over some of the details more quickly now. We've just reached the point where Bill is ready to set to work. For his first instruction he hires a print elf, who prints the word hell on your screen. Why hell and not hello? The answer is that when Bill hires a thing expert to evaluate the expression :word, the thing rules say that that expert must look *first* in Bill's pockets, *then* (if Bill didn't have a pocket named word) in Ann's pockets.

Bill then carries out the if instruction, which again has no effect. Then Bill is ready for the downup instruction. He hires a third downup elf, named Cathy. Bill puts the word hel in Cathy's pocket. There are now three elves, all with pockets named word, each with a different word.

Cathy is now ready to get to work. Don't forget, though, that Ann and Bill haven't finished their jobs. Bill is still working on his third instruction, waiting for Cathy to report the completion of her task. Similarly, Ann is waiting for Bill to finish.

Cathy evaluates her first instruction, printing `hel` on the screen. She evaluates the `if` instruction, with no effect. Then she's ready for the `downup` instruction, the third one in the procedure definition. To carry out this instruction, she hires David, a fourth `downup` expert. She puts the word `he` in his pocket.

David's career is like that of the other `downup` elves we've met so far. He starts by printing his input, the word `he`. He evaluates the `if` instruction, with no effect. (The `count` of the word `he` is still not equal to 1.) He then gets to the recursive invocation of `downup`, for which he hires a fifth expert, named Ellen. He puts the word `h` in Ellen's pocket.

Ellen's career is *not* quite like that of the other elves. It starts similarly: she prints her input, the word `h`, on your screen. Then she prepares to evaluate the `if` instruction. This time, though, the first input to `if` turns out to be the word `true`, since the `count` of `h` is, indeed, 1. Therefore, the `if` elf evaluates the instruction contained in its second input, the list `[stop]`. It hires a `stop` elf, whose job is to tell Ellen to stop working. (Why Ellen? Why not one of the other active elves? There are *seven* elves active at the moment: Ann, Bill, Cathy, David, Ellen, the `if` elf, and the `stop` elf. The rule is that a `stop` elf stops the *lowest-level invocation of a user-defined procedure.* `If` and `stop` are primitives, so they don't satisfy the `stop` elf. The remaining five elves are experts in `downup`, a user-defined procedure; of the five, Ellen is the lowest-level invocation.)

(By the way, the insistence of `stop` on a user-defined procedure to stop is one of the few ways in which Logo treats such procedures differently from primitive procedures. If you think about it, you'll see that it would be useless for `stop` to stop just the invocation of `if`. That would mean that the `if` instruction would never do anything of interest and there would be no way to stop a procedure of your own conditionally. But you can imagine other situations in which it would be nice to be able to `stop` a primitive. Here's one:

```
repeat 100 [print "hello if equalp random 5 0 [stop]]
```

If it worked, this instruction would print the word `hello` some number of times, up to 100, but with a 20 percent chance of stopping after each time. In fact, though, you can't use `stop` to stop a `repeat` invocation.)

Let's review what's been printed so far:

```
hello   printed by Ann
hell    printed by Bill
hel     printed by Cathy
he      printed by David
h       printed by Ellen
```

Ellen has just stopped. She reports back to David, the elf who hired her. He's been waiting for her; now he can continue with his own work. David is up to the fourth and final instruction in the definition of `downup`:

```
print :word
```

What word will David print? For David, `:word` refers to the contents of *his own* pocket named `word`. That is, when David hires a `thing` expert, that expert looks first in David's pockets, before trying Cathy's, Bill's, and Ann's. The word in David's `word` pocket is `he`. So that's what David prints.

Okay, now David has reached the end of his instructions. He reports back to his employer, Cathy. She's been waiting for him, so that she can continue her own work. She, too, has one more `print` instruction to evaluate. She has the word `hel` in her `word` pocket, so that's what she prints.

Cathy now reports back to Bill. He prints his own word, `hell`. He reports back to Ann. She prints her word, `hello`.

When Ann finishes, she reports back to the Chief Elf, who prints a question mark on the screen and waits for you to type another instruction.

Here is the complete effect of this `downup` instruction:

```
hello   printed by Ann
hell    printed by Bill
hel     printed by Cathy
he      printed by David
h       printed by Ellen
he      printed by David
hel     printed by Cathy
hell    printed by Bill
hello   printed by Ann
```

☞ You might want to see if the little person metaphor can help you understand the working of the `inout` procedure from Chapter 7. Remember that each elf carrying out the recursive procedure needs two pockets, one for each input.

Tracing

Many people find the idea of multiple, simultaneous invocations of a single procedure confusing. To keep track of what's going on, you have to think about several "levels" of evaluation at once. "Where is downup up to right now?" — "Well, it depends what you mean. The lowest-level downup invocation has just evaluated its first print instruction. But there are three other invocations of downup that are in the middle of evaluating their recursive downup instructions." This can be especially confusing if you've always been taught that the computer can only do one thing at a time. People often emphasize the *sequential* nature of the computer; what we've been saying about recursion seems to violate that nature.

If this kind of confusion is a problem for you, it may help to think about a procedure like downup by *tracing* its progress. That is, we can tell the procedure to print out extra information each time it's invoked, to help you see the sequence of events.

Just for reference, here's downup again:

```
to downup :word
print :word
if equalp count :word 1 [stop]
downup butlast :word
print :word
end
```

The trace command takes a procedure name (or a list of procedure names, to trace more than one) as its input. It tells Logo to notify you whenever that procedure is invoked:

```
? trace "downup
? downup "logo
( downup "logo )
logo
 ( downup "log )
log
  ( downup "lo )
lo
   ( downup "l )
l
   downup stops
lo
  downup stops
log
 downup stops
logo
downup stops
```

To make this result a little easier to read, I've printed the lines that are generated by the tracing in smaller letters than the lines generated by downup itself. Of course the actual computer output all looks the same.

Each line of tracing information is indented by a number of spaces equal to the number of traced procedure invocations already active—the *level* of procedure invocation. By looking only at the lines between one downup invocation and the equally-indented stopping line, you can see how much is accomplished by each recursive call. For example, the innermost invocation (at level 4) prints only the letter l.

Level and Sequence

The result of tracing downup is most helpful if you think about it two-dimensionally. If you read it *vertically*, it represents the *sequence* of instructions that fits the traditional model of computer programming. That is, the order of the printed lines represents the order of events in time. First the computer enters downup at level 1. Then it prints the word logo. Then it enters downup at level 2. Then it prints log. And so on. Each printed line, including the "official" lines as well as the tracing lines, represents a particular instruction, carried out at a particular moment. Reading the trace vertically will help you fit downup's recursive method into your sequential habits of thought.

On the other hand, if you read the trace *horizontally*, it shows you the hierarchy of *levels* of downup's invocations. To see this, think of the trace as divided into two overlapping columns. The left column consists of the official pattern of words printed by the original downup. In the right column, the pattern of entering and exiting from each level is shown. The lines corresponding to a particular level are indented by a number of spaces that corresponds to the level number. For example, find the line

```
 ( downup "log )
```

and the matching

```
 downup stops
```

Between these two lines you'll see this:

```
log
  ( downup "lo )
lo
   ( downup "l )
l
   downup stops
lo
  downup stops
log
```

What this shows is that levels 3 and 4 are *part of* level 2. You can see that the traced invocation and stopping lines for levels 3 and 4 begin further to the right than the ones for level 2. Similarly, the lines for level 4 are further indented than the ones for level 3. This variation in indentation is a graphic display of the superprocedure/subprocedure relationships among the various invocations.

There are two ways of thinking about the lines that aren't indented. One way is to look at all such lines within, say, level 2:

```
log
lo
l
lo
log
```

This tells you that those five lines are printed somehow within the activity of level 2. (In terms of the little people metaphor, those lines are printed by Bill, either directly or through some subordinate elf.) Another way to look at it is this:

```
 ( downup "log )
log
  ( downup "lo )
  ...
  downup stops
log
 downup stops
```

What this picture is trying to convey is that only the two `log` lines are *directly* within the control of level 2. The three shorter lines (`lo`, `l`, `lo`) are delegated to level 3.

We've seen three different points of view from which to read the trace, one vertical and two horizontal. The vertical point of view shows the sequence of events in time. The horizontal point of view can show either the *total* responsibility of a given level or the *direct* responsibility of the level. To develop a full understanding of recursion, the trick is to be able to see all of these aspects of the program at the same time.

☞ Try invoking the traced `downup` with a single-letter input. Make a point of reading the resulting trace from all of these viewpoints. Then try a two-letter input.

Instruction Stepping

Perhaps you are comfortable with the idea of levels of invocation, but confused about the particular order of instructions within `downup`. Why should the `if` instruction be where it is, instead of before the first `print`, for example? Logo's `step` command will allow you to examine each instruction line within `downup` as it is carried out:

```
? step "downup
? downup "ant
[print :word] >>>
ant
[if equalp count :word 1 [stop]] >>>
[downup butlast :word] >>>
[print :word] >>>
an
[if equalp count :word 1 [stop]] >>>
[downup butlast :word] >>>
[print :word] >>>
a
[if equalp count :word 1 [stop]] >>>
[print :word] >>>
an
[print :word] >>>
ant
```

After each of the lines ending with >>>, Logo waits for you to press the RETURN or ENTER key.

You can combine `trace` and `step`:

```
? step "downup
? trace "downup
? downup "ant
( downup "ant )
[print :word] >>>
ant
[if equalp count :word 1 [stop]] >>>
[downup butlast :word] >>>
 ( downup "an )
 [print :word] >>>
an
 [if equalp count :word 1 [stop]] >>>
 [downup butlast :word] >>>
  ( downup "a )
  [print :word] >>>
a
  [if equalp count :word 1 [stop]] >>>
  downup stops
 [print :word] >>>
an
 downup stops
[print :word] >>>
ant
downup stops
```

In this case, the `step` lines are indented to match the `trace` lines.

Once a procedure is `traced` or `stepped`, it remains so until you use the `untrace` or `unstep` command to counteract the tracing or stepping.

☞ Try drawing a vertical line extending between the line

```
( downup "an )
```

and the equally indented

```
downup stops
```

Draw the line just to the left of the printing, after the indentation. The line you drew should also touch exactly four instruction lines. These four lines make up the entire definition of the `downup` procedure. If we restrict our attention to one particular invocation of `downup`, like the one you've marked, you can see that each of `downup`'s instructions is, indeed, evaluated in the proper sequence. Below each of these instruction lines, you can see the effect of the corresponding instruction. The two `print` instructions each print one line in the left (unindented) column. (In this case, they both print the word `an`.) The `if` instruction has no visible effect. But the recursive invocation of `downup` has quite a large effect; it brings into play the further invocation of `downup` with the word `a` as input.

One way to use the stepping information is to "play computer." Pretend you are the Logo interpreter, carrying out a `downup` instruction. Exactly what would you do, step by step? As you work through the instructions making up the procedure definition, you can check yourself by comparing your activities to what's shown on the screen.

10 Turtle Geometry

Logo is best known as the language that introduced the *turtle* as a tool for computer graphics. In fact, to many people, Logo and turtle graphics are synonymous. Some computer companies have gotten away with selling products called "Logo" that provided nothing *but* turtle graphics, but if you bought a "Logo" that provided only the list processing primitives we've used so far, you'd probably feel cheated.

Historically, this idea that Logo is mainly turtle graphics is a mistake. As I mentioned at the beginning of Chapter 1, Logo's name comes from the Greek word for *word,* because Logo was first designed as a language in which to manipulate language: words and sentences. Still, turtle graphics has turned out to be a very powerful addition to Logo. One reason is that any form of computer graphics is an attention-grabber. But other programming languages had allowed graphics programming before Logo. In this chapter we'll look at some of the reasons why *turtle* graphics, specifically, was such a major advance in programming technology.

This chapter can't be long enough to treat the possibilities of computer graphics fully. My goal is merely to show you that the same ideas we've been using with words and lists are also fruitful in a very different problem domain. Ideas like locality, modularity, and recursion appear here, too, although sometimes in different guises.

A Review, or a Brief Introduction

I've been assuming that you've already been introduced to Logo turtle graphics, either in a school or by reading Logo tutorial books. If not, perhaps you should read one of those books now. But just in case, here is a very brief overview of the primitive procedures for turtle graphics. Although some versions of Logo allow more than one turtle, or allow *dynamic* turtles with programmable shapes and speeds, for now I'll only consider the traditional, single, static turtle.

Type the command `cs` (short for `clearscreen`), with no inputs. The effect of this command is to initiate Logo's graphics capability. A turtle will appear in the center of a graphics window. (Depending on which version of Logo you have, the turtle may look like an actual animal with a head and four legs or—as in Berkeley Logo—it may be represented as a triangle.) The turtle will be facing toward the top of the screen. Any previous graphic drawing will be erased from the screen and from the computer's memory.

The crucial thing about the turtle, which distinguishes it from other metaphors for computer graphics, is that the turtle is pointing in a particular direction and can only move in that direction. (It can move forward or back, like a car with reverse gear, but not sideways.) In order to draw in any other direction, the turtle must *first* turn so that it is facing in the new direction. (In this respect it is unlike a car, which must turn and move at the same time.)

The primary means for moving the turtle is the `forward` command, abbreviated `fd`. `Forward` takes one input, which must be a number. The effect of `forward` is to move the turtle in the direction it's facing, through a distance specified by the input. The unit of distance is the "turtle step," a small distance that depends on the resolution of your computer's screen. (Generally, one turtle step is the smallest line your computer can draw. This is slightly oversimplified, though, because that smallest distance may be different in different directions. But the size of a turtle step does *not* depend on the direction; it's always the same distance for any given computer.) Try typing the command

```
forward 80
```

Since the turtle was facing toward the top of the screen, that's the way it moved. The turtle should now be higher on the screen, and there should be a line behind it indicating the path that it followed.

The first turtles were actual robots that rolled along the floor. They got the name "turtle" because of the hard shells surrounding their delicate electronic innards. A robot turtle has a pen in its belly, which it can push down to the floor, or pull up inside itself. When the pen is down, the turtle draws a trace of its motion along the floor.

When talking about the screen turtle, it's customary to think of the screen as a kind of map, representing a horizontal floor. Therefore, instead of referring to the screen directions as "up," "down," "left," and "right," we talk about the compass headings North, South, West, and East. Your turtle is now facing North. Besides fitting better with the turtle metaphor, this terminology avoids a possible confusion: the word "left" could mean either the *turtle's* left or the *screen's* left. (They're the same direction right now, but they won't be the same after we turn the turtle.) To avoid this problem, we use "West" for the left edge of the screen, and reserve the word "left" for the direction to the left of whichever way the turtle is facing.

Logo provides primitive commands to raise and lower the turtle's pen. The command `penup` (abbreviated `pu`) takes no inputs; its effect is to raise the pen. In other words, after you use this command, any further turtle motion won't draw lines. Try it now:

```
penup
forward 30
```

Similarly, the command `pendown` (`pd`) takes no inputs, and lowers the pen. Here's a procedure you can try:

```
to dash :count
repeat :count [penup forward 4 pendown forward 4]
end

? clearscreen dash 14
```

The command `back` (or `bk`) takes one input, which must be a number. The effect of `back` is to move the turtle backward by the distance used as its input. (What do you think `fd` and `bk` will do if you give them noninteger inputs? Zero inputs? Negative inputs? Try these possibilities. Then look up the commands in the reference manual for your version of Logo and see if the manual describes the commands fully.)

To turn the turtle, two other commands are provided. `Left` (abbreviated `lt`) takes one input, which must be a number. Its effect is to turn the turtle toward the *turtle's* own left. The angle through which the turtle turns is the input; angles are measured in degrees, so `left 360` will turn the turtle all the way around. (In other words, that instruction has no real effect!) Another way of saying that the turtle turns toward its own left is that it turns *counterclockwise.* The command `right` (or `rt`) is just like `left`, except that it turns the turtle clockwise, toward its own right.

☞ Clear the screen and try this, the classic beginning point of Logo turtle graphics:

```
repeat 4 [forward 100 right 90]
```

This instruction tells Logo to draw four lines, each 100 turtle steps long, and to turn 90 degrees between lines. In other words, it draws a square.

There are many more turtle procedures provided in Logo, but these are the fundamental ones; with them you can go quite far in generating interesting computer graphics. If you haven't had much experience with turtle graphics before, you might enjoy spending some time exploring the possibilities. There are many introductory Logo turtle graphics books to help you. Because that part of Logo programming is so thoroughly covered elsewhere, I'm not going to suggest graphics projects here. Instead I want to go on to consider some of the deeper issues in computer programming that are illuminated by the turtle metaphor.

Local vs. Global Descriptions

Earlier we considered the difference between *local* variables, which are available only within a particular procedure, and *global* variables, which are used throughout an entire project. I've tried to convince you that the use of local variables is a much more powerful programming style than one that relies on global variables for everything. For one thing, local variables are essential to make recursion possible; in order for a single procedure to solve a large problem and a smaller subproblem simultaneously, each invocation of the procedure must have its own, independent variables. But even when recursion is not an issue, a complex program is much easier to read and understand if each procedure can be understood without thinking about the context in which it's used.

The turtle approach to computer graphics embodies the same principle of locality, in a different way. The fact that the turtle motion commands (`forward` and `back`) and the turtle turning commands (`left` and `right`) are all *turtle-relative* means that a graphics procedure need not think about the larger picture.

To understand what that means, you should compare the turtle metaphor with the other metaphor that is commonly used in computer graphics: *Cartesian coordinates.* This metaphor comes from analytic geometry, invented by René Descartes (1596–1650). The word "Cartesian" is derived from his name. Descartes' goal was to use the techniques of algebra in solving geometry problems by using *numbers* to describe *points.* In a two-dimensional plane, like your computer screen, you need two numbers to identify a point. These numbers work like longitude and latitude in geography: One tells how far the point is to the left or right and the other tells how high up it is.

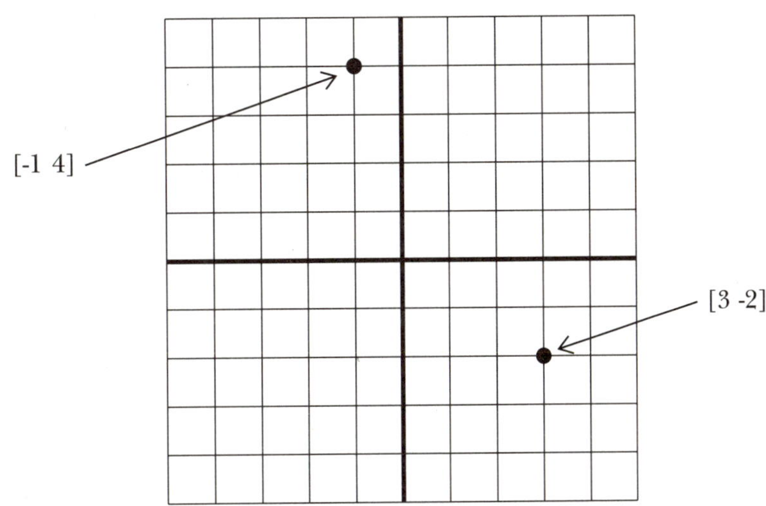

This diagram shows a computer screen with a grid of horizontal and vertical lines drawn on it. The point where the two heavy lines meet is called the *origin;* it is represented by the numbers `[0 0]`. For other points the first number (the *x-coordinate*) is the horizontal distance from the origin to the point, and the second number (the *y-coordinate*) is the vertical distance from the origin to the point. A positive x-coordinate means that the point is to the right of the origin; a negative x-coordinate means that the point is to the left of the origin. Similarly, a positive y-coordinate means that the point is above the origin; a negative y-coordinate puts it below the origin. Logo does allow you to refer to points by their Cartesian coordinates, using a list of two numbers. The origin is the point where the turtle starts when you clear the screen.

The primary tool for Cartesian-style graphics in Logo is the command `setpos` (for `set position`). `Setpos` requires one input, which must be a list of two numbers. Its effect is to move the turtle to the point on the screen at those coordinates. If the pen is down, the turtle draws a line as it moves, just as it does for `forward` and `back`. Here is how you might draw a square using Cartesian graphics instead of turtle graphics:

```
clearscreen
setpos [0 100]
setpos [100 100]
setpos [100 0]
setpos [0 0]
```

Do you see why I said that the Cartesian metaphor is global, like the use of global variables? Each instruction in this square takes into account the turtle's position within the screen as a whole. The "point of view" from which we draw the picture is that of an observer standing above the plane looking down on all of it. This observer sees not only the turtle but also the edges and center of the screen as part of what is relevant to drawing each line. By contrast, the turtle geometry metaphor adopts the point of view of the turtle itself; each line is drawn without regard to where the turtle is in global terms.

Using the turtle metaphor, we can draw our square (or any other figure we can program) anywhere on the screen at any orientation. First I'll write a `square` command:

```
to square :size
repeat 4 [forward :size right 90]
end
```

Now here's an example of how `square` can be used in different positions and orientations:

```
to face
pendown square 100
penup forward 20
right 90
forward 25
pendown forward 50
penup back 75
left 90
forward 65
right 90
forward 20
pendown square 15
penup forward 45
pendown square 15
penup back 15
right 90
forward 20
left 45
pendown square 20
end
```

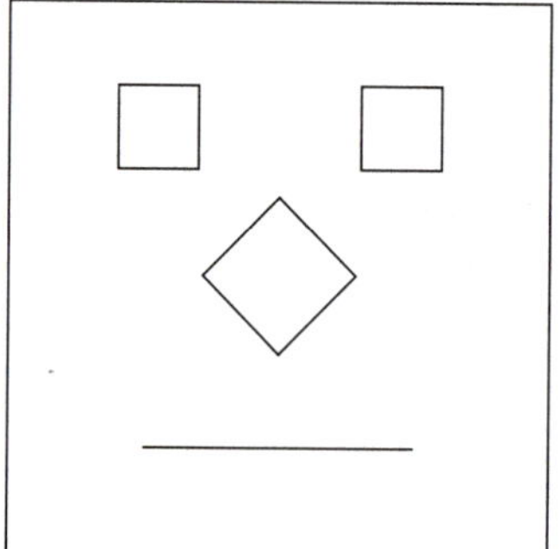

The head and the eyes are upright squares; the nose is a square at an angle (a diamond). To write this program using Cartesian graphics, you'd have to know the absolute coordinates of the corners of each of the squares. To draw a square at an unusual angle, you'd need trigonometry to calculate the coordinates.

☞ Here is another demonstration of the same point. Clear the screen and type this instruction:

```
repeat 20 [pendown square 12 penup forward 20 right 18]
```

You'll see squares drawn in several different orientations. This would not be a one-line program if you tried to do it using the Cartesian metaphor!

The Turtle's State

From a turtle's-eye point of view, drawing an upright square is the same as drawing a diamond. It's only from the global point of view, taking the borders of the screen into account, that there is a difference.

From the global point of view how can we think about that difference? How do we describe what makes the same procedure sometimes draw one thing (an upright square) and sometimes another (a diamond)? The answer, in the most general terms, is that the result of the `square` command depends on the past *history* of the turtle—its twists and turns before it got to wherever it may be now. That is, the turtle has a sort of memory of past events.

But what matters is not actually the turtle's entire past history. All that counts is the turtle's current *position* and its current *heading,* no matter how it got there. Those two things, the position and the heading, are called the turtle's *state.* It's a little like trying to solve a Rubik's Cube; you may have turned part of the cube 100 times already, but all that counts now is the current pattern of colors, not how you got there.

I've mentioned the `setpos` command, which sets the turtle's position. There is also a command `setheading` (abbreviated `seth`) to set the heading. `Setheading` takes one input, a number. The effect is to turn the turtle so that it faces toward the compass heading specified by the number. Zero represents North; the heading is measured in degrees clockwise from North. (For example, East is 90; West is 270.) The compass heading is different from the system of angle measurement used in analytic geometry, in which angles are measured counterclockwise from East instead of clockwise from North.

In addition to commands that set the turtle's state, Logo provides operations to find out the state. `Pos` is an operation with no inputs. Its output is a list of two numbers, representing the turtle's current position. `Heading` is also an operation with no inputs. Its output is a number, representing the turtle's current heading.

Remember that when you use these state commands and operations, you're thinking in the global (Cartesian) style, not the local (turtle) style. Global state is sometimes important, just as global variables are sometimes useful. If you want to draw a picture containing three widgets, you might use `setpos` to get the turtle into position for each widget. But the `widget` procedure, which draws each widget, probably shouldn't use `setpos`. (You might also use `setpos` extensively in a situation in which the Cartesian metaphor is generally more appropriate than the turtle metaphor, like graphing a mathematical function.) As in the case of global variables, you'll be most likely to overuse global graphics style if you're accustomed to BASIC computer graphics. A good rule of thumb, if you're doing something turtleish and not graphing a function, is that you shouldn't use `setpos` with the pen down.

☞ Do you see why?

Symmetry

Very young children often begin playing with Logo simply by moving the turtle around at random. The resulting pictures usually don't look very interesting. You can recapture the days of your youth by alternating `forward` and `right` commands with arbitrary inputs. Here is a sample, which I've embodied in a procedure:

```
to squiggle
forward 100
right 135
forward 40
right 120
forward 60
right 15
end
```

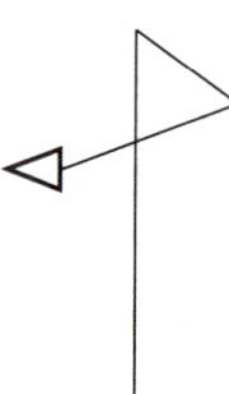

This isn't a very beautiful picture. But something interesting happens when you keep squiggling repeatedly:

```
repeat 20 [squiggle]
```

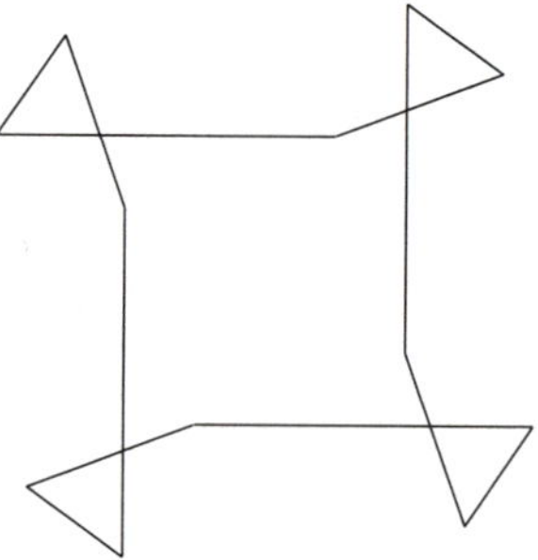

Instead of filling up the screen with hash, the turtle draws a symmetrical shape and repeats the same path over and over! Let's try another example:

```
to squaggle
forward 50
right 150
forward 60
right 100
forward 30
right 90
end
```

`squaggle`

`repeat 20 [squaggle]`

`Squiggle` turns into a sort of fancy square when you repeat it; `squaggle` turns into an 18-pointed pinwheel. Does every possible squiggle produce a repeating pattern this way? Yes. Sometimes you have to `repeat` the procedure many times, but essentially any combination of `forward` and `right` commands will eventually retrace its steps. (There's one exception, which we'll talk about shortly.)

To see why repetition brings order out of chaos, we have to think about a simpler Logo graphics procedure that is probably very familiar to you:

```
to poly :size :angle
forward :size
right :angle
poly :size :angle
end
```

Since this is a recursive procedure without a stop rule, it'll keep running forever. You'll have to stop it by pressing the BREAK key, or command-period, or whatever your particular computer requires. The procedure draws regular polygons; here are some examples to try:

```
poly 100 90
poly 80 60
poly 100 144
```

A little thought (or some experimentation) will show you that the `size` input makes the picture larger or smaller but doesn't change its shape. The shape is entirely controlled by the `angle` input.

☞ What angle would you pick to draw a triangle? A pentagon? How do you know?

The trick is to think about the turtle's state. When you finish drawing a polygon, the turtle must return to its original position *and its original heading* in order to be ready to retrace the same path. To return to its original heading, the turtle must turn through a complete circle, 360 degrees. To draw a square, for example, the turtle must turn through 360 degrees in four turns, so each turn must be 360/4 or 90 degrees. To draw a triangle, each turn must be 360/3 or 120 degrees.

☞ Now explain why an `angle` input of 144 draws a star!

Okay, back to our squiggles. Earlier, I said that the only thing we have to remember from the turtle's past history is the change in its state. It doesn't matter how that change came about. When you draw a `squiggle`, the turtle moves through a certain distance and turns through a certain angle. The fact that it took a roundabout path doesn't matter. As it happens, `squiggle` turns right through 135 + 120 + 15 degrees, for a total of 270. This is equivalent to turning left by 90 degrees. That's why repeating `squiggle` draws something shaped like a square.

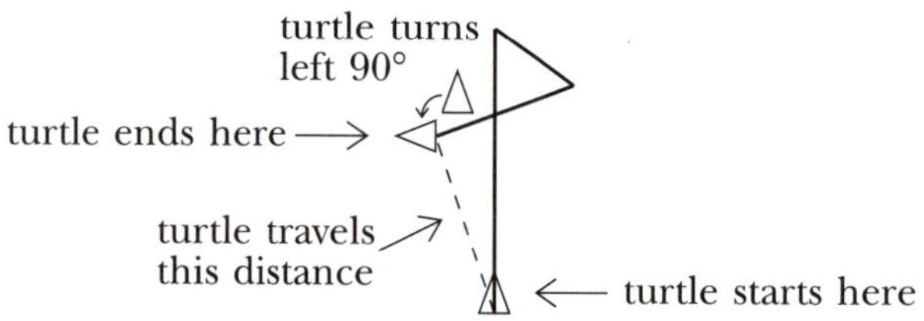

☞ What about `squaggle`? If repeating it draws a figure with 18-fold symmetry, then its total turning should be 360/18 or 20 degrees. Is it?

☞ Here's another bizarre shape. See if you can predict what kind of symmetry it will show *before* you actually repeat it on the computer.

```
to squoggle
forward 50
right 70
forward 10
right 160
forward 35
right 58
end
```

Suppose you like the shape of `squiggle`, but you want to draw a completed picture that looks triangular (3-fold symmetry) instead of square (4-fold). Can you do this? Of course; you can simply change the last instruction of the `squiggle` procedure so that the total turning is 120 degrees instead of 90. (Go ahead, try it. Be careful about left and right.)

But it's rather an ugly process to have to edit `squiggle` in order to change not what a squiggle looks like but how the squiggles fit into a larger picture. For one thing, it violates the idea of modularity. `Squiggle`'s job should just be drawing a squiggle, and there should be another procedure, something like `poly`, that combines squiggles into a symmetrical pattern. For another, people shouldn't have to do arithmetic; computers should do the arithmetic!

To clean up our act, I'm going to start by writing a procedure that can draw an arbitrary squiggle but without changing the turtle's heading. It's called `protect.heading` because it protects the heading against change by the squiggle procedure.

```
to protect.heading :squig
local "oldheading
make "oldheading heading
run :squig
setheading :oldheading
end
```

This procedure demonstrates the use of `heading` and `setheading`. We remember the turtle's initial heading in the local variable `oldheading`. Then we carry out whatever squiggle procedure you specify as the input to `protect.heading`. (The `run` command takes a Logo instruction list as input and evaluates it.) Here is how you can use it:

```
protect.heading [squiggle]
protect.heading [squaggle]
```

Notice that what is drawn on the screen is the same as it would be if you invoked `squiggle` or `squaggle` directly; the difference is that the turtle's final heading is the same as its initial heading.

`squiggle`　　　　`protect.heading [squiggle]`

Now we can use `protect.heading` to write the decorated-`poly` procedure that will let us specify the kind of symmetry we want:

```
to spin :turns :command
repeat :turns [protect.heading :command right 360/:turns]
end
```

☞ Try out `spin` with instructions like these:

```
spin 3 [squiggle]
spin 5 [squiggle]
spin 4 [squaggle]
spin 6 [squoggle]
spin 6 [fd 40 squoggle]
spin 5 [pu fd 50 pd squaggle]
```

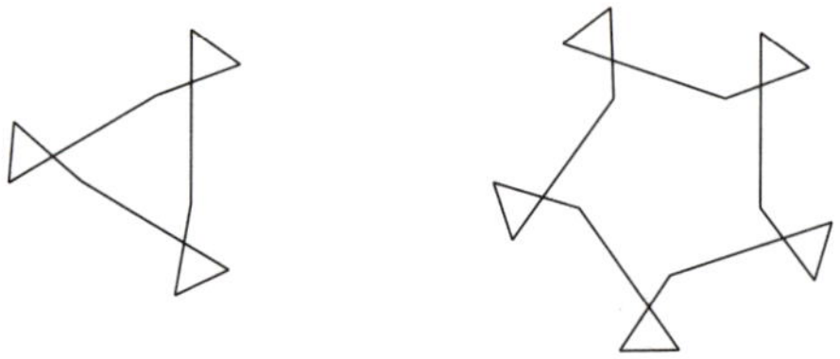

Isn't that better?

I mentioned that there is an exception to the rule that every squiggle will eventually retrace its steps if you repeat it. Here it is:

```
to squirrel
forward 40
right 90
forward 10
right 90
forward 15
right 90
forward 20
right 90
end
```

☞ Try repeating `squirrel` 20 times. You'll find that instead of turning around to its original position and heading, the turtle goes straight off into the distance. Why? (`Squiggle` had four-fold symmetry because its total turning was 90 degrees. What is the total turning of `squirrel`?) Of course, if you use `squirrel` in the second input to `spin`, it will perform like the others, because `spin` controls the turtle's heading in that case.

I've been using random squiggles with silly names to make the point that by paying attention to symmetry, Logo *can* make a silk purse from a sow's ear. But of course there is no reason not to apply `spin` to more carefully designed pieces. Here's one I like:

```
to fingers :size
penup forward 10 pendown
right 5
repeat 5 [forward :size right 170 forward :size left 170]
left 5
penup back 10 pendown
end
```

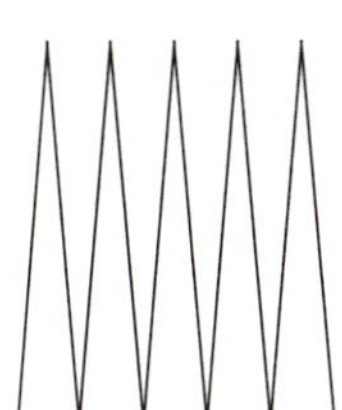

```
spin 4 [fingers 50]
spin 10 [fingers 30]
```

Fractals

I'd like to write a procedure to draw this picture of a tree:

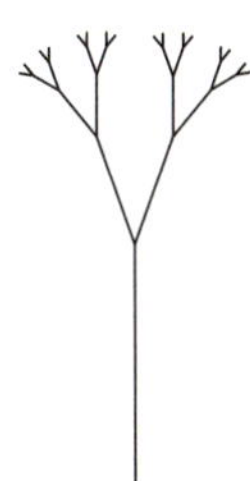

The trick is to identify this as a recursive problem. Do you see the smaller-but-similar subproblems? The tree consists of a trunk with two smaller trees attached.

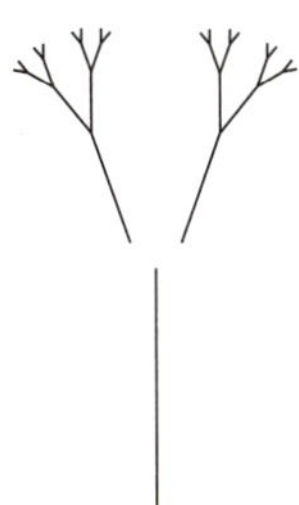

So a first approximation to the solution might look like this:

```
to tree :size
forward :size
left 20
tree :size/2
right 40
tree :size/2
end
```

If you try running this procedure, you'll see that we still have some work to do. But let me remind you that an unfinished procedure like this isn't a *mistake;* you shouldn't feel that you have to have every detail worked out before you first touch the keyboard. The first obvious problem is that there is no stop rule, so the procedure keeps trying to draw smaller and smaller subtrees. What should the limiting condition be? In this case there is no obvious end, like the `butfirst` of a word becoming empty.

There are two approaches we could take to limiting the number of branches of the tree. One approach would be to choose explicitly how deep we want to get in recursive invocations. We could do this by adding another input, called `depth`, that will be the number of levels of recursion to allow:

```
to tree :depth :size
if :depth=0 [stop]
forward :size
left 20
tree (:depth-1) :size/2
right 40
tree (:depth-1) :size/2
end
```

The other approach would be to keep letting the branches get smaller until they go below a reasonable minimum:

```
to tree :size
if :size<4 [stop]
forward :size
left 20
tree :size/2
right 40
tree :size/2
end
```

Either approach is reasonable. I'll choose the second one just because it seems a little simpler. The cost of that choice is somewhat less control over the final picture; I'm not sure if it'll have exactly the number of branches I originally planned.

The modified procedure does come to a halt now, but it still doesn't draw the tree I had in mind. The problem is that this version of `tree` is not *state-invariant:* it doesn't leave the turtle with the same position and heading that it had originally. That's important because when `tree` says

```
tree :size/2
right 40
tree :size/2
```

the assumption is that at the end of the first smaller tree the turtle will be back at the top of the main trunk, in position to draw the second subtree. We can fix the problem by making the turtle climb back down the trunk (of each subtree):

```
to tree :size
if :size<4 [stop]
forward :size
left 20
tree :size/2
right 40
tree :size/2
left 20
back :size
end
```

Voilà! If you try `tree 50` you'll see something like the picture I had in mind.

You're probably thinking that this "tree" doesn't look very tree-like. There are several things wrong with it: It's too symmetrical; it doesn't have enough branches; the branches should grow partway up the trunk as well as at the top. But all of these problems can be solved by adding a few more steps to the procedure:

```
to tree :size
if :size < 5 [forward :size back :size stop]
forward :size/3
left 30 tree :size*2/3 right 30
forward :size/6
right 25 tree :size/2 left 25
forward :size/3
right 25 tree :size/2 left 25
forward :size/6
back :size
end
```

We can embellish the tree as much as we want. The only requirement is that the procedure be state-invariant: The turtle's final position and heading must be the same as its beginning position and heading.

Because I chose to use a minimum length as the stopping condition, the shape of the tree depends on the size of its trunk. That's slightly unusual in turtle graphics programs, which usually draw the same shape regardless of the size.

A recursively-defined shape (one that contains smaller versions of itself) is called a *fractal.* Until the 1970s, hardly anybody explored fractals except for kids learning Logo and a few recreational mathematicians. Today, however, fractals have become important becase movie producers are using computer graphics as an alternative to expensive sets and models for fancy special effects. It turns out that programs like `tree` are the secret of drawing realistic clouds, mountains, and other natural backgrounds with a computer.

☞ If you want another challenging fractal project, try writing a program to produce these fractal snowflakes:

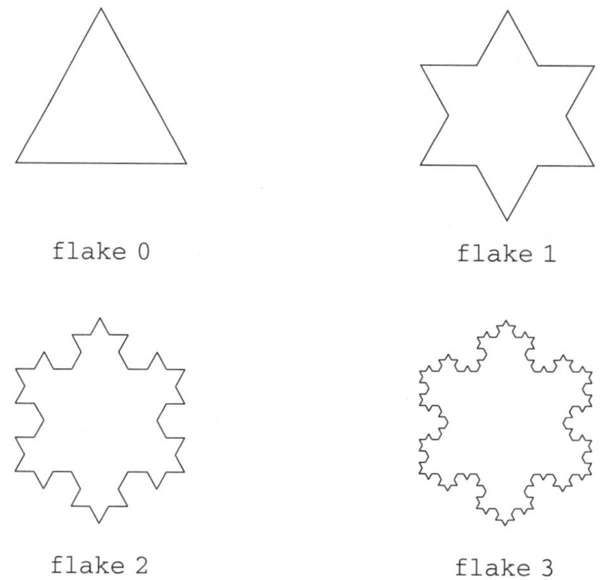

Further Reading

If you're interested in an intellectually rigorous exploration of turtle geometry, continuing along the lines I've started here, read *Turtle Geometry,* Abelson and diSessa (MIT Press, 1981). I learned many of the things in this chapter from them. It's a hard book but worth the effort.

The standard reference book on fractals is *The Fractal Geometry of Nature,* by Benoit Mandelbrot (W. H. Freeman, 1982). Dr. Mandelbrot gave fractals their name and was the first to see serious uses for them.

11 Recursive Operations

So far, the recursive procedures we've seen have all been commands, not operations. Remember that an operation is a procedure that has an *output* rather than an *effect*. In other words, an operation computes some value that is then used as the input to some other procedure. In the instruction

```
print first "hello
```

`print` is a command, because it does something: It prints its input (whatever that may be) on the screen. But `first` is an operation, because it computes something: With the word `hello` as input, it computes the letter `h`, which is the first letter of the input.

A Simple Substitution Cipher

I'm going to write a program to produce secret messages. The program will take an ordinary English sentence (in the form of a Logo list) and change each letter into some other letter. For example, we can decide to replace the letter E with the letter J every time it occurs in the message. The program will need two inputs: the message and the correspondence between letters. The latter will take the form of a word of 26 letters, representing the coded versions of the 26 letters in alphabetical order. For example, the word

```
qwertyuiopasdfghjklzxcvbnm
```

indicates that the letter A in the original text will be represented by Q in the secret version, B will be represented by W, and so on.

In order to encipher a sentence, we must go through it word by word. (Strictly speaking, what we're doing is called a *cipher* rather than a *code* because the latter is a system that substitutes something for an entire word at a time, like a foreign language, whereas we're substituting for a single letter at a time, like the Elvish alphabet in *The Lord of the Rings*.) In order to encipher a word we must go through it letter by letter. So I'll begin by writing a procedure to translate a single letter to its coded form.

```
to codelet :letter :code
output codematch :letter "abcdefghijklmnopqrstuvwxyz :code
end

to codematch :letter :clear :code
if emptyp :clear [output :letter]        ; punctuation character
if equalp :letter first :clear [output first :code]
output codematch :letter butfirst :clear butfirst :code
end
```

`Codelet` is an operation that takes two inputs. The first input must be a single-letter word, and the second must be a code, that is, a word with the 26 letters of the alphabet rearranged. The output from `codelet` is the enciphered version of the input letter. (If the first input is a character other than a letter, such as a punctuation mark, then the output is the same as that input.)

`Codelet` itself is a very simple procedure. It simply passes its two inputs on to a subprocedure, `codematch`, along with another input that is the alphabet in normal order. The idea is that `codematch` will compare the input letter to each of the letters in the regular alphabet; when it finds a match, it will output the letter in the corresponding position in the scrambled alphabet. Be sure you understand the use of the `output` command in `codelet`; it says that whatever `codematch` outputs should become the output from `codelet` as well.

The job of `codematch` is to go through the alphabet, letter by letter, looking for the particular letter we're trying to encode. The primary tool that Logo provides for looking at a single letter in a word is `first`. So `codematch` uses `first` to compare its input letter with the first letter of the input alphabet:

```
if equalp :letter first :clear ...
```

If the first input to `codematch` is the letter A, then `equalp` will output `true` and `codematch` will output the first letter of `:code` (Q in the example I gave earlier). But suppose the first input isn't an A. Then `codematch` has to solve a smaller subproblem: Find the input letter in the remaining 25 letters of the alphabet. Finding a smaller, similar subproblem means that we can use a recursive solution. `Codematch` invokes itself, but for its second and third inputs it uses the butfirsts of the original inputs because the first letter of the alphabet (A) and its corresponding coded letter (Q) have already been rejected.

Here is a trace of an example of codematch at work, to help you understand what's going on.

```
codematch "e "abcdefghijklmnopqrstuvwxyz "qwertyuiopasdfghjklzxcvbnm
   codematch "e "bcdefghijklmnopqrstuvwxyz "wertyuiopasdfghjklzxcvbnm
      codematch "e "cdefghijklmnopqrstuvwxyz "ertyuiopasdfghjklzxcvbnm
         codematch "e "defghijklmnopqrstuvwxyz "rtyuiopasdfghjklzxcvbnm
            codematch "e "efghijklmnopqrstuvwxyz "tyuiopasdfghjklzxcvbnm
            codematch outputs "t
         codematch outputs "t
      codematch outputs "t
   codematch outputs "t
codematch outputs "t
```

The fifth, innermost invocation of codematch succeeds at matching its first input (the letter E) with the first letter of its second input. That invocation therefore outputs the first letter of its third input, the letter T. Each of the higher-level invocations outputs the same thing in turn.

The pattern of doing something to the first of an input, then invoking the same procedure recursively with the butfirst as the new input, is a familiar one from recursive commands. If we only wanted to translate single letters, we could have written codelet and codematch as commands, like this:

```
to codelet :letter :code                               ;; command version
codematch :letter "abcdefghijklmnopqrstuvwxyz :code
end

to codematch :letter :clear :code                      ;; command version
if emptyp :clear [print :letter stop]
if equalp :letter first :clear [print first :code stop]
codematch :letter butfirst :clear butfirst :code
end
```

You may find this version a little easier to understand, because it's more like the recursive commands we've examined in the past. But making codelet an operation is a much stronger technique. Instead of being required to print the computed code letter, we can make that letter part of a larger computation. In fact, we have to do that in order to encipher a complete word. Each word is made up of letters, and the task of codeword will be to go through a word, letter by letter, using each letter as input to codelet. The letters output by codelet must be combined into a new word, which will be the output from codeword.

We could write codeword using the higher order function map:

```
to codeword :word :code                ;; using higher order function
output map [codelet ? :code] :word
end
```

But to help you learn how to write recursive operations, in this chapter we'll avoid higher order functions. (As it turns out, map itself is a recursive operation, written using the techniques of this chapter.)

Recall the structure of a previous procedure that went through a word letter by letter:

```
to one.per.line :word
if emptyp :word [stop]
print first :word
one.per.line butfirst :word
end
```

Compare this to the structure of the recursive codeword:

```
to codeword :word :code
if emptyp :word [output "]
output word (codelet first :word :code) (codeword butfirst :word :code)
end
```

There are many similarities. Both procedures have a stop rule that tests for an empty input. Both do something to the first of the input (either print or codelet), and each invokes itself recursively on the butfirst of the input. (Codeword has an extra input for the code letters, but that doesn't really change the structure of the procedure. If that's confusing to you, you could temporarily pretend that code is a global variable and eliminate it as an input.)

The differences have to do with the fact that codeword is an operation instead of a command. The stop rule invokes output rather than stop and must therefore specify what is to be output when the stop condition is met. (In this case, when the input word is empty, the output is also the empty word.) But the main thing is that the action step (the print in one.per.line) and the recursive call (the one.per.line instruction) are not two separate instructions in `codeword`. Instead they are expressions (the two in parentheses) that are combined by `word` to form the complete output. Here's a picture:

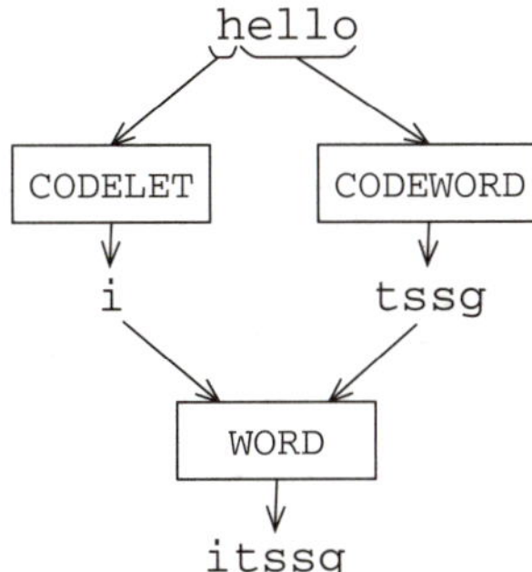

Remember what you learned in Chapter 2 about the way in which Logo instructions are evaluated. Consider the `output` instruction in `codeword`. Before `output` can be invoked, Logo must evaluate its input. That input comes from the output from `word`. Before `word` can be invoked, Logo must evaluate *its* inputs. There are two of them. The first input to `word` is the expression

```
codelet first :word :code
```

This expression computes the coded version of the first letter of the word we want to translate. The second input to `word` is the expression

```
codeword butfirst :word :code
```

This expression invokes `codeword` recursively, solving the smaller subproblem of translating a smaller word, one with the first letter removed. When both of these computations are complete, `word` can combine the results to form the translation of the complete input word. Then `output` can output that result.

Here's an example of how `codeword` is used.

```
? print codeword "hello "qwertyuiopasdfghjklzxcvbnm
itssg
```

Notice that we have to say `print`, not just start the instruction line with `codeword`; a complete instruction must have a command. Suppose you had the idea of saving all that typing by changing the `output` instruction in `codeword` to a `print`. What would happen? The answer is that `codeword` wouldn't be able to invoke itself recursively as an operation. (If you don't understand that, try it!) Also, it's generally a better idea to write an operation when you have to compute some result. That way, you aren't committed to printing the result; you can use it as part of a larger computation.

For example, right now I'd like to write a procedure code that translates an entire sentence into code. Like codeword, it will be an operation with two inputs, the second of which is a code (a word of 26 scrambled letters). The difference is that the first input will be a sentence instead of a word and the output will also be a sentence.

☞ Write code using a higher order function. Then see if you can write an equivalent recursive version.

Just as codeword works by splitting up the word into letters, code will work by splitting up a sentence into words. The structure will be very similar. Here it is:

```
to code :sent :code
if emptyp :sent [output []]
output sentence (codeword first :sent :code) (code butfirst :sent :code)
end
```

The main differences are that code outputs the empty list, instead of the empty word, for an empty input and that sentence is used as the combining operation instead of word. Here's an example of code at work.

```
? print code [meet at midnight, under the dock.] ~
             "qwertyuiopasdfghjklzxcvbnm
dttz qz dorfouiz, xfrtk zit rgea.
```

More Procedure Patterns

Code and codeword are examples of a very common pattern in recursive operations: They are like using map with a particular function. Here is the pattern that they fit.

```
to procedure :input
if emptyp :input [output :input]
output combiner (something first :input) (procedure butfirst :input)
end
```

The *combiner* is often word or sentence, although others are possible. In fact, when working with lists, the most common combiner is not sentence but another operation that we haven't used before, fput (First PUT). Fput takes two inputs. The first can be any datum, but the second must be a list. The output from fput is a list that is equal to the second input, except that the first input is inserted as a new first member. In other words the output from fput is a list whose first is the first input and whose butfirst is the second input.

```
? show sentence [hee hee hee] [ho ho ho]
[hee hee hee ho ho ho]
? show fput [hee hee hee] [ho ho ho]
[[hee hee hee] ho ho ho]
```

Fput is a good combiner because the two things we want to combine are the first and the butfirst of a list, except that each has been modified in some way. But the *shape* of the final result (a list of so many members) should be the same as the shape of the input, and that's what fput ensures.

When you're working with sentences—lists of words rather than lists of lists—sentence and fput will work equally well as the combiner. For example, code could have been written using fput instead of sentence. Not until some of the later examples, when we use tree-structured lists, will the choice really be important.

☞ Fput is actually a "more primitive" operation than sentence, in the sense that the Logo interpreter actually constructs lists by doing the internal equivalent of fput. As an exercise, you might like to try writing your own versions of list combiners like sentence and list out of fput, first, and butfirst. You should also be able to write last and butlast using only those three building blocks. (Actually you'll also need if, emptyp, wordp, and output, but you won't need any other primitive combiners.) Give your versions distinct names, such as my-sentence, since Logo won't let you redefine primitives.

☞ Another "less primitive" primitive is lput, an operation that takes two inputs. As for fput, the first can be any datum but the second must be a list. The output from lput is a list whose last is the first input and whose butlast is the second. Write my-lput using fput and the selectors first and butfirst.

It may seem silly to learn a recursive pattern for problems that can be solved using map. But sometimes we run into a problem that's *almost* like a map, but not exactly. For example, how would you write the following operation:

```
? show pairup [now here after glow worm hole]
[nowhere hereafter afterglow glowworm wormhole]
```

Instead of the usual map-like situation in which each word in the result is a function of one word of the input, this time each word of the result is a function of *two* neighboring input words. Map won't solve this problem, but the map-like recursion pattern will.

```
to pairup :words
if emptyp butfirst :words [output []]
output (sentence (word first :words first butfirst :words)
                 (pairup butfirst :words))
end
```

Compare this procedure with the general pattern on page 200; look for similarities and differences.

☞ One difference is in the test for the base case. Why is the version in `pairup` different from the one in the pattern?

☞ Write an operation that interchanges pairs of words in a sentence, like this:

```
? show swap [the rain in spain stays mainly on the plain]
[rain the spain in mainly stays the on plain]
```

Don't forget to think about that leftover word in an odd-length sentence!

The `Filter` Pattern

In Chapter 5 we saw this example:

```
? show filter "numberp [76 trombones, 4 calling birds, and 8 days]
[76 4 8]
```

To write a recursive operation `numbers` with the same result, we must handle three cases: the base case, in which the input is empty; the case in which the first word of the input is a number; and the case in which the first word isn't a number.

```
to numbers :sent
if emptyp :sent [output []]
if numberp first :sent ~
   [output sentence first :sent numbers butfirst :sent]
output numbers butfirst :sent
end
```

```
? show numbers [76 trombones, 4 calling birds, and 8 days]
[76 4 8]
```

Here's the general `filter` pattern:

```
to procedure :input
if emptyp :input [output :input]
if predicate first :input ~
   [output combiner first :input procedure butfirst :input]
output procedure butfirst :input
end
```

As in the case of the `map` pattern, this one is most useful in situations for which the higher order function won't quite do.

☞ Write an operation that looks for two equal words next to each other in a sentence, and outputs a sentence with one of them removed:

```
? show unique [Paris in the the spring is a joy joy to behold.]
Paris in the spring is a joy to behold.
```

What does your procedure do with *three* consecutive equal words? What should it do?

The Reduce Pattern

Other examples from Chapter 5 introduced the `reduce` higher order function.

```
? show reduce "word [C S L S]
CSLS
? show reduce "sum [3 4 5 6]
18
```

Recursive operations equivalent to these examples are very much like the `map` pattern except that the combiner function is applied to the members of the input directly, rather than to some function of the members of the input:

```
to wordify :sentence
if emptyp :sentence [output "]
output word (first :sentence) (wordify butfirst :sentence)
end

to addup :numbers
if emptyp :numbers [output 0]
output sum (first :numbers) (addup butfirst :numbers)
end
```

What are the differences between these two examples? There are two: the combiner used and the value output in the base case. Here is the pattern:

```
to procedure :input
if emptyp :input [output identity]
output combiner (first :input) (procedure butfirst :input)
end
```

The **identity** in this pattern depends on the combiner; it's the value that, when combined with something else, gives that something else unchanged as the result. Thus, zero is the identity for sum, but the identity for product would be one.

☞ Write a multiply operation that takes a list of numbers as its input and returns the product of all the numbers.

☞ You can make your multiply procedure more efficient, in some situations, by having it notice when one of the numbers in the input list is zero. In that case, you can output zero as the overall result without looking at any more numbers. The resulting procedure will, in a sense, combine aspects of the filter and reduce patterns.

Addup is one example of an important sub-category of reduce-like procedures in which the "combining" operation is arithmetic, usually sum. The simplest example is a procedure equivalent to the primitive count, which counts the members of a list or the letters of a word:

```
to length :thing
if emptyp :thing [output 0]
output 1+length butfirst :thing
end
```

In this procedure, as usual, we can see the reduction of a problem to a smaller subproblem. The length of any word or list is one more than the length of its butfirst. Eventually this process of shortening the input will reduce it to emptiness; the length of an empty word or list is zero.

Although count is a primitive, there are more complicated counting situations in which not every member should be counted. For example, here is a procedure to count the number of vowels in a word:

```
to vowelcount :word
if emptyp :word [output 0]
if vowelp first :word [output 1+vowelcount butfirst :word]
output vowelcount butfirst :word
end
```

```
to vowelp :letter
output memberp :letter [a e i o u]
end
```

(Actually, my predicate `vowelp` is somewhat oversimplified. The letter Y is a vowel in certain positions in the word, and even some other letters can sometimes play the role of a vowel. But this isn't a book on linguistics!)

You can see the similarities between `vowelcount` and `length`. The difference is that, in effect, `length` uses a predicate that is always `true`, so it always carries out the instruction inside the `if`. Here's the pattern:

```
to procedure :input
if emptyp :input [output 0]
if predicate first :input [output 1+procedure butfirst :input]
output procedure butfirst :input
end
```

☞ Try writing a procedure that will accept as input a word like `$21,997.00` and output the number of digits before the decimal point. (In this case the correct output is 5.) Don't assume that there *is* a decimal point; your program shouldn't blow up no matter what word it gets as input.

☞ Another counting problem is to output the position of a member in a list. This operation is the inverse to `item`, a Logo primitive, which outputs the member at a given position number. What I'm asking you to write is `index`, which works like this:

```
? print index "seven [four score and seven years ago]
4
? print index "v "aardvark
5
```

The `Find` Pattern

A variation of the `filter` pattern is for *selection* operations: ones that pick a single element out of a list. The general idea looks like this:

```
to procedure :input
if emptyp :input [output :input]
if predicate first :input [output something first :input]
output procedure butfirst :input
end
```

There will generally be extra inputs to these procedures, to indicate the basis for selection. For example, here is a program that translates English words into French.

```
to french :word
output lookup :word [[book livre] [computer ordinateur] [window fenetre]]
end

to lookup :word :dictionary
if emptyp :dictionary [output "]
if equalp :word first first :dictionary [output last first :dictionary]
output lookup :word butfirst :dictionary
end
```

```
? print french "computer
ordinateur
```

The expression

```
first first :dictionary
```

selects the English word from the first word-pair in the list. Similarly,

```
last first :dictionary
```

selects the French version of the same word. (Of course, in reality, the word list in `french` would be much longer than the three word-pairs I've shown.)

`Codematch`, in the example that started this chapter, follows the same pattern of selection. The only difference is that there are two inputs that are `butfirst`ed in parallel.

Somewhat similar to the selection pattern is one for a recursive *predicate;* the difference is that instead of

```
output something first :input
```

for a successful match, the procedure simply says

```
output "true
```

in that case. This pattern is followed by predicates that ask a question like "Does any member of the input do X?" For example, suppose that instead of counting the vowels in a word, we just want to know whether or not there is a vowel. Then we're asking the question "Is any letter in this word a vowel?" Here's how to find out.

```
to hasvowelp :word
if emptyp :word [output "false]
if vowelp first :word [output "true]
output hasvowelp butfirst :word
end
```

A more realistic example is also somewhat more cluttered with extra inputs and sometimes extra end tests. Here's a procedure that takes two words as input. It outputs `true` if the first word comes before the second in the dictionary.

```
to sort.beforep :word1 :word2
if emptyp :word1 [output "true]
if emptyp :word2 [output "false]
if (ascii first :word1) < (ascii first :word2) [output "true]
if (ascii first :word1) > (ascii first :word2) [output "false]
output sort.beforep butfirst :word1 butfirst :word2
end
```

The procedure will end on one of the `emptyp` tests if one of the input words is the beginning of the other, like `now` and `nowhere`. Otherwise, the procedure ends when two letters are unequal. The recursion step is followed when the beginning letters are equal. (The operation `ascii` takes a one-character word as input, and outputs the numeric value for that character in the computer's coding system, which is called the American Standard Code for Information Interchange.)

A combination of the translation kind of operation and the selection kind is an operation that selects not one but several members of the input. For example, you sometimes want to examine the words in a sentence in various ways but have trouble because the sentence includes punctuation as part of some words. But the punctuation isn't *really* part of the word. In Chapter 4, for instance, I defined a predicate `about.computersp` and gave this example of its use:

```
? print about.computersp [this book is about programming]
true
```

But if the example were part of a larger program, carrying on a conversation with a person, the person would probably have ended the sentence with a period. The last word would then have been `programming.` (including the period). That word, which is different from `programming` without the period, isn't in the procedure's list of relevant words, so it would have output `false`. The solution is to write a procedure that strips the punctuation from each word of a sentence. Of course that's a straightforward case of the translation pattern, applying a subprocedure to each word of the sentence:

```
to strip :sent
if emptyp :sent [output []]
output sentence (strip.word first :sent) (strip butfirst :sent)
end
```

`Strip.word`, though, is more interesting. It must select only the letters from a word.

```
to strip.word :word
if emptyp :word [output "]
if letterp first :word ~
   [output word (first :word) (strip.word butfirst :word)]
output strip.word butfirst :word
end

to letterp :char
output or (inrangep (ascii :char) (ascii "A) (ascii "Z)) ~
          (inrangep (ascii :char) (ascii "a) (ascii "z))
end

to inrangep :this :low :high
output and (:this > (:low-1)) (:this < (:high+1))
end
```

`Strip.word` is like the translation pattern in the use of the combining operation `word` in the middle instruction line. But it's also like the selection pattern in that there are two different choices of output, depending on the result of the predicate `letterp`.

☞ You might want to rewrite `about.computersp` so that it uses `strip`. Consider an initialization procedure.

Numerical Operations: The `Cascade` Pattern

Certain mathematical functions are defined in terms of recursive calculations. It used to be that computers were used *only* for numerical computation. They're now much more versatile, as you've already seen, but sometimes the old numerical work is still important.

The classic example in this category is the *factorial* function. The factorial of a positive integer is the product of all the integers from 1 up to that number. The factorial of 5 is represented as 5! so

$$5! = 1 \times 2 \times 3 \times 4 \times 5$$

We can use `cascade` to carry out this computation:

```
to fact :n                          ;; cascade version
output cascade :n [? * #] 1
end

? print fact 5
120
```

In this example I'm using a feature of `cascade` that we haven't seen before. The template (the second input to `cascade`) may include a number sign (`#`) character, which represents the number of times the template has been repeated. That is, it represents 1 the first time, 2 the second time, and so on.

Here is a recursive version of `fact` that takes one input, a positive integer, and outputs the factorial function of that number. The input can also be zero; the rule is that $0! = 1$.

```
to fact :n
if :n=0 [output 1]
output :n * fact :n-1
end
```

This procedure works because

$$5! = 5 \times 4!$$

That's another version of reducing a problem to a smaller subproblem.

☞ Chapter 5 gives the following example:

```
to power :base :exponent
output cascade :exponent [? * :base] 1
end
```

Write a version of `power` using recursion instead of using `cascade`.

Another classic example, slightly more complicated, is the Fibonacci sequence. Each number in the sequence is the sum of the two previous numbers; the first two numbers are 1. So the sequence starts

$$1, 1, 2, 3, 5, 8, 13, \ldots$$

A formal definition of the sequence looks like this:

$$F_0 = 1,$$
$$F_1 = 1,$$
$$F_n = F_{n-1} + F_{n-2}, \qquad n \geq 2.$$

Here's an operation `fib` that takes a number n as input and outputs F_n.

```
to fib :n
if :n<2 [output 1]
output (fib :n-1)+(fib :n-2)
end
```

That procedure will work, but it's quite seriously inefficient. The problem is that it ends up computing the same numbers over and over again. To see why, here's a trace of what happens when you ask for `fib 4`:

```
fib 4
  fib 3
    fib 2
      fib 1
      fib 0
    fib 1
  fib 2
    fib 1
    fib 0
```

Do you see the problem? `fib 2` is computed twice, once because `fib 4` needs it directly and once because `fib 4` needs `fib 3` and `fib 3` needs `fib 2`. Similarly, `fib 1` is computed three times. As the input to `fib` gets bigger, this problem gets worse and worse.

It turns out that a much faster way to handle this problem is to compute a *list* of all the Fibonacci numbers up to the one we want. Then each computation can take advantage of the work already done. Here's what I mean:

```
to fiblist :n
if :n<2 [output [1 1]]
output newfib fiblist :n-1
end
```

```
to newfib :list
output fput (sum first :list first butfirst :list) :list
end

? print fiblist 5
8 5 3 2 1 1
```

We can then define a faster `fib` in terms of `fiblist`:

```
to fib :n
output first fiblist :n
end
```

Convince yourself that the two versions of `fib` give the same outputs but that the second version is much faster. I'm purposely not going through a detailed explanation of this example; you should use the analytical techniques you learned in Chapter 8. What problem is `fiblist` trying to solve? What is the smaller subproblem?

The hallmark of numerical recursion is something like `:n-1` in the recursion step. Sometimes this kind of recursion is combined with the `butfirst` style we've seen in most of the earlier examples. Logo has a primitive operation called `item`, which takes two inputs. The first is a positive integer, and the second is a list. The output from `item` is the *n*th member of the list if the first input is *n*. (Earlier I suggested that you write `index`, the opposite of `item`.) If Logo didn't include `item`, here's how you could write it:

```
to item :n :list
if equalp :n 1 [output first :list]
output item :n-1 butfirst :list
end
```

Pig Latin

When I was growing up, every kid learned a not-very-secret "secret" language called Pig Latin. When I became a teacher, I was surprised to find out that kids apparently didn't learn it any more. But more recently it seems to have come back into vogue. Translating a sentence into Pig Latin is an interesting programming problem, so I'm going to teach it to you.

Here's how it works. For each word take any consonants that are at the beginning (up to the first vowel) and move them to the end. Then add "ay" at the end. So "hello" becomes "ellohay"; "through" becomes "oughthray"; "aardvark" just becomes "aardvarkay." (Pig Latin is meant to be spoken, not written. You're supposed to practice so that you can do it and understand it really fast.)

By now you can write in your sleep the operation `piglatin`, which takes a sentence and outputs its translation into Pig Latin by going through the sentence applying a subprocedure `plword` to each word. (It's just like `code`, only different.) It's `plword` that is the tricky part. The stop rule is pretty straightforward:

```
if vowelp first :word [output word :word "ay]
```

If the first letter *isn't* a vowel, what we want to do is move that letter to the end and try again. Here's the complete procedure.

```
to plword :word
if vowelp first :word [output word :word "ay]
output plword word butfirst :word first :word
end
```

What makes this tricky is that the recursion step doesn't seem to make the problem smaller. The word is still the same length after we move the first letter to the end. This would look more like all the other examples if the recursion step were

```
output plword butfirst :word
```

That would make the procedure easier to understand. Unfortunately it would also give the wrong answer. What you have to see is that there *is* something that is getting smaller about the word, namely the "distance" from the beginning of the word to the first vowel. Trace through a couple of examples to clarify this for yourself.

By the way, this will work better if you modify `vowelp` (which we defined earlier) so that `y` is considered a vowel. You'll then get the wrong answer for a few strange words like `yarn`, but on the other hand, if you consider `y` a consonant, you'll get no answer at all for words like `try` in which `y` is the only vowel! (Try it. Do you understand what goes wrong?)

☞ Some people learned a different dialect of Pig Latin. According to them, if the word starts with a vowel in the first place, you should add "way" at the end instead of just "ay." Modify `plword` so that it speaks that dialect. (I think the idea is that some words simply sound better with that rule.) Hint: You'll want an initialization procedure.

☞ The top-level procedure `piglatin`, which you wrote yourself, is a good candidate for careful thought about punctuation. You don't want to see

```
? print piglatin [what is he doing?]
atwhay isway ehay oing?day
```

A good first attempt would be to modify `piglatin` to use `strip`, to get rid of the punctuation altogether. But even better would be to remove the punctuation from each word, translate it to Pig Latin, then put the punctuation back! Then we could get

```
atwhay isway ehay oingday?
```

That's the right thing to do for punctuation at the end of a word, like a period or a comma. On the other hand, the apostrophe inside a word like `isn't` should be treated just like a letter.

The project I'm proposing to you is a pretty tricky one. Here's a hint. Write an operation `endpunct` that takes a word as input and outputs a *list* of two words, first the "real" word full of letters, then any punctuation that might be at the end. (The second word will be empty if there is no such punctuation.) Then your new `plword` can be an initialization procedure that invokes a subprocedure with `endpunct`'s output as its input.

A Mini-project: Spelling Numbers

Write a procedure `number.name` that takes a positive integer input, and outputs a sentence containing that number spelled out in words:

```
? print number.name 5513345
five million five hundred thirteen thousand three hundred forty five
? print number.name (fact 20)
two quintillion four hundred thirty two quadrillion nine hundred two
trillion eight billion one hundred seventy six million six hundred
forty thousand
```

There are some special cases you will need to consider:

- Numbers in which some particular digit is zero
- Numbers like 1,000,529 in which an entire group of three digits is zero.
- Numbers in the teens.

Here are two hints. First, split the number into groups of three digits, going from right to left. Also, use the sentence

```
[thousand million billion trillion quadrillion quintillion
 sextillion septillion octillion nonillion decillion]
```

You can write this bottom-up or top-down. To work bottom-up, pick a subtask and get that working before you tackle the overall structure of the problem. For example, write a procedure that returns the word `fifteen` given the argument `15`.

To work top-down, start by writing `number.name`, freely assuming the existence of whatever helper procedures you like. You can begin debugging by writing *stub* procedures that fit into the overall program but don't really do their job correctly. For example, as an intermediate stage you might end up with a program that works like this:

```
? print number.name 1428425              ;; intermediate version
1 million 428 thousand 425
```

Advanced Recursion: `Subsets`

We've seen that recursive operations can do the same jobs as higher order functions, and we've seen that recursive operations can do jobs that are similar to the higher order function patterns but not quite the same. Now we'll see that recursive operations can do jobs that are quite outside the bounds of any of the higher order functions in Chapter 5.

I'd like to write an operation `subsets` that takes a word as input. Its output will be a sentence containing all the words that can be made using letters from the input word, in the same order, but not necessarily using all of them. For example, the word `lit` counts as a subset of the word `lights`, but `hit` doesn't count because the letters are in the wrong order. (Of course the procedure won't know which words are real English words, so `iht`, which has the same letters as `hit` in the right order, *does* count.)

☞ How many subsets does `lights` have? Write them all down if you're not sure. (Or perhaps you'd prefer to count the subsets of a shorter word, such as `word`, instead.)

A problem that follows the `map` pattern is one in which the size of the output is the same as the size of the input, because each member of the input gives rise to one member of the output. A problem that follows the `filter` pattern is one in which the output is smaller than the input, because only some of the members are selected. And the `reduce` pattern collapses all of the members of the input into one single result. The `subsets` problem is quite different from any of these; its output will be much *larger* than its input.

If we can't rely on known patterns, we'll have to go back to first principles. In Chapter 8 you learned to write recursive procedures by looking for a smaller, similar subproblem within the problem we're trying to solve. What is a smaller subproblem that's similar to finding the subsets of `lights`? How about finding the subsets of its butfirst? This idea is the same one that's often worked for us before. So imagine that we've already found all the subsets of `ights`.

Some of the subsets of `lights` *are* subsets of `ights`. Which ones aren't? The missing subsets are the ones that start with the letter L. What's more, the other letters in such a subset form a subset of `ights`. For example, the word `lits` consists of the letter L followed by `its`, which is a subset of `ights`.

```
to subsets :word                        ;; incomplete
local "smaller
make "smaller subsets butfirst :word
output sentence :smaller (map [word (first :word) ?] :smaller)
end
```

This procedure reflects the idea I've just tried to explain. The subsets of a given word can be divided into two groups: the subsets of its butfirst, and those same subsets with the first letter of the word stuck on the front.

The procedure lacks a base case. It's tempting to say that if the input is an empty word, then the output should be an empty sentence. But that isn't quite right, because every word is a subset of itself, so in particular the empty word is a subset (the only subset) of itself. We must output a sentence containing an empty word. That's a little tricky to type, but we can represent a quoted empty word as `"` and so a sentence containing an empty word is `(sentence ")`.

```
to subsets :word
if emptyp :word [output (sentence ")]
local "smaller
make "smaller subsets butfirst :word
output sentence :smaller (map [word (first :word) ?] :smaller)
end
```

Why did I use the local variable `smaller` and a `make` instruction? It wasn't strictly necessary; I could have said

```
output sentence (subsets butfirst :word) ~
                (map [word (first :word) ?] (subsets butfirst :word))
```

The trouble is that this would have told Logo to compute the smaller similar subproblem twice instead of just once. It may seem that that would make the program take twice as long, but in fact the problem is worse than that, because each smaller subproblem has a smaller subproblem of its own, and those would be computed four times—twice for each of the two computations of the first smaller subproblem! As in the case of the Fibonacci sequence we studied earlier, avoiding the duplicated computation makes an enormous difference.

Problems like this one, in which the size of the output grows extremely quickly for small changes in the size of the input, tend to be harder to program than most. Here are a couple of examples. Like `subsets`, each of these has a fairly short procedure definition that hides a very complex computation.

☞ On telephone dials, most digits have letters associated with them. In the United States, for example, the digit 5 is associated with the letters J, K, and L. (The correspondence is somewhat different in other countries.) You can use these letters to spell out words to make your phone number easier to remember. For example, many years ago I had the phone number 492-6824, which spells I-WANT-BH. Write a procedure that takes a number as its input, and outputs a sentence of all the words that that number can represent. You may want to test the program using numbers of fewer than seven digits!

☞ In the game of Boggle^{TM}, the object is to find words by connecting neighboring letters in a four by four array of letters. For example, the array

```
BEZO
URND
AKAJ
WEOE
```

contains the words ZEBRA, DONE, and DARK, but not RADAR, because each letter can be used only once. Write a predicate procedure that takes a word and an array of letters (in the form of a sentence with one word for each row) as inputs, and outputs `true` if and only if the given word can be found in the given array.

```
? print findword "zebra [bezo urnd akaj weoe]
true
? print findword "radar [bezo urnd akaj weoe]
false
```

A Word about Tail Recursion

What I want to talk about in the rest of this chapter isn't really very important, so you can skip it if you want. But *some* people think it's important, so this is for those people.

Every procedure invocation takes up a certain amount of computer memory, while the procedure remains active, to hold things like local variables. Since a recursive procedure can invoke itself many times, recursion is a fairly "expensive" technique to allow in a programming language. It turns out that if the only recursion step in a procedure is the very last thing the procedure does, the interpreter can handle that procedure in a special way that uses memory more efficiently. You can then use as many levels of recursive invocation as you want without running out of space. Such a procedure is called *tail recursive.* It doesn't make any difference to you as a programmer; it's just a matter of what's happening inside the Logo interpreter.

A tail recursive command is very easy to recognize; the last instruction is an invocation of the same procedure. Tail recursive commands are quite common; here are a couple of examples we've seen before.

```
to one.per.line :thing
if emptyp :thing [stop]
print first :thing
one.per.line butfirst :thing
end

to poly :size :angle
forward :size
right :angle
poly :size :angle
end
```

The thing is, many people are confused about what constitutes a tail recursive operation. It *isn't* one that is invoked recursively on the last instruction line! Instead, the rule is that the recursive invocation must be used *directly* as the input to `output`, not as part of a larger computation. For example, this is a tail recursive operation:

```
to lookup :word :dictionary
if emptyp :dictionary [output "]
if equalp :word first first :dictionary [output last first :dictionary]
output lookup :word butfirst :dictionary
end
```

But this is *not* tail recursive:

```
to length :thing
if emptyp :thing [output 0]
output 1+length butfirst :thing
end
```

It's that `1+` that makes the difference.

It's sometimes possible to change a nontail recursive operation into a tail recursive one by tricky programming. For example, look again at `fact`:

```
to fact :n
if :n=0 [output 1]
output :n * fact :n-1
end
```

This is not tail recursive because the input to the final `output` comes from the multiplication, not directly from `fact`. But here is a tail recursive version:

```
to fact :n
output fact1 :n 1
end

to fact1 :n :product
if :n=0 [output :product]
output fact1 (:n-1) (:n*:product)
end
```

Indeed, this version can, in principle, compute the factorial of larger numbers than the simpler version without running out of memory. In practice, though, the largest number that most computers can understand is less than the factorial of 70, and any computer will allow 70 levels of recursion without difficulty. In fact, not every Logo interpreter bothers to recognize tail recursive operations. It's a small point; I only mention it because some people *both* make a big fuss about tail recursion *and* misunderstand what it means!

12 Example: Playfair Cipher

Program file for this chapter: `playfair`

This project investigates a cipher that is somewhat more complicated than the simple substitution cipher of Chapter 11. In the Playfair cipher, there is not a single translation of each letter of the alphabet; that is, you don't just decide that every B will be turned into an F. Instead, *pairs* of letters are translated into other pairs of letters.

Here is how it works. To start, pick a *keyword* that does not contain any letter more than once. For example, I'll pick the word `keyword`. Now write the letters of that word in the first squares of a five by five matrix:

K	E	Y	W	O
R	D			

Then finish filling up the remaining squares of the matrix with the remaining letters of the alphabet, in alphabetical order. Since there are 26 letters and only 25 squares, we assign I and J to the same square.

K	E	Y	W	O
R	D	A	B	C
F	G	H	IJ	L
M	N	P	Q	S
T	U	V	X	Z

(Actually, when choosing the keyword, besides making sure that no letter appears twice you must make sure that I and J do not both appear. For example, `juice` wouldn't do as a keyword.)

To encipher a message, divide it into pairs of letters. Pay no attention to punctuation or to spaces between words. For example, the sentence "Why, don't you?" becomes

```
WH YD ON TY OU
```

Now, find each pair of letters in the matrix you made earlier. Most pairs of letters will form two corners of a smaller square or rectangle within the matrix. For example, in my matrix, the first pair of letters (`WH`) are at two corners of a two-by-three rectangle also containing `Y`, `A`, `B`, and `IJ`. The enciphering of the pair `WH` is the pair at the two other corners of this rectangle, namely `YI`. (I could also have chosen `YJ`, in this case.) It's important to be consistent about the order of the new pair: the one that comes first is the one on the same *row* as the first of the original pair. In this case, `Y` is on the same row as `W`. We can continue to translate the remaining pairs of letters in the same way, ending up with

```
YI EA ES VK EZ
```

Notice that the letter `Y` turned into `E` in the second pair of letters, but it turned into `K` in the fourth pair.

Part of the strategy for keeping a code secret is to hide even the *kind* of code being used. Pairs of letters, to a cryptographer, are a dead giveaway that a Playfair cipher was used, so it's traditional to insert irrelevant spacing and punctuation in the actual written version of the message, like this:

```
Yie ae, svkez.
```

Of course the recipient of the message, knowing how the message was encoded, ignores this spacing and punctuation.

As an illustration of some of the special cases that complicate this scheme, consider the message, "Come to the window." First we divide it up into pairs:

```
CO ME TO TH EW IN DO W
```

The first problem is that the message has an odd number of letters. To solve this problem we simply add an extra letter at the end, generally `Q`. In this example, the final `W` becomes a pair `WQ`.

If you look up the first pair of letters, `CO`, in my matrix, you'll find that they do not determine a rectangle, because they are in the same column. (Strictly speaking, they *do* determine a one-by-two rectangle, but the two diagonals are the same, so that `CO` would be encoded as `CO` if we followed the usual rule.) For two letters in the same column, the rule is to replace each letter by the one below it, so `CO` becomes `LC`. (If one of the letters is at the end of the column, it is replaced by the top letter. So, for example, `OZ` would become `CO`.) Similarly, for two letters in the same row, each is replaced by the letter to its right. We can now translate the entire message:

```
LC NK ZK VF YO GQ CE BX
```

The pair `EW`, on a single row, has become `YO`; the final pair `WQ`, on a single column, has become `BX`.

The final exceptional case is the one in which the same letter appears twice in a pair. For example, the phrase "the big wheel" divides into

```
TH EB IG WH EE LQ
```

The pair `EE` is treated specially. It could be translated into `YY` (treating it as two letters in the same row) or into `DD` (if you think of it as two letters in the same column). Instead, though, the rule is to break up the pair by inserting a `Q` between the two letters. This changes all the pairings after that one in the message. The new version is

```
TH EB IG WH EQ EL
```

This version can now be translated into

```
VF WD LH YJ WN OG
```

(Notice that I chose to translate WH into YJ instead of into YI. You should use some of each when coding a message. A cipher with no Js at all, or one with a simple pattern of I and J alternating, is another giveaway that the Playfair cipher was used.)

What about the frequencies of letters in a Playfair-encoded message? You can't simply say that the most common letters are likely to represent E or T or A, because a letter doesn't represent a single letter that way. But it is still possible to say that a common letter in the coded version is likely to *be on the same row* as one of the frequent letters in English. For example, here is a well-known text in Playfair-coded form:

```
ZK DW KC SE XM ZK DW VF RV LQ VF WN ED MZ LW QE GY VF KD XF MP WC GO
BF MU GY QF UG ZK NZ IM GK FK GY ZS GQ LN DP AB BM CK OQ KL EZ KF DH
YK ZN LK FK EU YK FK KZ RY YD FT PC HD GQ MZ CP YD KL KF EZ CI ON DP
AC WK QS SY QL UN DU RU GY NS
```

The most commonly occurring letters in this coded text are K (19 times), F (12 times), D and Z (tied at 11), and Y (10 times). K is on the same row as both E and O, and can also represent T in the same-column case. Y is also on the same row. F can represent I (especially in the common pair IT); D can represent A; Z can represent T. Of all the letters that might represent E, why should K and Y be the popular ones? The answer is that they have common letters in their columns as well. In order for W to represent E, for example, the other letter of the (cleartext) pair must be B, I, J, Q, or X. Of these, only I is particularly common, and Q and X are downright rare.

If you were trying to break a Playfair cipher, one approach you might take would be to count the frequencies of *pairs* of letters. For example, in the message above, the only pairs that occur more than twice are GY, four times, and FK, VF, and ZK, three times each. It's a good guess that each of these corresponds to a commonly occurring pair of letters in English text. In fact, as it turns out, GY corresponds to HE, which is not only a word by itself but also part of the, them, then, and so on. VF corresponds to TH, an extremely common pair; ZK corresponds to TO, which is again a word in itself as well as a constituent of many other words. The other pair that occurs three times in the text, FK, corresponds to RT. This is not such a common English pair, although it does come up in words like worth. But it turns out that in the particular sample text I'm using, this pair of letters comes up mostly as parts of two words, as in the combination or to.

If you want to know more about how to break a Playfair cipher, you can see an example in *Have His Carcase,* a mystery novel by Dorothy L. Sayers. In this project, I'm less ambitious: the program merely enciphers a message, given the keyword and the cleartext as inputs. The first input to `playfair` must be a word, the keyword. The second input must be a list of words, the text. The keyword must meet the criterion of no duplicated letters, and the cleartext input must contain only words of letters, without punctuation. Here is an example:

```
? print playfair "keyword [come to the window]
lcnkzkvfyogqcebx
```

`Playfair` is an operation whose output is a single word containing the enciphered letters of the original text.

Data Redundancy

In writing this program, the first question I thought about was how to represent in a Logo program the matrix of letters used in the coding process. The most natural structure is a two-dimensional array—that is, an array with five members, each of which is an array of five letters.* So if the keyword is `keyword` then the program will, in effect, do this:

```
make "matrix {{k e y w o} {r d a b c} {f g h i l}
              {m n p q s} {t u v x z}}
```

The position of a letter in the matrix is represented as a list of two numbers, the row and the column. The Berkeley Logo procedure library includes an operation `mditem` that takes such a list as an input, along with a multi-dimensional array, and outputs the desired member:

```
to letter :rowcol
output mditem :rowcol :matrix
end
```

* In the tic-tac-toe program, I used a one-dimensional array to represent the board, even though a tic-tac-toe board is drawn in two dimensions. I could have used an array of three arrays of three numbers each, but that wouldn't really have fit with the way that program labels the board. In tic-tac-toe, the nine squares are named 1 to 9. You ask to move in square 8, for example, not in row 3, column 2. But in the Playfair program, the row and column numbers are going to be very important.

(The actual procedure listed at the end of this section includes a slight complication to deal with the case of `I` and `J`, but that's not important right now.)

The Playfair process goes like this: The program is given two letters. It finds each letter in the matrix, determines each letter's row and column numbers, then rearranges those numbers to make new row and column numbers, then looks in the matrix again to find the corresponding letters. For example, suppose we are given the keyword `keyword` and the letters `T` and `A`. The first step is to translate `T` into the row and column list `[5 1]`, and to translate `A` into `[2 3]`. Then the program must combine the row of one letter with the column of the other, giving the new lists `[5 3]` and `[2 1]`. Finally, the `letter` procedure shown above will find the letters `V` and `R` in the matrix.

`Letter` handles the last step of the translation process, but what about the first step? We need the inverse operation of `letter`, one that takes a letter as input and provides its row and column.

It would be possible to write a `row.and.column` procedure that would examine each letter in the matrix until it located the desired letter. But that procedure would be both slow and complicated. Instead, I decided to keep *redundant* information about the matrix in the form of 26 variables, one for each letter, each of which contains the coordinates of that letter. That is, the variables take the form

```
make "a [2 3]
make "w [1 4]
make "z [5 5]
```

and so on. (As in the case of the variable named `matrix` above, these `make` instructions are just illustrative. The actual program does not contain explicit data for this particular matrix, using this particular keyword!)

The letter variables contain the same information as the variable `matrix`. Strictly speaking, they are not needed. By creating the redundant variables for the letters, I've made a *space/time tradeoff;* the extra variables take up room in the computer's memory, but the program runs faster. One of the recurring concerns of a professional programmer is deciding which way to make such tradeoffs. It depends on the amounts of space and time required and the amounts available. In this case, the extra space required is really quite small, compared to the memory of a modern computer, so the decision is clear-cut. For larger programming problems it is sometimes harder to decide.

Composition of Functions

Earlier I showed a `make` instruction to put a particular coding matrix into the variable `matrix`. How does the program create a matrix for any keyword given as input? Here are two of the relevant procedures:

```
to playfair :keyword :message
local [matrix a b c d e f g h i j k l m n o p q r s t u v w x y z]
setkeyword jtoi lowercase :keyword
output encode (reduce "word :message)
end

to setkeyword :word
make "matrix reorder word :word (remove :word "abcdefghiklmnopqrstuvwxyz)
make "j :i
end
```

The keyword that is provided by the user as one of the inputs to the toplevel procedure `playfair` goes through several stages as it is transformed into a matrix.

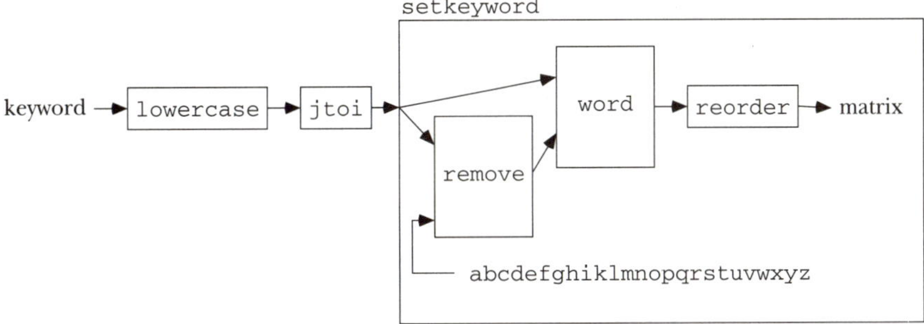

This *dataflow* diagram is very similar to a plumbing diagram from Chapter 2 turned on its side. The format is a little different to put somewhat more emphasis on the inputs and outputs, so you can follow the "flow" of information through the arrows.

In English, here's what the diagram tells us. The keyword given by the user must be converted to lower case letters. (I could have chosen to use capital letters instead; the goal is to have some uniform convention.) If the keyword happens to contain a `J`, it will be represented within the program as an `I` instead. Then, to make the matrix, we combine (with `word`) two words: the keyword and the result of removing the keyword's letters from the alphabet (leaving out `J`). Finally, that combined word must be rearranged into a five-by-five square.

The advantage of a view such as this one is that each of the small boxes in the diagram has a relatively simple task. Indeed, `lowercase` and `word` are primitive operations in Berkeley Logo. `Jtoi` is trivial:

```
to jtoi :word
output map [ifelse equalp ? "j ["i] [?]] :word
end
```

`Remove` is a straightforward recursive operation that outputs the result of removing one group of letters from another group of letters.

```
to remove :letters :string
if emptyp :string [output "]
if memberp first :string :letters [output remove :letters bf :string]
output word first :string remove :letters bf :string
end
```

The job of `reorder` is somewhat messier. It must keep track of what row and column it's up to, so `reorder` is just an initialization procedure for the recursive helper `reorder1` that does the real work. `Reorder` also creates the two-dimensional Logo array to provide another input to its helper procedure.

```
to reorder :string
output reorder1 :string (mdarray [5 5]) 1 1
end

to reorder1 :string :array :row :column
if :row=6 [output :array]
if :column=6 [output reorder1 :string :array :row+1 1]
mdsetitem (list :row :column) :array first :string
make first :string (list :row :column)
output reorder1 (butfirst :string) :array :row :column+1
end
```

If I were filling in a matrix by hand, instead of writing a computer program, I'd use a very different approach. I'd handle one letter at a time. First I'd go through the keyword a letter at a time, stuffing each letter into the next available slot in the matrix. (If necessary, I'd convert upper to lower case and `J` to `I` in the process.) Then I'd go through the alphabet a letter at a time, saying "If this letter isn't in the keyword, then stuff it into the matrix."

Many people would find it natural to use that same technique in writing a computer program, also:

```
to playfair :keyword :message          ;; sequential version
local [matrix a b c d e f g h i j k l m n o p q r s t u v w x y z]
make "matrix mdarray [5 5]
local [row column]
make "row 1
make "column 1
foreach :keyword [stuff jtoi lowercase ?]
foreach "abcdefghiklmnopqrstuvwxyz ~
        [if not memberp ? jtoi :keyword [stuff ?]]
make "j :i
output encode (reduce "word :message)
end

to stuff :letter
mdsetitem (list :row :column) :matrix :letter
make :letter (list :row :column)
make "column :column+1
if :column=6 [make "row :row+1  make "column 1]
end
```

In this version, the first `foreach` instruction handles the letters of the keyword. The second `foreach` instruction handles the rest of the alphabet. The `not memberp` test handles the removal of the keyword letters from the alphabet.

My intent in writing this alternate version was to model my idea of how the problem would be solved without a computer, processing one letter at a time. So, for example, in the template

```
[stuff jtoi lowercase ?]
```

it's worth noting that the operations `jtoi` and `lowercase` are being applied to single-letter inputs, even though those operations were designed to accept words of any length as a unit. I cheated, though, by applying `jtoi` to the entire keyword in the second `foreach` instruction. I was trying to make the program more readable; the honest version would be

```
foreach "abcdefghiklmnopqrstuvwxyz ~
        [if (ifelse equalp ? "i
                    [not (or (memberp "i :keyword)
                             (memberp "j :keyword))]
                    [not memberp ? :keyword])
            [stuff ?]]
```

Why am I subjecting you to this? My point is that what may seem to be the most natural way to think about a problem—in this case, handling one letter at a time—may not be the easiest, most elegant, or most efficient programming solution.

What makes the dataflow-structured version of `playfair` possible is the use of *operations* in Logo, and the *composition* of these operations by using the output from one as the input to another. This is an important technique, but one that doesn't seem to come naturally to everyone. If you're not accustomed to writing operations, I think it really pays to train yourself into that habit.

Conversational Front End

It's inconvenient to type a long message into the computer in the form of an input to a procedure. Another approach would be a *conversational front end.* This is a procedure that reads the cleartext message using `readlist`, perhaps accepting the message over several lines. It's not hard to write:

```
to encode.big.message
local [keyword cleartext]
print [Welcome to the Playfair enciphering program.]
print [What keyword would you like to use?]
make "keyword first readlist
print [Now please enter your message, using as many lines as needed.]
print [When you're done, enter a line containing only a period (.).]
make "cleartext []
read.big.message
print [Here is the enciphered version:]
print []
print playfair :keyword :cleartext
end

to read.big.message
local "line
make "line readlist
if equalp :line [.] [stop]
make "cleartext sentence :cleartext :line
read.big.message
end
```

Such a top-level procedure may be justified in a project like this, in which a very large block of text may be used as a datum. But don't get carried away. Programming languages that don't emphasize composition of functions encourage this sort of programming style, to the point where the part of the program that prompts the user and reads the data gets to be longer than the part that does the actual computation. This preoccupation with verbose conversation between the program and the user is sometimes justified by the idea of "good human engineering," but I don't think that's necessarily true. To take an extreme case, consider the standard elementary school Logo procedure to draw a square:

```
to square :size
repeat 4 [forward :size right 90]
end
```

Compare that to this "human engineered" version:

```
to square
local "size
print [Brian's square program copyright 1985]
print [What size square would you like me to draw?]
make "size first readlist
repeat 4 [forward :size right 90]
print [Thank you, please come again.]
end
```

Not only is the first version (in my opinion) much more pleasant to use, but it is also more powerful and flexible. The second version can be used *only* as a top-level program, carrying on a conversation with a human user. The first version can be run at top level, but it can also be used as a subprocedure of a more complicated drawing program. If it's used at top level, some person types in a number, the size, as the input to `square` on the instruction line. If it's used inside another procedure, that procedure can *compute* the input.

Further Explorations

I haven't described the part of the program that actually transforms the message: the procedure `encode` and its subprocedures. Read the listing at the end of the chapter, then answer these questions:

☞ Why does `encode` need two base cases?

☞ What purpose is served by the four invocations of `thing` at the beginning of procedure `paircode`?

Of course this program can be improved in many ways.

☞ One straightforward improvement to this program would be to "bulletproof" it so that it doesn't die with a Logo error message if, for example, the user provides a bad keyword. (Instead, the program should give its own message, making it clear what the problem is. It's better for the user to see

```
Keywords may not have any letter repeated.
```

than

```
t has no value  in paircode
```

after making that mistake.) Also, what if the cleartext input contains words with characters other than letters? The program should just ignore those characters and process the letters in the words correctly.

☞ Another fairly straightforward improvement would be to take the one long word output by `playfair` and turn it into a list of words with spacing and punctuation thrown in at random. The goal is to have the result look more or less like an actual paragraph of English text, except for the scrambled letters.

Another direction would be to work on deciphering a Playfair-coded message. There are two problems here: the easy one, in which you know what the keyword is, and the hard one, in which you know only that a Playfair cipher was used.

☞ The procedure `playfair` itself will almost work in the first case. It would work perfectly were it not for the special cases of letters in the same row and column. It's a simple modification to handle those cases correctly. An interesting extension would be to try to restore the original spacing by using a dictionary to guess where words end.

☞ The much harder problem is to try to guess the keyword. I mentioned earlier some ideas about the approaches you'd have to take, such as exploring the frequencies of use of pairs of letters. If you want more advice, you'll have to study books on cryptography.

Program Listing

```
to playfair :keyword :message
local [matrix a b c d e f g h i j k l m n o p q r s t u v w x y z]
setkeyword jtoi lowercase :keyword
output encode (reduce "word :message)
end
```

```
;; Prepare the code array

to setkeyword :word
make "matrix ~
     reorder word :word (remove :word "abcdefghiklmnopqrstuvwxyz)
make "j :i
end

to remove :letters :string
if emptyp :string [output "]
if memberp first :string :letters [output remove :letters bf :string]
output word first :string remove :letters bf :string
end

to reorder :string
output reorder1 :string (mdarray [5 5]) 1 1
end

to reorder1 :string :array :row :column
if :row=6 [output :array]
if :column=6 [output reorder1 :string :array :row+1 1]
mdsetitem (list :row :column) :array first :string
make first :string (list :row :column)
output reorder1 (butfirst :string) :array :row :column+1
end

;; Encode the message

to encode :message
if emptyp :message [output "]
if emptyp butfirst :message [output paircode first :message "q]
if equalp (jtoi first :message) (jtoi first butfirst :message) ~
   [output word (paircode first :message "q) (encode butfirst :message)]
output word (paircode first :message first butfirst :message) ~
            (encode butfirst butfirst :message)
end
```

```
to paircode :one :two
local [row1 column1 row2 column2]
make "row1 first thing :one
make "column1 last thing :one
make "row2 first thing :two
make "column2 last thing :two
if :row1 = :row2 ~
   [output letters (list :row1 rotate (:column1+1)) ~
                   (list :row1 rotate (:column2+1))]
if :column1 = :column2 ~
   [output letters (list rotate (:row1+1) :column1)  ~
                   (list rotate (:row2+1) :column1)]
output letters (list :row1 :column2) (list :row2 :column1)
end

to rotate :index
output ifelse :index = 6 [1] [:index]
end

to letters :one :two
output word letter :one letter :two
end

to letter :rowcol
output itoj mditem :rowcol :matrix
end

;; I and J conversion

to jtoi :word
output map [ifelse equalp ? "j ["i] [?]] :word
end

to itoj :letter
if :letter = "i [if (random 3) = 0 [output "j]]
output :letter
end
```

13 Planning

Program file for this chapter: `poker`

The picture on page 234 shows some of the architecture on the University of California campus at Berkeley. At the left of the picture is South Hall, one of the original campus buildings, with red brick, ivy, and many chimneys. The white brick clock tower that dominates the center of the picture is Sather Tower, popularly called the Campanile after the building in Venice, Italy, on which it is modeled. Just to its left is Evans Hall, the concrete fortress that houses the Mathematics Department. Andrews Hall, at the very front of the picture, is a small, one-floor building with an unusually shaped roof. Stephens Hall, mostly hidden by the trees behind Andrews, is a yellow-green zigzag.

Page 235 shows a similar view of the Stanford University campus in Palo Alto, California. Compared to the Berkeley buildings, the ones you see here look very uniform. At the left in the first photo is a corner of the Quadrangle, the central building complex of the campus. The School of Education, down the path on the left, follows the same pattern of rough tan stone with a sloping orange roof. The Meyer Library, at the rear of the photo, follows the same color scheme, even though it's obviously a more recent building. The second photo shows the new School of Law. In this building the architect has clearly worked to combine the same tan stone, orange roof theme with more modern details: the texture of the stone is more uniform and the arches are less ornate.

Both of these campuses are the result of architectural planning, but they illustrate two different *styles* of planning. The Stanford campus was planned *top-down;* first came an overall concept and then the details to fill in that concept. The Berkeley campus was planned *bottom-up;* each new building was designed to fit its architect's idea of the immediate, local situation. Some of the individual buildings are quite beautiful, but it's those buildings, rather than the campus as a unit, that attract attention.

(I'm oversimplifying, of course. In a strictly top-down approach, the entire campus would be laid out on paper before any building was built. Adding new buildings later,

University of California, Berkeley

Stanford University

even if they're made to fit in with the old ones, means that the original plan was defective. Instead of patching it up, a top-down purist would have the architects begin all over again, allowing for more buildings from the beginning of the design process. And in fact the original Berkeley campus was much more uniform than the campus today, but very rapid growth led to widespread changes in the original plan. Still, the difference in architectural planning styles is striking and suggestive.)

The same two planning strategies are possible in computer programming. Suppose you want to write a program to play tic-tac-toe, as I did in Chapter 6. You can start by saying, "Let's see if I can draw the board." You'd write a procedure to draw the four lines that make up the tic-tac-toe grid. Then you might write procedures to draw an X and an O in the right size for the boxes you've made. And so on. That would be a bottom-up design. Alternatively, you might start by deciding on the major tasks that your program will have to carry out. You might then write a top-level procedure like this:

```
to ttt
drawboard
choose.x.o
playgame
end

to playgame
move "x
if winp "x [stop]
move "o
if winp "o [stop]
playgame
end
```

In writing `ttt` and `playgame`, I've freely used subprocedures that I haven't written yet. Later I could fill in the gaps, writing procedures that will do exactly what's needed to fill their places in the main procedure.

Structured Programming

In recent years the majority of computer scientists have adopted a school of thought called structured programming. This phrase—the title of a 1972 book by O. J. Dahl, Edsger Dijkstra, and C. A. R. Hoare—describes an uncompromising top-down philosophy of programming. Structured programming is more than just the top-down idea, though; it also includes rules for each step in the program development process. For example, one potential problem with top-down programming is that it's hard to test a procedure you've written until its subprocedures are written also. (By contrast, a subprocedure can be tested before its superprocedures are written.) Structured programming solves this problem by recommending the use of *stubs*—preliminary versions of the subprocedures that don't really do the job but provide some result that allows the higher-level procedures to be tested. For example, an operation that hasn't been written yet might be replaced by a stub that always outputs zero, or the empty list, or some other simple, appropriate value.

More importantly, the structured programming approach tells us not to write any procedures at all until we've first written a detailed specification of the how the program should behave, and then a detailed plan of how it will be organized to achieve that goal.

The programming language Pascal was designed by Niklaus Wirth in 1970 to promote a programming style and philosophy like that of structured programming. Pascal is meant to teach a top-down structured style by providing just the tools needed for that approach but making it hard to program in other styles. The widespread use of Pascal in college programming courses reflects the popularity of the structured programming approach.

(As I am preparing the second edition of this book in 1995, Pascal is just beginning to lose ground as a teaching language; several competing schools of thought about programming have led to diverse language choices. The best known right now is the language C++, which exemplifies an *object oriented* approach to program structure. Others are Ada and Modula, two languages more or less in the Pascal tradition, and Scheme, which is, like Logo, a dialect of Lisp and represents the artificial intelligence tradition.)

Critique of Structured Programming

One area of computer science in which the top-down approach has not been accepted so enthusiastically is artificial intelligence. AI researchers try to program computers to carry out ill-defined, complex tasks (playing chess is a prototypical example) for which there is no single, obvious method. In that kind of research project you can't start by writing down on paper a complete specification of how the finished program will be organized. Instead you start with a more or less vague idea, you try programming it, and then you play around with it to try to improve the results. That's one reason why the majority of AI programs are written in Lisp, a language that is interactive, so it encourages you to "program at the keyboard." Pascal, on the other hand, was designed to be a *compiled* language, in which you must write an entire program before you can carry out a single instruction.

Logo, a dialect of Lisp, was developed by artificial intelligence researchers. Their idea was to see if they could use some of their experience with the problem of trying to get computers to think in order to help human beings learn to think more effectively—at least about certain kinds of problems. You shouldn't be surprised, therefore, to learn that Logoites tend not to be enthusiastic about structured programming.

It's not that we're against planning. On the contrary! Planning is one of the most fundamental problem-solving skills. But there are many kinds of planning. The kind in which every part of your program's behavior is written down before you begin programming isn't very realistic in many contexts. Even in the large-scale business or government projects that structured programmers like to talk about, it's very common that the ultimate users of a program change their minds about how it should work, once they have some experience with using it. The wise programmer will anticipate these changing requirements in the original planning process. Still, one never anticipates everything; a sensible person faced with an unexpected change in requirements will be flexible enough to modify the initial plan, not start all over again. And it's even more true for people like you, who are just learning to program, that the "goal" of a programming project is exploratory rather than predetermined.

Sometimes human lives depend on the correct operation of a computer program. In one famous example, just about the time that the first edition of this book was published, one person died and others were injured because the program controlling a medical X-ray machine gave patients massive overdoses of radiation. Certainly, any programming techniques that can help prevent such accidents are valuable. Still, the techniques applicable to life-or-death programming situations are not necessarily the best techniques for beginning learners, nor even for experienced researchers who are exploring a new area rather than writing production programs.

A Sample Project: Counting Poker Hands

To make all this more concrete, I'd like to show you an actual planning process for a programming project. I'm going to write a Logo program and tell you what I'm doing as I go along. I am sitting at a rather crowded desk; on my left is a microcomputer running Logo, and on my right is the terminal with which I call up the large computer I use for text editing. I'll switch back and forth as I work.* Please understand that I'm not showing

* Home computers have become more powerful since I wrote that in 1984. I can now run Logo in one window and edit the book in another window on the same computer.

you the Official Logo Programming Style. I'm showing you one way in which one Logo programmer approaches a particular project.

The project I have in mind is to announce the value of a poker hand. That is, the program should behave something like this:

```
? pokerhand [3s qc 3d 3h qd]
full house (threes and queens)
? pokerhand [4c 7h 5d 3c 6d]
straight (seven high)
? pokerhand [2h 10d 5s 6s 10s]
pair of tens
?
```

In imagining this sample dialogue, I'm doing a kind of top-down planning. I've specified, for example, the form in which I intend to represent a hand (a list of five cards) and a card (a word combining a rank from

```
[a 2 3 4 5 6 7 8 9 10 j q k]
```

with a suit from

```
[h s d c]
```

standing for hearts, spades, diamonds, and clubs). I suppose that means that I've decided we're playing five-card draw poker rather than seven-card stud. But later I may want to think again about that choice. I've also written down a few of the specific messages the program can print, although I'm much less certain about these. I may or may not actually bother with the details in parentheses, for example.

Okay, how will the program work? I envision a series of tests for particular kinds of poker hands. So in my head there is a vague procedure template like this:

```
to pokerhand :cards
if royal.flushp :cards [print [royal flush] stop]
if fourp :cards [print [four of a kind] stop]
if straight.flushp :cards [print [straight flush] stop]
...
print [I suggest you fold.]
end
```

This isn't something I'm ready to type into my computer. I'm still thinking about how the details are likely to work out. One thing that comes to mind is that, as it stands, there will be a great duplication of effort. The test for a royal flush is just like the test for a straight flush, plus a particular special condition (ace high). I shouldn't really make that test twice. For that matter the test for a straight flush is the test for a straight combined with the test for a flush. I shouldn't have another instruction starting `if straightp` repeating the same test.

An Initialization Procedure

I also shouldn't read through the list representing the hand a million times, each time pulling out the rank without the suit or vice versa. It seems that I should begin by going through the hand *once,* extracting various kinds of information into a bunch of variables. I'll probably have `ranks` and `suits`, along with things like `pairs`, which will list the ranks that appear twice in the hand. I'm not sure exactly what variables I'll need, but I am now impatient to start programming. What I'm going to do is write an initialization procedure to set up all this information.

In revising this chapter for the second edition, I find that I have very different ideas about how to write this initialization procedure. But I think that it's worthwhile, since this is a chapter about planning a program and not about the finished product, to preserve my original version and the reasoning that led me to write it. In the next section I'll show another approach.

```
to poker.init :cards                         ;; first edition version
make "ranks []
make "suits []
make "pairs []
make "threes []
make "fours []
read.cards :cards
end
```

`Read.cards`, when I write it, will insert new members into the lists that `poker.init` sets up as empty lists. Why `pairs`, `threes`, and `fours` but not, for example, `straights` and `flushes`? Pairhood is a property of just part of a hand, whereas straighthood is a property of the entire hand. It doesn't make sense to say that three of the five cards form a straight. But the lists `:ranks` and `:suits` will help in determining whether the hand is a straight or a flush, respectively. For instance, a flush is a hand in which there is only one suit, so if `:suits` turns out to be a list of length one, the hand is a flush. A full house is a hand with one rank listed in `:threes` and another listed in `:pairs`.

I seem to be violating my own rules here, with all these explicit assignments to variables that are not made `local`. But of course the whole point of an initialization procedure is that the variables will be used later by some other procedure, not this one or one of its subprocedures. In a large project, it's typical for an initialization procedure to assign values to nonlocal variables. If I'm being careful, when I get around to writing the top-level `pokerhand` I'll probably put `local` instructions for these variables there.

I can write `read.cards` without thinking about it at all, and I hope you can too. It's one of the standard templates: "Do something to each member of a list."

```
to read.cards :cards
foreach :cards "read.card
end
```

It's not obvious what goes inside `read.card`, but I can imagine some of the instructions. So I'll start writing it anyway.

```
to read.card :card
make "ranks fput butlast :card :ranks
make "suits fput last :card :suits
...
```

Okay, time to do some thinking. I can see that there are going to be a lot of those `make`, `fput` instructions. I should have a subprocedure to handle it.

```
to read.card :card
insert butlast :card "ranks
insert last :card "suits
...
```

(By the way, do you see why I extract the rank of a card with `butlast` rather than `first`? It wouldn't matter, except for the tens where the rank is two digits. That is, the ten of spades is represented by the word `10s`. The `first` of that word is the single digit `1`; its `butlast` is `10`, the number we really want.)

I know that the second input to `insert` has to be the name of the variable (like `"ranks`) and not the value of the variable (like `:ranks`) because I've used techniques like this before. That input is going to be used, among other things, as the first input to a `make` invocation. `Make` needs the *name* of the variable in order to be able to change its value. Although this particular notation is specific to Logo, most programming languages have some way to distinguish between *call by value* (`:ranks`) and *call by name* (`"ranks`) or some similar mechanism to handle the special cases in which a subprocedure must be able to modify a superprocedure's variable.

What about `pairs` and so on? The idea is that if I've seen this particular rank before, I should insert it in `pairs`:

```
if memberp butlast :card :ranks [insert butlast :card "pairs]
```

But there's a bug. If I put that instruction after the ones I've already written, the rank will *always* be found in `:ranks` because I've just put it there! Instead I have to put this instruction *before* the one that inserts into `:ranks`. In fact, the same problem will arise with the other lists. I have to start by testing `:threes` and inserting into `:fours`, and work my way down to `:ranks`. This illustrates a general rule: *Always make the most restrictive test first.* I learned that rule through hours of debugging earlier projects; now I recognize the situation right away. Here's the finished procedure:

```
to read.card :card
insert last :card "suits
if memberp butlast :card :threes [insert butlast :card "fours stop]
if memberp butlast :card :pairs [insert butlast :card "threes stop]
if memberp butlast :card :ranks [insert butlast :card "pairs stop]
insert butlast :card "ranks
end
```

The `stop` commands are just for efficiency. Suppose I've found a particular rank three times already in this poker hand, and the card I'm looking at now is the fourth of the same rank. Then the first `if` will succeed, since the rank was already a member of `:threes`. If the `stop` command were omitted, I'd go on to the next `if` instruction, which would find the rank in `:pairs` and therefore insert it into `:threes`. But that's unnecessary; if I've found the rank in `:threes`, there is no need to insert it there again! In other words, if I'm about to insert this card in the list of `fours`, there is no need to check to see if it's in the lists of smaller runs of the same rank. (Of course, it's sort of funny having `threes` and `fours` as lists, since there can't be more than one of them in a five-card poker hand! But this structure makes the instructions pleasingly similar.)

I notice another potential bug. When I add a rank to, for example, `:threes`, I don't remove it from `:pairs`. So my data base will claim that I have a pair as well as three of a kind. I could write a `remove` procedure analogous to `insert`, but my guess is that it won't be necessary. If I follow the "most restrictive test first" principle later in the program, I'll know I have three of a kind before I ever look at `:pairs`. If it turns out to be a problem later, I'll fix it then.

I'm slightly annoyed that this procedure computes `butlast :card` so many times. Perhaps it should be

```
to read.card :card
local "rank
make "rank butlast :card
...
```

But in fact I haven't bothered making that change.

Finally, here is the missing subprocedure `insert`:

```
to insert :item :list
if memberp :item thing :list [stop]
make :list fput :item thing :list
end
```

The first instruction is there to ensure that nothing is added to the same list twice. The `stop` commands I mentioned earlier ought to ensure the same thing, except for the list `:suits`. But since I need the instruction for that case anyway, I'll take a "belt and suspenders" approach for all the lists.

The input that I've called `item` here used to be called `thing`, because I was thinking, "Insert a thing into a list." But I found that using the procedure `thing` next to the variable `thing` looked too confusing to me, even though it wouldn't have bothered the Logo interpreter.

I hope you noticed that the second instruction starts with `make :list` rather than `make "list`. This is the indirect assignment technique that I mentioned briefly in Chapter 3. Remember that the variable `list` contains the *name* of another variable, such as `threes`. It is that second variable whose value is changed. For example,

```
insert butlast :card "fours
```

invokes `insert` with an input whose name is `list` and whose value is `fours`. In this case, the `make` instruction inside `insert` is equivalent to

```
make "fours fput :item thing "fours
```

or

```
make "fours fput :item :fours
```

Second Edition Second Thoughts

I wrote the first edition using versions of Logo without higher order functions. These functions can be written in Logo, and in fact I did write them later in the book, but I wasn't using them in this chapter. But in retrospect, the style of creating a variable named `ranks` whose value is an empty list, and then adding the rank of each card by reassigning a new value to the variable, seems much harder to understand than this:

```
to poker.init :cards
make "ranks map "butlast :cards
make "suits remdup map "last :cards
...
```

`Remdup` is an operation, primitive in Berkeley Logo, whose output is the same as its input, but with duplicate members removed.

As for `pairs`, `threes`, and `fours`, I think they are most easily replaced by an array that keeps track of the number of times each rank appears in the hand.

```
to poker.init :cards                               ;; second edition version
make "ranks map [ranknum butlast ?] :cards
make "suits remdup map "last :cards
make "rankarray {0 0 0 0 0 0 0 0 0 0 0 0 0}
foreach :ranks [setitem ? :rankarray (item ? :rankarray)+1]
end

to ranknum :rank                                   ;; turn rank to number
if :rank = "a [output 1]
if :rank = "j [output 11]
if :rank = "q [output 12]
if :rank = "k [output 13]
output :rank
end
```

Since I want to use the card's rank as an index into an array, I have to use a number from 1 to 13 to represent the ranks inside the program, even though the person using the program will still represent a rank in the more human-readable form of A for ace and so on.

Where the first version of the program would test for four of a kind with

```
if not emptyp :fours ...
```

this new version will say

```
if memberp 4 :rankarray ...
```

Notice that my second thoughts are about low-level details of the program. I haven't changed my mind about the big idea, which is to have a procedure `poker.init` that examines the hand and converts the information into a format in which the rest of the program can use it more easily. This is the same idea I used in the tic-tac-toe program of Chapter 6, in which I converted a human-readable "position" such as

```
{x o 3 x x 6 7 8 o}
```

into an internal list of "triples":

```
[xo3 xx6 78o xx7 ox8 36o xxo 3x7]
```

From now on, I won't show two versions of every procedure. I'll use the revised data representation, even though the chapter tells the story of how I wrote the older version of the program.

Planning and Debugging

Ideally, according to structured programming, you should never have to do any debugging. You should start with a complete, clear program specification. Then you should use the approved style to translate that specification into a program. Then you should be able to *prove* mathematically that your program is correct! Debugging is a relic of the dark ages.

That's not the Logo approach. I've already done some debugging in this project. Programming is sort of like real life: you don't always get it right the first time. Structured programmers don't get it right the first time either; the difference is that Logoites aren't embarrassed about it. We think of debugging as part of the process of solving problems in general.

If you're a student in a school, the odds are that you aren't often encouraged to accept debugging as valuable. When you hand in a paper or a quiz, the teacher doesn't point out errors and invite you to try again. Instead he marks your errors in red ink and takes off points for them. You're taught that your work has to be perfect the first time. One of the strong contributions that computer programming in general, and Logo in particular, has made to education is to provide one context in which you are shown a more realistic approach to making and correcting mistakes.

Classifying Poker Hands

The main thing remaining to be done in my project is the collection of predicates like `fourp` and `royal.flushp` to check for particular kinds of poker hands. I decided to write some of the easy ones, namely the ones for multiples of the same rank.

```
to fourp
output memberp 4 :rankarray
end

to threep
output memberp 3 :rankarray
end

to pairp
output memberp 2 :rankarray
end

to full.housep
output and threep pairp
end
```

These are all pretty obvious. Notice, though, that one thing has changed since my initial idea: these procedures don't take `:cards` as an input. They don't examine the poker hand directly; they examine the variables set up by the initialization procedure.

Now I want to start putting all these pieces together, so I'm going to write a preliminary version of `pokerhand`.

```
to pokerhand :cards
poker.init :cards
if fourp [print [four of a kind] stop]
if full.housep [print [full house] stop]
if threep [print [three of a kind] stop]
if pairp [print ifelse paircount = 1 [one pair] [two pairs] stop]
print [something else]
end
```

```
to paircount
output count locate 2 1
end

to locate :number :index
if :index > 13 [output []]
if (item :index :rankarray) = :number ~
   [output fput :index (locate :number :index+1)]
output locate :number :index+1
end
```

If there's a pair, I can't simply use `memberp` to find out how many pairs are in the hand. Instead, the procedure `locate` looks at each member of `:rankarray` and outputs a list of all the ranks of which there are exactly two cards in the hand. For this purpose I could have had `locate` output the number of pairs, which would be a little easier than computing the list of ranks of pairs. But I recall that I want to be able to say things like "pair of sevens," and for that I'll need the actual ranks.

Let's try it:

```
? pokerhand [ah 2c 4d 2s 6h]
I don't know how  to one  in pokerhand
[if pairp [print ifelse paircount = 1 [one pair] [two pairs] stop]]
```

Looks like a bug. (This really happened; I'm not just making it up to be able to talk about debugging!) The first step in solving a problem like this is to read the error message carefully. This message tells me that when the error happened, the immediately active procedure was `pokerhand`. So that's where I should look for a mistake. (The exact form of the message will be different in different versions of Logo, but they'll all give you that piece of information. In Berkeley Logo, the error message also includes the instruction line in which the error occurred.) I then edited `pokerhand` and looked for the word `one`. I found it in the list

```
[one pair]
```

which is one of the inputs to an `ifelse` operation. Aha! The trouble is that `ifelse` *evaluates* whichever input is selected by its predicate input, so it's trying to evaluate that list as a Logo expression. What I meant was this:

```
if pairp [print ifelse paircount = 1 [[one pair]] [[two pairs]] stop]
```

Now it should evaluate `[[one pair]]` and come up with the value `[one pair]` to use as the input to `print`. Let's try again:

```
? pokerhand [ah 2c 4d 2s 6h]
one pair
? pokerhand [2h 5d 2s 2c 7d]
three of a kind
? pokerhand [2h 5d 2s 2c 5h]
full house
? pokerhand [3h 4h 5h 6h 7h]
something else
```

So far so good, but of course there is more work to do. We need to write `straightp`, `flushp`, and their combinations: straight flush and royal flush. I think I shouldn't have an instruction in `pokerhand` testing `royal.flushp` as I originally planned; instead I should test for `straightp` and, if that's true, look for special cases within that.

```
to flushp
output emptyp butfirst :suits
end
```

It's not so obvious how to write `straightp`. Here's my plan: First, find the lowest-rank card in the hand. Then, in order to have a straight, the next four ranks must also be present in the hand.

☞ This isn't the only possible way to test for a straight; can you think of, and implement, another?

```
to straightp
output nogap (reduce "min :ranks) 5
end

to min :a :b
output ifelse :a < :b [:a] [:b]
end

to nogap :smallest :howmany
if :howmany=0 [output "true]
if not equalp (item :smallest :rankarray) 1 [output "false]
output nogap :smallest+1 :howmany-1
end
```

Nogap starts with the smallest rank in the hand and checks that there is exactly one card in each of that and the next four ranks. It takes advantage of the fact that I'm representing ranks internally as numbers; it can just add 1 to a rank to get the next one in sequence. If :howmany reaches zero, it means that we have indeed found all five consecutive ranks in the hand. If one of the five desired ranks isn't in the hand, or if the hand has more than one card in any of the ranks, then the hand isn't a straight.

There is one problem with this approach. The ace can be used either high card (10-J-Q-K-A) or low card (A-2-3-4-5) in a straight. Straightp thinks that the ace can only be the low card. We'll fix that later.

Now let's try some other cases. I've just added the line

```
if straightp [print [straight] stop]
```

to pokerhand. It doesn't much matter where I put that line, because there is no danger of a straight also being found as a multiple of any one rank. This instruction will be changed, eventually, because we want to test for straight flush and so on. But for now this will make it possible to debug straightp.

```
? pokerhand [3h 6d 7h 5c 4d]
straight
? pokerhand [3h 6d 7h 5c 8d]
something else
```

I picked those examples pretty much at random. It's a good idea, when testing a procedure, to pick test cases "near the boundaries" of what the program is supposed to accept. For example, what about an ace-low straight, or a king-high? What about a hand in which "the next four ranks" don't exist, because the lowest card is a Jack?

```
? pokerhand [ah 2d 3c 4c 5h]
straight
? pokerhand [9d 10c jh qh kh]
straight
? pokerhand [js jh qs qh kd]
two pairs
```

(Actually, that last example may never invoke straightp at all, if the test for pairp comes first in pokerhand.) Anyway, it looks okay. I could try more examples but I think I believe it. I now decide that the instruction I just put into pokerhand should be

```
if straightp [print ifelse flushp [[straight flush]] [[straight]] stop]
```

and that it should be followed by

```
if flushp [print [flush] stop]
```

(The `if flushp` instruction has to come second because of the principle of "most restrictive first." If that test came first, a straight flush would be reported as just a flush.) Time for more tests:

```
? pokerhand [3h 6h ah kh 7h]
flush
? pokerhand [3h 6h ad kh 7h]
something else
? pokerhand [3h 6h 4h 5h 7h]
straight flush
? pokerhand [3h 6h 4h 5s 7h]
straight
```

Now it's time to solve the problem of the ace-high straight. It turns out to be easy; if the hand has an ace, then I can use `nogap`, the subprocedure of `straightp` that checks for consecutive ranks, to check for the four ranks from 10 to king.

```
to ace.highp
if not equalp (item 1 :rankarray) 1 [output "false]
output nogap 10 4
end
```

That's the end of the categories of poker hands, but to put it all together requires a little editing of `pokerhand`:

```
to pokerhand :cards
local [ranks suits rankarray]
poker.init :cards
if fourp [print [four of a kind] stop]
if full.housep [print [full house] stop]
if threep [print [three of a kind] stop]
if pairp [print ifelse paircount = 1 [[one pair]] [[two pairs]] stop]
if ace.highp [print ifelse flushp [[royal flush]] [[straight]] stop]
if straightp [print ifelse flushp [[straight flush]] [[straight]] stop]
if flushp [print [flush] stop]
print [nothing!]
end
```

Embellishments

I've now done more or less what I set out to do. It took 14 procedures. I hope you have a feeling for the process of switching back and forth between thinking about a particular subproblem and thinking about the overall structure of the program.

I haven't done every detail of what I first suggested. In particular, I don't have the information about particular ranks in what I print. I think perhaps that's more effort than this project seems worth to me. (I'm not just being cute by saying "to me"; the point is that a real poker enthusiast might want to spend a lot of time on this program and make it as beautiful as possible.) But just to show how a completed program can be modified, I'll make it print things like `pair of sixes` instead of just `one pair`.

First I have to be able to find words like "`sixes`" starting with a rank indicator like `6`.

```
to plural :rank
output item :rank [aces twos threes fours fives sixes
                   sevens eights nines tens jacks queens kings]
end
```

The next step is to change one instruction in `pokerhand` to use this new tool:

```
if pairp [print ifelse paircount = 1
                       [sentence [pair of] plural first locate 2 1]
                       [[two pairs]]
          stop]
```

(If you were confused about the double square brackets around `one pair` and `two pairs` before, seeing this new version in which one of the possibilities is the output from a procedure, not a literal list, might help.)

```
? pokerhand [ah 7s 3d 10c 7c]
pair of sevens
```

☞ If you're motivated, you can modify the messages for other categories to include the specific rank information. You might want to change "`nothing`" to "`queen high`," for example.

☞ What if you wanted to use this program on a seven-card-stud hand? In other words, instead of a list of five cards, you'd be given a list of seven, from which you'd have to pick the best five. The main thing I can think of is that you'd have to be more careful about the order of the `if` instructions in `pokerhand`. I've said that you can test `threep` either before or after `straightp` because they can't both be true. But that's not the case for a seven-card hand:

```
[3h 3s 3d 4d 5s 6h 7c]
```

If you try this challenge, make sure your program announces

```
[8s 9s 10s js qs kh ad]
```

as a straight flush, not as an ace-high straight.

Putting the Project in a Context

I wrote this program because I was looking for an example for this book that would be not too long, not too short. That's kind of an artificial reason for starting a project. In real life, if I wrote a program like this one, it would be part of a larger program that would actually *play* poker.

In that context the problem would become very different. We wouldn't want merely to print the designation of a hand; we'd want to be able to compare several hands and announce a winner. To do that, we'd have to attach something like a numerical ranking to the hand, which might become the output from `pokerhand`. But it can't be just a single number; there are too many possible hands to have a list of all of them in rank order. Instead, the ranking of a hand might be a list of numbers. `[5 7 10]` might mean that the hand is a full house (I'm guessing that that would rank about fifth in value), with three sevens and two tens. To compare two lists of numbers, compare their `first`s; if those are equal, go on to compare the next members.

The point is that I'm now back to something approaching top-down planning. As the scale of the project becomes a lot bigger, that kind of advance planning seems necessary. But this isn't really top-down because comparing two hands is just one subproblem of playing poker. Really, according to the top-down view, I should start by designing the top-level procedure `poker`. Perhaps a first attempt might look like this:

```
to poker
deal.cards
bid
draw.more.cards
bid
pokerhand
end
```

But it would be premature to type this into a computer. We have to think about issues like these: Is the computer a player or does it just deal and bank for the other players? How many people can play? What is a good strategy for bidding?

In the end it might turn out that the pokerhand we've just written wouldn't fit into the larger project; it might have to be rewritten for that context. To a structured programmer, the effort we've put in would then be wasted. But I think that even if every procedure had to be edited, I'd benefit from having taken the time to understand how to solve this subproblem.

Program Listing

```
to pokerhand :cards
local [ranks suits rankarray]
poker.init :cards
if fourp [print [four of a kind] stop]
if full.housep [print [full house] stop]
if threep [print [three of a kind] stop]
if pairp [print ifelse paircount = 1 [[one pair]] [[two pairs]] stop]
if ace.highp [print ifelse flushp [[royal flush]] [[straight]] stop]
if straightp [print ifelse flushp [[straight flush]] [[straight]] stop]
if flushp [print [flush] stop]
print [nothing!]
end

to poker.init :cards
make "ranks map [ranknum butlast ?] :cards
make "suits remdup map "last :cards
make "rankarray {0 0 0 0 0 0 0 0 0 0 0 0 0}
foreach :ranks [setitem ? :rankarray (item ? :rankarray)+1]
end

to ranknum :rank
if :rank = "a [output 1]
if :rank = "j [output 11]
if :rank = "q [output 12]
if :rank = "k [output 13]
output :rank
end

to fourp
output memberp 4 :rankarray
end
```

```
to threep
output memberp 3 :rankarray
end

to pairp
output memberp 2 :rankarray
end

to full.housep
output and threep pairp
end

to paircount
output count locate 2 1
end

to locate :number :index
if :index > 13 [output []]
if (item :index :rankarray) = :number ~
   [output fput :index (locate :number :index+1)]
output locate :number :index+1
end

to flushp
output emptyp butfirst :suits
end

to straightp
output nogap (reduce "min :ranks) 5
end

to min :a :b
output ifelse :a < :b [:a] [:b]
end

to nogap :smallest :howmany
if :howmany=0 [output "true]
if not equalp (item :smallest :rankarray) 1 [output "false]
output nogap :smallest+1 :howmany-1
end

to ace.highp
if not equalp (item 1 :rankarray) 1 [output "false]
output nogap 10 4
end
```

14 Example: Pitcher Problem Solver

Program file for this chapter: `pour`

You have probably seen puzzles like this one many times:

> You are at the side of a river. You have a three-liter pitcher and a seven-liter pitcher. The pitchers do not have markings to allow measuring smaller quantities. You need two liters of water. How can you measure two liters?

These puzzles are used in some IQ tests, so many people come across them in schools. To solve the problem, you must pour water from one pitcher to another. In this particular problem, there are six steps in the shortest solution:

1. Fill the three-liter pitcher from the river.
2. Pour the three liters from the three-liter pitcher into the seven-liter pitcher.
3. Fill the three-liter pitcher from the river again.
4. Pour the three liters from the three-liter pitcher into the seven-liter pitcher (which now contains six liters).
5. Fill the three-liter pitcher from the river yet again.
6. Pour from the three-liter pitcher into the seven-liter pitcher until the latter is full. This requires one liter, since the seven-liter pitcher had six liters of water after step 4. This step leaves two liters in the three-liter pitcher.

This example is a relatively hard pitcher problem, since it requires six steps in the solution. On the other hand, it doesn't require pouring water back into the river, and it doesn't have any unnecessary pitchers. An actual IQ test has several such problems, starting with really easy ones like this:

> You are at the side of a river. You have a three-liter pitcher and a seven-liter pitcher. The pitchers do not have markings to allow measuring smaller quantities. You need four liters of water. How can you measure four liters?

and progressing to harder ones like this:

> You are at the side of a river. You have a two-liter pitcher, a five-liter pitcher, and a ten-liter pitcher. The pitchers do not have markings to allow measuring smaller quantities. You need one liter of water. How can you measure one liter?

The goal of this project is a program that can solve these problems. The program should take two inputs, a list of pitcher sizes and a number saying how many liters we want. It will work like this:

```
? pour [3 7] 4
Pour from river to 7
Pour from 7 to 3
Final quantities are 3 4
? pour [2 5 10] 1
Pour from river to 5
Pour from 5 to 2
Pour from 2 to river
Pour from 5 to 2
Final quantities are 2 1 0
```

How do *people* solve these problems? Probably you try a variety of special-purpose techniques. For example, you look at the sums and differences of the pitcher sizes to see if you can match the goal that way. In the problem about measuring four liters with a three-liter pitcher and a seven-liter pitcher, you probably recognized right away that $7 - 3 = 4$. A more sophisticated approach is to look at the remainders when one pitcher size is divided by another. In the last example, trying to measure one liter with pitchers of two, five, and ten liters, you might notice that the remainder of $5/2$ is 1. That means that after removing some number of twos from five, you're left with one.

Such techniques might or might not solve any given pitcher problem. Mathematicians have studied ways to solve such problems in general. To a mathematician, a pitcher problem is equivalent to an algebraic equation in which the variables are required to take on integer (whole number) values. For example, the problem at the beginning of this chapter corresponds to the equation

$$3x + 7y = 2$$

In this equation, x represents the number of times the three-liter pitcher is filled and y represents the number of times the seven-liter pitcher is filled. A positive value means that the pitcher is filled from the river, while a negative value means that it's filled from another pitcher.

An equation with two variables like this one can have infinitely many solutions, but not all the solutions will have integer values. One integer-valued solution is $x = 3$ and $y = -1$. This solution represents filling the three-liter pitcher three times from the river (for a total of nine liters) and filling the seven-liter pitcher once from the three-liter pitcher. Since the seven-liter pitcher is bigger than the three-liter pitcher, it has to be filled in stages. Do you see how this analysis corresponds to the sequence of steps I gave earlier?

An equation with integer-valued variables is called a *Diophantine* equation. In general, a Diophantine equation will have infinitely many solutions, but they won't all be practical as solutions to the original problem. For example, another solution to the equation we've been considering is $x = -4$ and $y = 2$. This solution tells us to fill the seven-liter pitcher from the river twice, and the three-liter pitcher from the seven-liter pitcher four times. Here's how that works out as a sequence of steps:

1. Fill the seven-liter pitcher from the river.
2. Fill the three-liter pitcher from the seven-liter pitcher. (This leaves four liters in the seven-liter pitcher.)
3. Empty the three-liter pitcher into the river.
4. Fill the three-liter pitcher from the seven-liter pitcher. (This leaves one liter in the seven-liter pitcher.)
5. Empty the three-liter pitcher into the river.
6. Pour the contents of the seven-liter pitcher (one liter) into the three-liter pitcher.
7. Fill the seven-liter pitcher from the river (for the second and last time).
8. Fill the three-liter pitcher (which already had one liter in it) from the seven-liter pitcher. (This leaves five liters in the seven-liter pitcher.)
9. Empty the three-liter pitcher into the river.
10. Fill the three-liter pitcher from the seven-liter pitcher. This leaves the desired two liters in the seven-liter pitcher.

This solution works, but it's more complicated than the one I used in the first place.

One way to solve Diophantine equations is graphically. For example, consider the problem about measuring one liter of water with pitcher capacities two, five, and ten liters. It turns out that the ten-liter pitcher is not actually needed, so let's forget it for now and consider the simpler but equivalent problem of using just the two-liter and the five-liter pitchers. This problem gives rise to the equation

$$2x + 5y = 1$$

For the moment, never mind that we are looking for integer solutions. Just graph the equation as you ordinarily would. The graph will be a straight line; probably the easiest way to draw the graph is to find the x-intercept (when $y = 0$, $2x = 1$ so $x = 1/2$) and the y-intercept (when $x = 0$, $y = 1/5$).

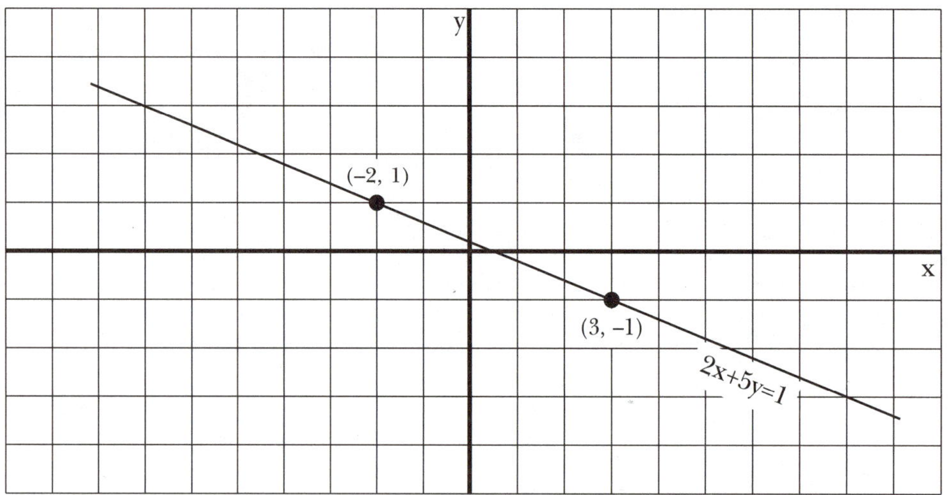

Once you've drawn the graph, you can look for places where the line crosses the grid points of the graph paper. In this case, two such points of intersection are $(-2, 1)$ and $(3, -1)$. The first of these points represents the solution shown earlier, in which the five-liter pitcher is filled from the river and then used as a source of water to fill the two-liter pitcher twice. The second integer solution represents the method of filling the two-liter pitcher from the river three times, then pouring the water from the two-liter pitcher to the five-liter pitcher each time. (On the third such pouring, the five-liter pitcher fills up after only one liter is poured, leaving one liter in the two-liter pitcher.)

What about the original version of this problem, in which there were three pitchers?

In this case, we have a Diophantine equation with three variables:

$$2x + 5y + 10z = 1$$

The graph of this equation is a plane in a three-dimensional coordinate system. An example of a solution point that uses all three pitchers is $(-2, -1, 1)$. How would you interpret this as a series of pouring steps?

By the way, not all pitcher problems have solutions. For example, how could you measure one liter with a two-liter pitcher and a ten-liter pitcher? The answer is that you can't; since both pitchers hold an even number of liters, any amount of water measurable with them will also be even.*

Tree Search

My program does not solve pitcher problems by manipulating Diophantine equations. Instead, it simply tries every possible sequence of pouring steps until one of the pitchers contains the desired amount of water. This method is not feasible for a human being, because the number of possible sequences is generally quite large. Computers are better than people at doing large numbers of calculations quickly; people have the almost magical ability to notice the one relevant pattern in a problem without trying all the possibilities. (Some researchers attribute this human ability to "parallel processing"—the fact that the human brain can carry on several independent trains of thought all at once. They are beginning to build computers designed for parallel processing, and hope that these machines will be able to perform more like people than traditional computers.)

The possible pouring steps for a pitcher problem form a *tree.* The root of the tree is the situation in which all the pitchers are empty. Connected to the root are as many branches as there are pitchers; each branch leads to a node in which one of the pitchers has been filled from the river. Each of those nodes has several branches connected to it, corresponding to the several possible pouring steps. Here is the beginning of the tree for the case of a three-liter pitcher and a seven-liter pitcher. Each node is represented in the diagram by a list of numbers indicating the current contents of the three-liter pitcher and the seven-liter pitcher; for example, the list `[3 4]` means that the three-liter pitcher is full and the seven-liter pitcher contains four liters.

* You can find a computational algorithm to solve (or show that there are no solutions to) any linear Diophantine equation with two variables on page 50 of Courant and Robbins, *What Is Mathematics?* (Oxford University Press, 1941).

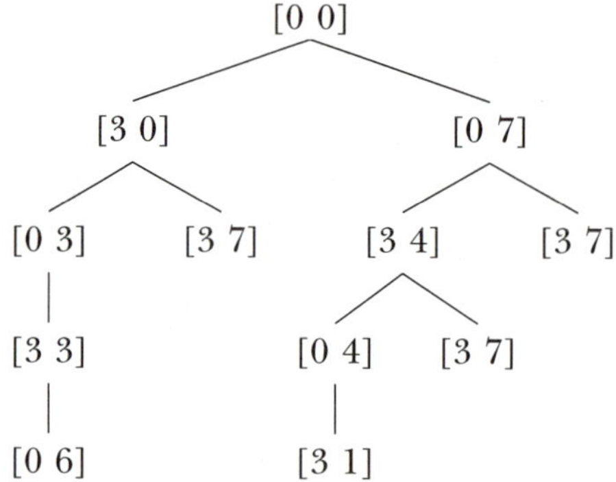

Actually, I have simplified this tree by showing only the meaningful pouring steps. The program must consider, and of course reject, things like the sequence

1. Fill the three-liter pitcher from the river.
2. Empty the three-liter pitcher into the river.

and individual meaningless steps like pouring from a pitcher into itself, pouring from an empty pitcher, and pouring into a full pitcher. For a two-pitcher problem there are three possible sources of water (the two pitchers and the river) and three possible destinations, for a total of nine possible pouring steps. Here is the top of the full tree:

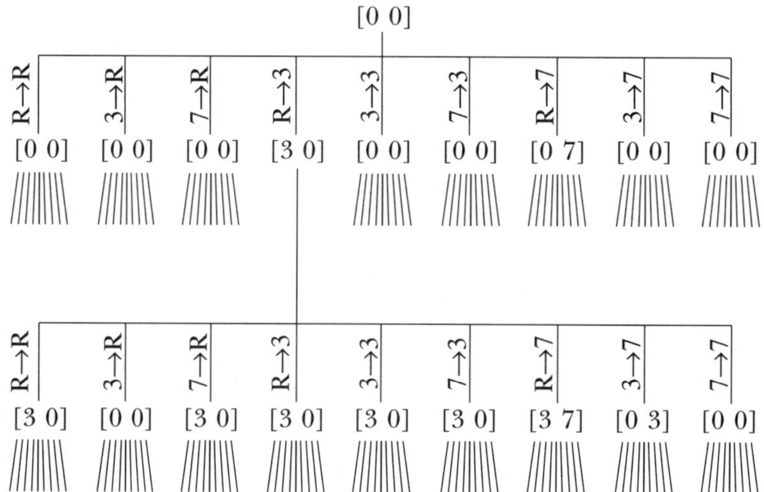

At each level of the tree, the number of nodes is multiplied by nine. If we're trying to measure two liters of water, a six-step problem, the level of the tree at which the solution is found will have 531,441 nodes! You can see that efficiency will be an important consideration in this program.

In some projects, a tree is represented within the program by a Logo list. That's not going to be the case in this project. The tree is not explicitly represented in the program at all, although the program will maintain a list of the particular nodes of the tree that are under consideration at a given moment. The entire tree can't be represented as a list because it's infinitely deep! In this project, the tree diagram is just something that should be in your mind as a model of what the program is doing: it's *searching* through the tree, looking for a node that includes the goal quantity as one of its numbers.

Depth-first and Breadth-first Searching

Many programming problems can be represented as searches through trees. For example, a chess-playing program has to search through a tree of moves. The root of the tree is the initial board position; the second level of the tree contains the possible first moves by white; the third level contains the possible responses by black to each possible move by white; and so on.

There are two general techniques for searching a tree. These techniques are called *depth-first search* and *breadth-first search.* In the first technique, the program explores all of the "descendents" of a given node before looking at the "siblings" of that node. In the chess example, a depth-first search would mean that the program would explore all the possible outcomes (continuing to the end of the game) of a particular opening move, then go on to do the same for another opening move. In breadth-first search, the program examines all the nodes at a given level of the tree, then goes on to generate and examine the nodes at the next level. Which technique is more appropriate will depend on the nature of the problem.

In a programming language like Logo, with recursive procedures and local variables, it turns out that depth-first search leads to a simpler program structure. Suppose that we are given an operation called `children` that takes a node as input and gives us as its output a list of all the children (one level down) of that node. Suppose we also are given a command called `process` that takes a node as input and does whatever the program needs to do for each node of the tree. (You can just use `print` in place of `process` if you want to see what's in the tree.) Here is how to do a depth-first search:

```
to depth.first :node
process :node
foreach (children :node) "depth.first
end
```

In this program, the structure of the tree is reflected in the structure of recursive invocations of `depth.first.`

It might be worthwhile to consider a specific example of how this program works. One of the suggested activities in Chapter 11 was to write a program that takes a telephone number as input and prints out all possible spellings of that number as letters. (Each digit can represent any of three letters. To keep things simple, I'm going to ignore the problem of the digits zero and one, which don't represent any letters on telephone dials in the United States.) Here is a partial picture of the tree for a particular telephone number. Each node contains some letters and some digits. (In the program, a node will be represented as a Logo list with two members, a word of letters and a word of digits.) The root node is all digits; the "leaf" nodes will be all letters.

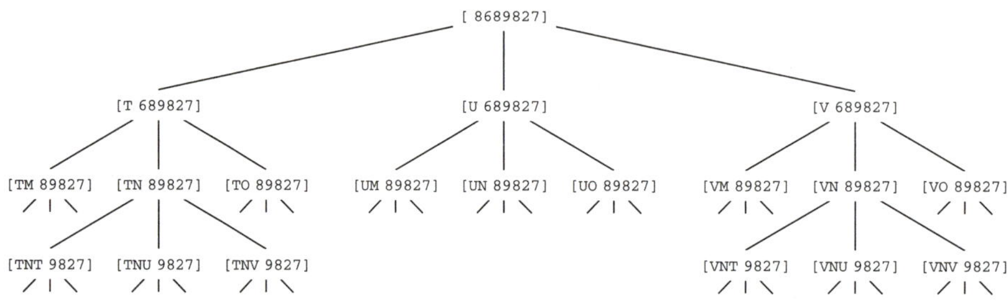

The operation `children` must output a list of three nodes, selecting each of the three possible letters for the first remaining digit. If the input to `children` is a leaf node (one with all letters), it must output the empty list to indicate that there are no children for that node.

```
to children :node
if emptyp last :node [output []]
output map [child (first :node) ? (butfirst last :node)] ~
           letters first last :node
end

to letters :digit
output item :digit [[] abc def ghi jkl mno prs tuv wxy]
end

to child :letters :this :digits
output list (word :letters :this) :digits
end

?show children [tnt 9827]
[[tntw 827] [tntx 827] [tnty 827]]
```

The top-level procedure has to turn a number into a root node and invoke a depth-first search:

```
to spell :number
depth.first list " :number
end
```

What about the `process` command? The program wants to print only leaf nodes:

```
to process :node
if emptyp last :node [print :node]
end
```

☞ Try this program. To get the tree illustrated above, use the instruction

```
spell 8689827
```

Then try again, but investigate the order in which the program searches the nodes of the tree by using a different version of `process`:

```
to process :node
print :node
end
```

This will let you see the order in which the program encounters the nodes of the tree.

Writing a breadth-first search is a little more complicated because the program must explicitly arrange to process all the nodes of a given level before processing those at the next level. It keeps track of the nodes waiting to be processed in a *queue,* a list in which new nodes are added at the right and the next node to be processed is taken from the left. Here is the program:

```
to breadth.first :root
breadth.descend (list :root)
end

to breadth.descend :queue
if emptyp :queue [stop]
process first :queue
breadth.descend sentence (butfirst :queue) ~
                         (children first :queue)
end
```

This breadth-first search program uses the same `children` and `process` subprocedures as the depth-first version. You can try a breadth-first listing of telephone number spellings simply by changing the top-level `spell` procedure to invoke `breadth.first` instead of `depth.first`. What you'll find is that (with the version of `process` that only prints leaf nodes) the two versions produce the same results, but the depth-first program trickles the spellings out one by one, while the breadth-first version prints nothing for a long time and then spits out all the spellings at once. If you use the version of `process` that prints all the nodes, you can see why.

The telephone number speller is an unusual example of a tree-search program for two reasons. First, the tree is finite; we know in advance that it extends seven levels below the root node, because a telephone number has seven digits. Second, the goal of the program requires searching the *entire* tree. It's more common that the program is looking for a solution that's "good enough" in some sense, and when a solution is found, the program stops looking. For example, in the pitcher problem program, once we find a sequence of steps to measure the desired amount of water, we don't care if there is also a second way to do it.

For the pitcher problem solver, I decided that a breadth-first search is appropriate. The main reason is that I wanted to present the *shortest* possible solution. To do that, first I see if any one-step sequences solve the problem, then I see if any two-step sequences solve it, and so on. This is a breadth-first order.

Data Representation

At first, I thought that I would represent each node of the tree as a list of numbers representing the contents of the pitchers, as in the diagram I showed earlier. I called this list of quantities a *state.* This information is enough to be able to generate the children of a node. Later, though, I realized that when I find a winning solution (one that has the goal quantity as one of the quantities in the state list) I want to be able to print not only the final quantities but also the sequence of pouring steps used to get there. In a depth-first search, this information is implicitly contained in the local variables of the procedure invocations leading to the winning solution. In a breadth-first search, however, the program doesn't keep track of the sequence of events leading to a given node. I had to remember this information explicitly.

The solution I chose was to have an extra member in the list representing a state, namely a list of *pourings.* A pouring is a list of two numbers representing the source and the destination of the water being poured. Zero represents the river; numbers greater than zero are pitcher numbers. (A pitcher number is not the same as the size of the pitcher. If you enter the instruction

```
pour [2 5 10] 1
```

then the two-liter pitcher is pitcher number 1, the five-liter is number 2, and the ten-liter is number 3.) The list of pourings is the first member of the expanded state list; pourings are added to that list at the front, with `fput`. For example, in the interaction

```
?pour [3 7] 4
Pour from river to 7
Pour from 7 to 3
Final quantities are 3 4
```

the extended state information for the final solution state is

```
[[[2 1] [0 2]] 3 4]
```

In this list, the sublist `[0 2]` represents pouring water from the river into pitcher number 2, which is the seven-liter pitcher. The sublist `[2 1]` represents pouring water from pitcher number 2 into pitcher number 1.

Abstract Data Types

Up to this point I've continued to call this expanded data structure a *state.* That's what I did in the program, also, until I found that certain procedures needed the new version, while other procedures dealt with what I had originally considered a state, with only the final quantities included in the list. As a result, my program had local variables named `state` in several procedures, some of which contained the old kind of state, and some the new kind. I thought this might be confusing, so I did what I should have done in the first place: I invented a new name for the expanded data structure. It's now called a *path*; when you read the program you can confidently assume that `:state` represents a list like

```
[3 4]
```

while `:path` represents a list like

```
[[[2 1] [0 2]] 3 4]
```

The trouble with using a list of lists of lists in a program is that it can become very complicated to keep track of all the uses of selectors like `first` and constructors like `fput`. For example, suppose the value of the variable `oldpath` is a path, and we decide to pour water from pitcher number `:from` to pitcher number `:to`. We now want to construct a new path, which will include a new state (computed from the old state and the two pitcher numbers) and a new list of moves, with the new move added to the existing ones. We'd end up saying

```
make "newpath fput (fput (list :from :to) first :oldpath) ~
                   (newstate butfirst :oldpath :from :to)
```

assuming that we have a procedure `newstate` that computes the new state. This instruction is hard to read! The two invocations of `fput` have quite different purposes. One adds a new move to a list of moves, while the other connects a list of moves to a state in order to form a path. We can clarify instructions like this one if we make up synonyms for procedures like `first` and `fput` to be used in particular contexts. For example, we make a new path using `fput`, but we'll call it `make.path` when we're using it for that purpose. Just as `fput` is a constructor, and `first` a selector, for lists, we can invent constructors and selectors for *abstract* data types (ones that we make up, rather than ones built into Logo) such as paths:

```
to make.path :moves :state
output fput :moves :state
end

to path.moves :path
output first :path
end

to path.state :path
output butfirst :path
end
```

That unreadable instruction shown earlier would now be written this way:

```
make "newpath make.path (fput (list :from :to) path.moves :oldpath) ~
                        (newstate (path.state :oldpath) :from :to)
```

At first glance this may not seem like much of an improvement, since the new names are longer and less familiar than the old ones. But we can now read the instruction and see that it calls a constructor `make.path` with two inputs, one that seems to have to do with moves, and the other that seems to have to do with states. If we remember that a path has two parts, a list of moves and a state, this makes sense.

☞ Invent a constructor and selectors for a *move* data type.

Sentence as a Combiner

The general breadth-first search program I showed earlier contains this procedure:

```
to breadth.descend :queue
if emptyp :queue [stop]
process first :queue
breadth.descend sentence (butfirst :queue) (children first :queue)
end
```

The most common use of `sentence` is in generating English sentences. In that use, the input and output lists are *sentences* or flat lists. You're supposed to think, "`Sentence` takes two words or sentences as inputs; its output is a sentence containing all the words of the inputs." In this program, we're using `sentence` in a different way, more like what is called `append` in Lisp. Here you're supposed to think, "`Sentence` takes two lists as inputs; its output is a list containing the members of the inputs." Those members could be words or lists, but in this case they'll be lists, namely paths.

Recursive procedures that manipulate non-flat lists generally use `fput` as the combiner. That wouldn't work here for two reasons. First, the queue structure that we need to implement breadth-first search requires that we add new entries at the opposite end of the list from where we look for the next node to process. If we use `first` to select a node and `fput` to add new candidate nodes, then instead of a queue we'd be using a *stack,* in which the newest entries are processed first instead of the oldest ones first. That would give us a depth-first tree search algorithm. We could solve that problem by using `lput` as the combiner, but the second reason for choosing `sentence` is that we don't generate new entries one at a time. Instead, `children` gives us several children to add to the queue at once. That means we must append the list output by `children` to the list that represents the nodes already queued.

Finding the Children of a Node

`Pour` is going to work essentially by invoking `breadth.first` on a root node containing zeros for all the current quantities. But in this case we want to pick a single node that satisfies the conditions of the problem, so we must modify `breadth.first` to make it an *operation* that outputs the first such node:

```
to breadth.first :root
output breadth.descend (list :root)
end

to breadth.descend :queue
if emptyp :queue [output []]
if winnerp first :queue [output first :queue]
output breadth.descend sentence (butfirst :queue) ~
                                (children first :queue)
end
```

The predicate `winnerp` will output `true` if its input is a node that satisfies the problem conditions:

```
to winnerp :path
output memberp :goal path.state :path
end
```

If `breadth.first` runs out of nodes without finding a solution, it returns an empty list to indicate failure.

Here is a simplified version of `pour`:

```
to pour :sizes :goal
win breadth.first make.path [] all.empty :sizes
end

to all.empty :list
output map [0] :list
end
```

`All.empty` is an operation that outputs a state in which all of the values are zeros. The number of zeros in the list is equal to the number of members in its input, which is the number of pitchers. `Pour` combines this initial state with an empty list of moves to produce the first path.

To allow `breadth.first` to work, we must have an operation called `children` that outputs a list of the children of a node. Starting from a particular state, what are the possible outcomes of a single pouring? As I mentioned earlier, the source of a pouring can be the river or any of the pitchers, and the destination can also be the river or any of the pitchers. If there are n pitchers, then there are $n+1$ sources, $n+1$ destinations, and therefore $(n+1)^2$ possible pourings. Here is how the program structure reflects this. I'm assuming that we've created (elsewhere in the program) a variable called `pitchers` whose value is a list of all the integers from zero to n.

```
to children :path
output map.se [children1 :path ?] :pitchers
end

to children1 :path :from
output map.se [child :path :from ?] :pitchers
end

to child :path :from :to
output (list make.path (fput (list :from :to) path.moves :path)
                       (newstate (path.state :path) :from :to))
end
```

The version of `child` presented here is simpler than the one in the actual project, but the other procedures are the real versions. We'll see later how `child` is expanded. The immediately important point is to see how `children` and `children1` ensure that every possible source (`:from`) and destination (`:to`) from zero to the number of pitchers are used.

You should be wondering, at this point, why `children1` uses `sentence` as a combiner. (That's what it means to use `map.se` rather than `map`.) It makes sense for `children` to combine using `sentence` because, as I discussed earlier, the things it's combining are lists of nodes, the outputs from invocations of `children1`. But `children1` is not combining lists of nodes; it's combining the outputs from invocations of `child`. Each invocation of `child` computes a single child node. It would be more straightforward to write the program this way:

```
to children1 :path :from                          ;; simplified
output map [child :path :from ?] :pitchers
end

to child :path :from :to                          ;; simplified
output make.path (fput (list :from :to) path.moves :path) ~
                 (newstate (path.state :path) :from :to)
end
```

This also eliminates the use of `list` in `child`, needed in the other version to turn a single node into a singleton (one-member) list of nodes, which is what `sentence` needs to function properly as a combiner.

The reason for the use of `sentence` in `children1` is that we are later going to modify `child` so that sometimes it rejects a possible new node for efficiency reasons. For example, it makes no sense to have nodes for pourings in which the source and the destination are the same. When it wants to reject a node, `child` will output the empty list. Using `sentence` as the combiner, this empty list simply doesn't affect the accumulated list of new nodes. Here is a version of `child` modified to exclude pourings to and from the same place:

```
to child :path :from :to
if equalp :from :to [output []]
output (list make.path (fput (list :from :to) path.moves :path)
                       (newstate (path.state :path) :from :to))
end
```

With this version of `child`, the use of `sentence` in `children1` may seem more sensible to you.

To create the variable `pitchers` we modify the top-level `pour`:

```
to pour :sizes :goal
local "pitchers
make "pitchers fput 0 (map [#] :sizes)
win breadth.first make.path [] all.empty :sizes
end
```

Here we are taking advantage of a feature of `map` that I haven't mentioned earlier. The number sign (`#`) can be used in a `map` template to represent the position in the input, rather than the value, of a member of the input data list. That is, `#` is replaced by 1 for the first member, 2 for the second, and so on. In this example, these position numbers are all we care about; the template does not contain the usual question mark to refer to the values of the data.

Computing a New State

The job of `child` is to produce a new child node, that is to say, a new path. Its inputs are an old path and the source and destination of a new pouring. The new path consists of a new state and a new list of pourings. The latter is easy; it's just the old list of pourings with the new one inserted. `Child` computes that part itself, with the expression

```
fput (list :from :to) path.moves :path
```

The new state is harder to compute. There are four cases.

1. If the destination is the river, then the thing to do is to empty the source pitcher.
2. If the source is the river, then the thing to do is to fill the destination pitcher to its capacity.
3. If source and destination are pitchers and the destination pitcher has enough empty space to hold the contents of the source pitcher, then the thing to do is to add the entire contents of the source pitcher to the destination pitcher, setting the contents of the source pitcher to zero.
4. If both are pitchers but there is not enough room in the destination to hold the contents of the source, then the thing to do is fill the destination to its capacity and subtract that much water from the source.

Here is the procedure to carry out these computations:

```
to newstate :state :from :to
if riverp :to [output replace :state :from 0]
if riverp :from [output replace :state :to (size :to)]
if (water :from) < (room :to) ~
   [output replace2 :state ~
                    :from 0 ~
                    :to ((water :from)+(water :to))]
output replace2 :state ~
                :from ((water :from)-(room :to)) ~
                :to (size :to)
end
```

Each instruction of this procedure straightforwardly embodies one of the four numbered possibilities.

Helper procedures are used to compute a new list of amounts of water, replacing either one or two old values from the previous list:

```
to replace :list :index :value
if equalp :index 1 [output fput :value butfirst :list]
output fput first :list (replace butfirst :list :index-1 :value)
end
```

```
to replace2 :list :index1 :value1 :index2 :value2
if equalp :index1 1 ~
   [output fput :value1 replace butfirst :list :index2-1 :value2]
if equalp :index2 1 ~
   [output fput :value2 replace butfirst :list :index1-1 :value1]
output fput first :list ~
            replace2 butfirst :list :index1-1 :value1 :index2-1 :value2
end
```

Replace takes as inputs a list, a number representing a position in the list, and a value. The output is a copy of the first input, but with the member selected by the second input replaced with the third input. Here's an example:

```
?show replace [a b c d e] 4 "x
[a b c x e]
```

Replace2 has a similar purpose, but its output has *two* members changed from their values in the input list.

Remember that newstate has as one of its inputs a state, that is, a list of numbers representing quantities of water. Newstate uses replace to change the amount of water in one of the pitchers. The second input to replace is the pitcher number, and the third is the new contents of that pitcher. For example, if the destination is the river then we want to empty the source pitcher. This case is handled by the instruction

```
if riverp :to [output replace :state :from 0]
```

If the destination is the river, the output state is the same as the input state except that the pitcher whose number is :from has its contents replaced by zero. The other cases are handled similarly, except that two replacements are necessary if both source and destination are pitchers.

More Data Abstraction

The instructions in newstate use some procedures I haven't written yet, such as riverp to test whether a source or destination is the river, and room to find the amount of empty space in a pitcher. If we think of a pitcher as an abstract data type, then these can be considered selectors for that type. Here they are:

```
to riverp :pitcher
output equalp :pitcher 0
end

to size :pitcher
output item :pitcher :sizes
end

to water :pitcher
output item :pitcher :state
end

to room :pitcher
output (size :pitcher)-(water :pitcher)
end
```

To underscore the importance of data abstraction, here is what `newstate` would look like without these selectors. (I actually wrote it this way at first, but I think you'll agree that it's unreadable.)

```
to newstate :state :from :to
if equalp :to 0 [output replace :state :from 0]
if equalp :from 0 [output replace :state :to (item :to :sizes)]
if ((item :from :state) < ((item :to :sizes)-(item :to :state))) ~
   [output replace2 :state ~
                    :from 0 ~
                    :to ((item :from :state)+(item :to :state))]
output replace2 :state ~
                :from ((item :from :state)-
                       ((item :to :sizes)-(item :to :state))) ~
                :to (item :to :sizes)
end
```

Printing the Results

When `breadth.first` finds a winning path, the top-level procedure `pour` invokes `win` with that path as its input. `Win`'s job is to print the results. Since the list of moves is kept in reverse order, `win` uses the Logo primitive operation `reverse` to ensure that the moves are shown in chronological order.

```
to win :path
if emptyp :path [print [Can't do it!] stop]
foreach (reverse path.moves :path) "win1
print sentence [Final quantities are] (path.state :path)
end

to win1 :move
print (sentence [Pour from] (printform first :move)
                [to] (printform last :move))
end

to printform :pitcher
if riverp :pitcher [output "river]
output size :pitcher
end
```

Efficiency: What Really Matters?

The `pour` program as described so far would run extremely slowly. The rest of the commentary in this chapter will be on ways to improve its efficiency. The fundamental problem is one I mentioned earlier: the number of nodes in the tree grows enormously as the depth increases. In a problem with two pitchers, the root level has one node, the next level nine nodes, the third level 81, the fourth level 729, the fifth level 6561, and the sixth level 59049. A six-step problem like

```
pour [3 7] 2
```

would strain the memory capacity of many computers as well as taking forever to run!

When you're trying to make a program more efficient, the easiest improvements to figure out are not usually the ones that really help. The easy things to see are details about the computation within some procedure. For example, the `newstate` procedure described earlier calls the `room` procedure twice to compute the amount of room available in the destination pitcher. Each call to `room` computes the quantity

```
(item :to :sizes)-(item :to :state)
```

This expression represents the amount of empty space in the destination pitcher. Perhaps it would be faster to compute this number only once, and store it in a variable? I haven't bothered trying to decide, because the effect is likely to be small either way. Improving the speed of computing each new node is much less important than cutting down the *number* of nodes we compute. The reason is that eliminating one node also eliminates all its descendants, so that the effect grows as the program moves to lower levels of the tree.

The best efficiency improvement is likely to be a complete rethinking of the algorithm. For example, I've mentioned that a numerical algorithm exists for solving two-variable linear Diophantine equations. This algorithm would be a *much* faster way to solve two-pitcher problems than even the best tree search program. I haven't used that method because I wanted a simple program that would work for any number of pitchers, but if I really had to solve such problems in practice, I'd use the Diophantine equation method wherever possible.

Avoiding Meaningless Pourings

We have already modified `child` to avoid one kind of meaningless pouring, namely ones in which the source is the same as the destination. Two other avoidable kinds of meaningless pourings are ones from an empty source and ones to a full destination. In either case, the quantity of water poured will be zero, so the state will not change. Here is a modified version of `child` that avoids these cases:

```
to child :path :from :to
local "state
if equalp :from :to [output []]
make "state path.state :path
if not riverp :from ~
   [if equalp (water :from) 0 [output []]]
if not riverp :to ~
   [if equalp (water :to) (size :to) [output []]]
output (list make.path (fput list :from :to path.moves :path)
                       (newstate :state :from :to))
end
```

The local variable `state` is set up because the procedure `water` needs it. (`Water` relies on Logo's dynamic scope to give it access to the `state` variable provided by its caller.)

The important changes are the two new `if` instructions. The first avoids pouring from an empty pitcher; the second avoids pouring into a full one. In both cases, the test makes sense only for actual pitchers; the river does not have a size or a current contents.

To underscore what I said earlier about what's important in trying to improve the efficiency of a program, notice that these added tests *slow down* the process of computing each new node, and yet the overall effect is beneficial because the number of nodes is dramatically reduced.

Eliminating Duplicate States

It's relatively easy to find individual pourings that are absurd. A harder problem is to avoid *sequences* of pourings, each reasonable in itself, that add up to a state we've already seen. The most blatant examples are like the one I mentioned a while back about filling a pitcher from the river and then immediately emptying it into the river again. But there are less blatant cases that are also worth finding. For example, suppose the problem includes a three-liter pitcher and a six-liter pitcher. The sequence

```
Pour from river to 6
Pour from 6 to 3
```

leads to the same state (`[3 3]`) as the sequence

```
Pour from river to 3
Pour from 3 to 6
Pour from river to 3
```

The latter isn't an absurd sequence of pourings, but it's silly to pursue any of its children because they will have the same states as the children of the first sequence, which is one step shorter. Any solution that could be found among the descendents of the second sequence will be found one cycle earlier among the descendents of the first.

To avoid pursuing these duplicate states, the program keeps a list of all the states found so far. This strategy requires changes to `pour` and to `child`.

```
to pour :sizes :goal
local [oldstates pitchers]
make "oldstates (list all.empty :sizes)
make "pitchers fput 0 (map [#] :sizes)
win breadth.first make.path [] all.empty :sizes
end
```

```
to child :path :from :to
local [state newstate]
if equalp :from :to [output []]
make "state path.state :path
if not riverp :from ~
   [if equalp (water :from) 0 [output []]]
if not riverp :to ~
   [if equalp (water :to) (size :to) [output []]]
make "newstate (newstate :state :from :to)
if memberp :newstate :oldstates [output []]
make "oldstates fput :newstate :oldstates
output (list make.path (fput list :from :to path.moves :path) :newstate)
end
```

The change in `pour` is simply to initialize the list of already-seen states to include the state in which all pitchers are empty. There are two important new instructions in `child`. The first rejects a new node if its state is already in the list; the second adds a new state to the list. Notice that it is duplicate *states* we look for, not duplicate *paths*; it's in the nature of a tree-search program that there can never be duplicate paths.

Stopping the Program Early

The breadth-first search mechanism we're using detects a winning path as it's *removed* from the front of the queue. If we could detect the winner as we're about to *add* it to the queue, we could avoid the need to compute all of the queue entries that come after it: children of nodes that are at the same level as the winning node, but to its left.

It's not easy to do this elegantly, though, because we add new nodes to the queue several at a time, using the procedure `children` to compute them. What we need is a way to let `child`, which constructs the winning node, prevent the computation of any more children, and notify `breadth.first` that a winner has been found.

The most elegant way to do this in Berkeley Logo uses a primitive called `throw` that we won't meet until the second volume of this series. Instead, in this chapter I'll use a less elegant technique, but one that works in any Logo implementation. I'll create a variable named won whose value is initially `false` but becomes `true` as soon as a winner is found. Here are the necessary modifications:

```
to pour :sizes :goal
local [oldstates pitchers won]
make "oldstates (list all.empty :sizes)
make "pitchers fput 0 (map [#] :sizes)
make "won "false
win breadth.first make.path [] all.empty :sizes
end

to breadth.descend :queue
if emptyp :queue [output []]
if :won [output last :queue]
op breadth.descend sentence (butfirst :queue) ~
                            (children first :queue)
end

to child :path :from :to
local [state newstate]
if :won [output []]
if equalp :from :to [output []]
make "state path.state :path
if not riverp :from ~
   [if equalp (water :from) 0 [output []]]
if not riverp :to
   [if equalp (water :to) (size :to) [output []]]
make "newstate (newstate :state :from :to)
if memberp :newstate :oldstates [output []]
make "oldstates fput :newstate :oldstates
if memberp :goal :newstate [make "won "true]
output (list make.path (fput list :from :to path.moves :path) :newstate)
end
```

The procedure `winnerp` is no longer used; we are now checking a state, rather than a path, for the goal amount.

Further Explorations

☞ Is it possible to eliminate more pieces of the tree by more sophisticated analysis of the problem? For example, in all of the specific problems I've presented, the best solution never includes pouring from pitcher A to pitcher B and then later pouring from B to A. Is this true in general? If so, many possible pourings could be rejected with an instruction like

```
if memberp list :to :from path.moves :path [output []]
```

in `child`.

☞ Do some research into Diophantine equations and the techniques used to solve them computationally. See if you can devise a general method for solving pitcher problems with any number of pitchers, based on Diophantine equations.

☞ Think about writing a program that would mimic the way people actually approach these problems. The program would, for example, compute the differences and remainders of pairs of pitcher sizes, looking for the goal quantity.

☞ What other types of puzzles can be considered as tree searching problems?

Program Listing

```
;; Initialization

to pour :sizes :goal
local [oldstates pitchers won]
make "oldstates (list all.empty :sizes)
make "pitchers fput 0 (map [#] :sizes)
make "won "false
win breadth.first make.path [] all.empty :sizes
end

to all.empty :list
output map [0] :list
end

;; Tree search

to breadth.first :root
op breadth.descend (list :root)
end

to breadth.descend :queue
if emptyp :queue [output []]
if :won [output last :queue]
op breadth.descend sentence (butfirst :queue) ~
                            (children first :queue)
end
```

```
;; Generate children

to children :path
output map.se [children1 :path ?] :pitchers
end

to children1 :path :from
output map.se [child :path :from ?] :pitchers
end

to child :path :from :to
local [state newstate]
if :won [output []]
if equalp :from :to [output []]
make "state path.state :path
if not riverp :from ~
   [if equalp (water :from) 0 [output []]]
if not riverp :to ~
   [if equalp (water :to) (size :to) [output []]]
make "newstate (newstate :state :from :to)
if memberp :newstate :oldstates [output []]
make "oldstates fput :newstate :oldstates
if memberp :goal :newstate [make "won "true]
output (list make.path (fput list :from :to path.moves :path) :newstate)
end

to newstate :state :from :to
if riverp :to [output replace :state :from 0]
if riverp :from [output replace :state :to (size :to)]
if (water :from) < (room :to) ~
   [output replace2 :state ~
                    :from 0 ~
                    :to ((water :from)+(water :to))]
output replace2 :state ~
                :from ((water :from)-(room :to)) ~
                :to (size :to)
end

;; Printing the result

to win :path
if emptyp :path [print [Can't do it!] stop]
foreach (reverse path.moves :path) "win1
print sentence [Final quantities are] (path.state :path)
end
```

```
to win1 :move
print (sentence [Pour from] (printform first :move)
                [to] (printform last :move))
end

to printform :pitcher
if riverp :pitcher [output "river]
output size :pitcher
end

;; Path data abstraction

to make.path :moves :state
output fput :moves :state
end

to path.moves :path
output first :path
end

to path.state :path
output butfirst :path
end

;; Pitcher data abstraction

to riverp :pitcher
output equalp :pitcher 0
end

to size :pitcher
output item :pitcher :sizes
end

to water :pitcher
output item :pitcher :state
end

to room :pitcher
output (size :pitcher)-(water :pitcher)
end
```

```
;; List processing utilities

to replace :list :index :value
if equalp :index 1 [output fput :value butfirst :list]
output fput first :list (replace butfirst :list :index-1 :value)
end

to replace2 :list :index1 :value1 :index2 :value2
if equalp :index1 1 ~
   [output fput :value1 replace butfirst :list :index2-1 :value2]
if equalp :index2 1 ~
   [output fput :value2 replace butfirst :list :index1-1 :value1]
output fput first :list ~
            replace2 butfirst :list :index1-1 :value1 :index2-1 :value2
end
```

15 Debugging

I haven't talked much, until now, about how to find and fix mistakes in the programs you write. Except for the chapter-length examples in Chapters 6, 12, and 14, it hasn't been much of a problem because the sample programs I've shown you have been so small. That doesn't mean you can't make a mistake in a small program! But mistakes are relatively easy to find when the entire program is one procedure with just a few instruction lines. In a real programming project, which might have 20 or 200 procedures, it's harder to locate an error.

Using Error Messages

At one point in Chapter 13 I saw the error message

```
I don't know how  to one  in pokerhand
```

Logo's error messages were deliberately designed to use an informal, smooth, low-key style so that beginning programmers won't find them intimidating. But there is a lot of information in that message if you learn how to find it. The message tells me three things. First, it tells me what *kind* of error is involved. In this particular message, the phrase "I don't know how" suggests that a procedure is missing, and the words "to one" subtly suggest how the problem could be fixed. Second, the message tells me the *specific* expression that was in error: the word `one`. Third, it tells me that the error was detected while Logo was carrying out the procedure named `pokerhand`.

The precise form of the message may be different in different situations. If you make a mistake in a top-level instruction (that is, one that you type to a question mark prompt, not inside a procedure), the part about `in pokerhand` won't be included.

One very important thing to remember is that the place where an error is *found* may not be the place where the error really *is*. That's a little vague, so let's think about the I don't know how error. All the Logo interpreter knows is that it has been asked to invoke a procedure that doesn't exist. But there can be several possible reasons for that. The most common reason is that you've just misspelled the name of a procedure. When the message is

```
I don't know how  to forwrad  in poly
```

you can be pretty sure, just from reading the message, that the problem is a misspelling of forward. In this case the mistake is in poly, just as the message tells you.

On the other hand you might get a message like this about a procedure that really should exist. For example, I might have seen

```
I don't know how  to straight  in pokerhand
```

If I had been confronted with that message, I might have looked at pokerhand, and indeed I would have found an instruction that invokes a procedure named straight. But that's not an error; there *should* be such a procedure. One of two things would be wrong: either I'd forgotten to define straight altogether or else I made a spelling mistake in the title line of straight rather than in an instruction line of pokerhand. To find out, I would type the command pots (which, as you recall, stands for Print Out TitleS) and look for a possible misspelling of straight.

Another way to get the same error message is to write a program using one version of Logo and then transfer it to another version with somewhat different primitives. For example, Berkeley Logo includes higher order functions such as map that are not primitive in most other Logo dialects. If you write a program that uses map and then try to run it in another version of Logo, you'll get a message saying I don't know how to map. In that case you'd have to write your own version of map or rewrite the program to avoid using it—for example, by using a recursive operation instead.

The mistake I actually made in Chapter 13 wasn't a misspelling, a missing definition, or a nonexistent primitive. Instead, I failed to quote a list with square brackets. The particular context in which I did it, in an input to ifelse, is a fairly obscure one. But here is a common beginner's mistake, especially for people who are accustomed to other programming languages:

```
? print "How are you?"
How
i don't know how  to are
```

The moral of all this is that the error message *does* give you some valuable help in finding your bug, but it *doesn't* tell you the whole story. You have to read the message intelligently.

Invalid Data

I've spent a lot of time on the `I don't know how` message because it's probably the most common one. Another very common kind of message, which will merit some analysis here, is

```
procedure doesn't like datum as input
```

In general, this means that you've violated the rules about the kinds of data that some primitive procedure requires as input. (Recall that the type of input is one of the things I've been insisting that you mention as part of the description of a procedure.) For example, `word` requires words as inputs, so:

```
? print word "hello, [old buddy]
word doesn't like [old buddy] as input
```

There are several special cases, however, that come up more often than something as foolish as using a list as an input to `word`. The most common message of this form is this one:

```
butfirst doesn't like [] as input
```

This almost invariably means that you've left out the stop rule in a recursive procedure. The offending input to `butfirst` isn't an explicit empty list but instead is the result of evaluating a variable, usually an input to the procedure you're writing, that's `butfirsted` in the recursive invocation. This is a case where the error isn't really in the instruction that caused the message. Usually there is nothing wrong with the actual invocation of `butfirst`; the error is a missing instruction earlier in the procedure. If the input is a word instead of a list, this message will take the possibly confusing form

```
butfirst doesn't like  as input
```

That's an invisible empty word between `like` and `as`!

I said that this message is almost always caused by a missing stop rule. You have to be careful about the "almost." For example, recall this practical joke procedure from Chapter 1:

```
to process :instruction
test emptyp :instruction
iftrue [type "|? | process readlist stop]
iffalse [print sentence [|I don't know how  to|] first :instruction]
end
```

This is not a recursive procedure, and the question of stop rules doesn't arise. But its input might be empty, because the victim enters a blank line. If I hadn't thought of that, and had written

```
to process :instruction
print sentence [|I don't know how  to|] first :instruction
end
```

the result would be

```
first doesn't like [] as input  in process
```

Another case that sometimes comes up in programs that do arithmetic is

```
/ doesn't like 0 as input
```

For example, if you write a program that takes the average of a bunch of numbers and you try to use the program with an empty list of numbers as input, you'll end up trying to divide zero by zero. The solution is to insert an instruction that explicitly tests for that possibility.

As always, the procedure that provokes the error message may not actually be the procedure that is in error. Consider this short program:

```
to second :thing
output first butfirst :thing
end

to swap :list
output list (second :list) (first :list)
end
```

```
? print swap [watch pocket]
pocket watch
? print swap [farewell]
first doesn't like [] as input  in second
[output first butfirst :thing]
```

Although the error was caught during the invocation of `second`, there is nothing wrong with `second` itself. The error was in the top-level instruction, which provided a bad input to `swap`. That instruction doesn't even include an explicit reference to `second`. In this small example it's easy to see what happened. But in a more complicated program it can be hard to find errors like this one.

There are two ways you can protect yourself against this kind of difficulty. The first is *defensive programming.* I could have written the program this way:

```
to swap :list
if emptyp :list [pr [empty input to swap] stop]
if emptyp butfirst :list [pr [singleton input to swap] stop]
output list (second :list) (first :list)
end
```

This version checks for bad inputs and gives a more helpful error message.* It would also be possible to figure out an appropriate output for these cases and not consider them errors at all:

```
to swap :list
if emptyp :list [output []]
if emptyp butfirst :list [output :list]
output list (second :list) (first :list)
end
```

This version manages to produce an output for any input at all. How should you choose between these two defensively written versions? It depends on the context in which you'll be using `swap`. If you are writing a program in which `swap` should always get a particular kind of list as input, which should always have two members, then you should use the first defensive version, which will let you know if you make an error in the input to `swap`.

---

* Actually, when you invoke this version of `swap` with a bad input, you'll see *two* error messages. The procedure itself will print an error message. Then, since it `stop`s instead of `output`ting something to its superprocedure, you'll get a `didn't output` error message from the Logo interpreter.

But if `swap` is intended as a general tool, which might be used in a variety of situations, it might be better to accept any input.

The second protective technique, besides defensive programming, is tracing, the technique we used in Chapter 9. If you get an error message from a utility procedure like `second` and you have no idea how it was invoked, you can find out by tracing the entry into all of your procedures.

Another way to get the `doesn't like` message is to forget the order of inputs to a procedure, either a primitive or one that you've written. For example, `lput` is a primitive operation that requires two inputs. The first input can be any datum, but the second must be a list. The output from `lput` is a list that contains all the members of the second input, plus one more member at the end equal to the first input.

```
? show lput "c [a b]
[a b c]
```

`Lput` takes its inputs in the same order as `fput`, with the new member first and then the old list. But you might get confused and want the inputs to appear left-to-right as they appear in the result:

```
? show lput [a b] "c
lput doesn't like c as input
```

Incorrect Results

Beginning programmers are often dismayed when they see an error message, but more experienced programmers are relieved. They know that the bugs that cause such messages are the easy ones to find! Much harder are the bugs that allow a program to run to completion but produce the wrong answer. In that kind of situation you don't have the advantage of knowing which procedure tickled the error message, so it's hard to know where to begin looking.

Here's a short program with a couple of bugs in it. `Arabic` is an operation that takes one input, a word that is a Roman numeral. The output from `arabic` is the number represented by that Roman numeral in ordinary (Arabic numeral) notation.

```
to arabic :num
output addup map "digit :num
end
```

```
to digit :digit
output lookup :digit [[I 1] [V 5] [X 10] [L 50] [C 100] [D 500] [M 1000]]
end

to lookup :word :dictionary
if emptyp :dictionary [output "]
if equalp :word first first :dictionary [output last first :dictionary]
output lookup :word bf :dictionary
end

to addup :list
if emptyp :list [output 0]
if emptyp bf :list [output first :list]
if (first :list) < (first bf :list) ~
   [output sum ((first bl :list)-(first :list)) addup bf bf :list]
output sum first :list addup bf :list
end
```

`Arabic` uses two non-primitive subprocedures, dividing its task into two parts. First `digit` translates each letter of the Roman numeral into the number it represents: `C` into 100, `M` into 1000. The result is a list of numbers. Then `addup` translates that list into a single number, adding or subtracting each member as appropriate. The rule is that the numbers are added, except that a smaller number that appears to the left of a larger one is subtracted from the total. For example, in the Roman numeral `CLIV` all the letters are added except for the `I`, which is to the left of the `V`. Since `I` represents 1 and `V` represents 5, and 1 is less than 5, the `I` is subtracted. The result is 100 + 50 + 5 − 1 or 154.

Here's what happened the first time I tried `arabic`:

```
? print arabic "MLXVI
13
```

This is a short enough program that you may be able to find the bug just by reading it. But even if you do, let's pretend that you don't, because I want to use this example to talk about some ways of looking for bugs systematically.

The overall structure of the program is that `digit` is invoked for each letter, and the combined output from all the calls to `digit` is used as the input to `addup`. The first step is to try to figure out which of the two is at fault. Which should we try first? Since `addup` depends on the work of `digit`, whereas `digit` doesn't depend on `addup`, it's probably best to start with `digit`. So let's try looking at the output from `digit` directly.

```
? print digit "M
1000
? print digit "V
5
```

So far so good. Perhaps the problem is in the way `map` is used to combine the results from `digit`:

```
? show map "digit "MLXVI
1000501051
```

Aha! I wanted a list of numbers, one for each Roman digit, but instead I got all the numbers combined into one long word. I had momentarily forgotten that if the second input to `map` is a word, its output will be a word also. As soon as I see this, the solution is apparent to me: I should use `map.se` instead of `map`.

```
? show map.se "digit "MLXVI
[1000 50 10 5 1]

to arabic :num
output addup map.se "digit :num
end

? print arabic "MLXVI
1066
```

This time I got the answer I expected. On to more test cases:

```
? print arabic "III
3
? print arabic "XVII
17
? print arabic "CLV
155
? print arabic "CLIV
150
?
```

Another error! The result was 150 instead of the correct 154. Since the other three examples are correct, the program is not completely at sea; it's a good guess that the bug has to do with the case of subtracting instead of adding. Trying a few more examples will help confirm that guess.

```
? print arabic "IV
0
? print arabic "MCM
1000
? print arabic "MCMLXXXIV
1080
? print arabic "MDCCLXXVI
1776
?
```

Indeed, numbers that involve subtraction seem to fail, while ones that are purely additive seem to work. If you look carefully at exactly *how* the program fails, you may notice that the letter that should be subtracted and the one after it are just ignored. So in the numeral `MCMLXXXIV`, which represents 1984, the `CM` and the `IV` don't contribute to the program's result.

Once again, we must find out whether the bug is in `digit` or in `addup`, and it makes sense to start by checking the one that's called first. (If you read the instructions in the definitions of `digit` and `addup`, you'll see that `digit` handles each digit in isolation, whereas `addup` is the one that looks at two consecutive digits to decide whether or not to subtract. But at first I'm not reading the instructions at all; I'm trying to be sure that I understand the *behavior* of each procedure before I look inside any of them. For a simple problem like this one, the approach I'm using is more ponderous than necessary. But it would pay off for a larger program with more subtle bugs.)

```
? show map.se "digit "VII
[5 1 1]
? show map.se "digit "MDCCLXXVI
[1000 500 100 100 50 10 10 5 1]
```

I've started with Roman numerals for which the overall program works. Why not just concentrate on the cases that fail? Because I want to see what the *correct* output from mapping `digit` over the Roman numeral is supposed to look like. It turns out to be a list of numbers, one for each letter in the Roman numeral.

You may wonder why I need to investigate the correct behavior of `digit` experimentally. If I've planned the program properly in the first place, I should *know* what it's supposed to do. There are several reasons why I might feel a need for this sort of experiment. Perhaps it's someone else's program I'm debugging, and I don't know what the plan was. Perhaps it's a program I wrote a long time ago and I've forgotten. Finally, since there is a bug after all, perhaps my understanding is faulty even if I do think I know what `digit` is supposed to do.

Now let's try digit for some of the buggy cases.

```
? show map.se "digit "IV
[1 5]
? show map.se "digit "MCMLXXXIV
[1000 100 1000 50 10 10 10 1 5]
?
```

Digit still does the right thing: It outputs the number corresponding to each letter. The problem must be in addup.

Now it's time to take a look at addup. There are four instructions in its definition. Which is at fault? It must be one that comes into play only for the cases in which subtraction is needed. That's a clue that it will be one of the if instructions, although instructions that aren't explicitly conditional can, in fact, depend on earlier if tests. (In this procedure, for example, the last instruction doesn't look conditional. But it is carried out only if none of the earlier instructions results in an output being evaluated.)

Rather than read every word of every line carefully, we should start by knowing the purpose of each instruction. The first one is an end test, detecting an empty numeral. The second is also an end test, detecting a single-digit numeral. (Why are two end tests necessary? How would the program fail if each one were eliminated?) The third instruction deals with the subtraction case, and the fourth with the addition case. The bug, then, is probably in the third instruction. Here it is again:

```
if (first :list) < (first bf :list) ~
   [output sum ((first bl :list)-(first :list)) addup bf bf :list]
```

At this point a careful reading of the instruction will probably make the error obvious. If not, look at each of the expressions used within the instruction, like

```
first :list
```

and

```
bf bf :list
```

What number or list does each of them represent?

(If you'd like to take time out for a short programming project now, you might try writing roman, an operation to translate in the opposite direction, from Arabic to Roman numerals. The rules are that I can be subtracted from V or X; X can be subtracted from

L or C; and C can be subtracted from D or M. You should never need to repeat any symbol more than three times. For example, you should use IV rather than IIII.)

Tracing and Stepping

In Chapter 9 we used the techniques of *tracing* and *stepping* to help you understand how recursive procedures work. The same techniques can be very valuable in debugging. Tracing a procedure means making it print an indication of when it starts and stops. Stepping a procedure means making it print each of its instructions and waiting for you to type something before evaluating the instruction.

Berkeley Logo provides primitive commands trace and step that automatically trace or step procedures for you. Trace and step take one input, which can be either a word or a list. If the input is a word, it must be the name of a procedure. If a list, it must be a list of words, each of which is the name of a procedure. The effect of trace is to modify the procedure or procedures named in the input to identify the procedure and its inputs when it is invoked. The effect of step is to modify the named procedure(s) so that each instruction is printed before being evaluated.

Tracing a procedure is particularly useful in the annoying situation in which a program just sits there forever, never stopping, but never printing anything either. This usually means that there is an error in a recursive procedure, which invokes itself repeatedly with no stop rule or with an ineffective one. If you trace recursive procedures, you can find out how you got into that situation.

Pausing

When a program fails, either with an error message or by printing the wrong result, it can be helpful to examine the values of the variables used within the program. Of course, you understand by now that "the variables used within the program" may be a complicated idea; if there are recursive procedures with local variables, there may be several variables with the same name, one for each invocation of a procedure.

Once a program is finished running, the local variables created by the procedures within the program no longer exist. You can examine global variables individually by printing their values or all at once with the pons command. (Pons stands for Print Out NameS; it takes no inputs and prints the names and values of all current variables.) But it's too late to examine local variables after a program stops.

To get around this problem, Berkeley Logo provides a `pause` command. This command takes no inputs. Its effect is to stop, temporarily, the procedure in which it appears. (Like `stop` and `output`, `pause` is meaningless at top level.) Logo prints a question mark prompt (along with the name of the paused procedure to remind you that it's paused), and you can enter instructions to be evaluated as usual. But the paused procedure is *still active;* its local variables still exist. (Any superprocedures of the paused procedure, naturally, are also still active.) The instructions you type while the procedure is paused can make use of local variables, just as if the instructions appeared within the procedure definition.

The main use of `pause` is for debugging. If your program dies with an error message you don't understand, you can insert a `pause` command just before the instruction that gets the error. Then you can examine the variables that will be used by that instruction.

Better yet, you can ask Logo to pause *automatically* whenever an error occurs. In fact, you can ask Logo to carry out any instructions you want, whenever an error occurs, by creating a variable named `erract` (short for error action) whose value is an instruction list. If you want your program to pause at any error, say

```
? make "erract [pause]
```

before you run the program. To undo this request, you can erase the variable name `erract` with the `ern` (erase name) command:

```
? ern "erract
```

Once you've examined the relevant variables, you may want to continue running the program. You'll certainly want to continue if this pause wasn't the one you're waiting for, just before the error happens. Logo provides the command `continue` (abbreviated `co`) for this purpose. If you type `continue` with no input, Logo will continue the evaluation of the paused procedure where it left off.

It is also possible to use `continue` with an input, turning the `pause` command into an operation by providing a value for it to output. Whether or not that's appropriate depends on which error message you get. If the message complains about a missing value, you may be able to provide one to allow the program to continue:

```
to demo.error
print first :nonesuch
end
```

```
? make "erract [pause]
? demo.error
nonesuch has no value  in demo.error
[print first :nonesuch]
Pausing...
demo.error? continue "hello
h
```

If, after examining variables, you figure out the reason for the bug, you may not want to bother continuing the buggy procedure. Instead you'll want to forget about it, edit the definition to fix the bug, and try again. But you shouldn't just forget about it because the procedure is still active. If you don't want to continue it, you should `stop` it instead, to get back to the "real" top level with no procedures active. (Instead of `stop`, a more definitive way to stop all active procedures is with the instruction

```
throw "toplevel
```

For now just think of this as a magic incantation; we'll talk more about `throw` in the second volume.)

Berkeley Logo also has a special character that you can type on the keyboard to cause an immediate pause. The character depends on which computer you're using; see Appendix A. This is not as useful a capability as you might think because it's hard to synchronize your typing with the activity of the program so that it gets paused in the right *context* (that is, with the right procedures active and the right local variables available). But it can be useful if you can see that the program is repeating the same activities over and over, for example; pausing just about anywhere during that kind of *loop* is likely to give you useful information.

Final Words of Wisdom

You may be feeling a frustrating sense of incompleteness about this chapter. After the chapter on variables, for example, you really knew everything there is to know about variables. (I suppose that's not strictly true, since you hadn't thought about recursion yet, but it's true enough.) But you certainly don't know everything there is to know about debugging. That's because there isn't a complete set of rules that will get you through every situation. You just have to do a lot of programming, meet a lot of bugs, and develop an instinct for them.

As a beginner, you'll probably meet bugs with a different flavor from the ones I've been discussing. You'll put a space after a quotation mark or a colon, before the word to which it should be attached. You'll leave out a left or right parenthesis or bracket. (Perhaps you'll get confused about when to use parentheses and when brackets!) All of these simple errors will quickly get you error messages, and you can probably find your mistake just by reading the offending instruction. Later, as your programs get more complicated, you'll start having the more interesting bugs that require analysis to find and fix.

It's a good idea to program with a partner. Sometimes you can find someone else's bugs more easily than your own—when you read your own program, you know too well what you *meant* to say. This advice is not just for beginners; even experienced programmers often benefit from sharing their bugs with a friend. Another advantage of such a partnership is that trying to explain your program to someone else will often help you understand it more clearly yourself. I've often discovered a persistent bug halfway through explaining the problem to someone.

The main point, I think, is one I've made in earlier chapters: there is nothing shameful about a bug in your program. As a teacher, I've been astonished to see students react to a simple bug by angrily erasing an entire program, which they'd spent hours writing! Teach yourself to expect bugs and approach them with a good-natured spirit.

On the other hand, you can minimize your debugging time by writing the program in a reasonable style in the first place. If your program is one long procedure, you should know that you're making it harder to locate an offending instruction. If all your variables are named `x` and `y`, you deserve whatever happens to you! And if you can't figure out, yourself, which procedure does what, then perhaps you should stop typing in procedures and spend a little time with paper and pencil listing the tasks each procedure needs to carry out.

Appendices

A Running Berkeley Logo

One of my reasons for writing a second edition of these books was that all of the Logo interpreters described in the first edition are now obsolete. Current commercial Logo implementations are quite different in their user interface from those traditional versions. Those differences make newer Logo implementations more immediately accessible to children who want to produce animated graphics, but in many cases the changes have made the kind of programming I do in these books harder.

My solution has been to produce, along with some of my students, a Logo interpreter that is available free of charge for most popular computers. The design goal of Berkeley Logo has been that a program written for one kind of computer should run entirely unchanged on any other kind. Still, there are slight differences in the user interface and in the installation process, and this appendix discusses those differences. Since Berkeley Logo is distributed with source files, I hope that as new computers and operating systems come along, some enthusiast will make Berkeley Logo available for them even if I don't catch them all.

Still, people who are using some other version of Logo for other purposes might well want to use these books to help them learn more advanced Logo ideas. The programs in this first volume can be adapted to current commercial Logo dialects with some effort. In the later volumes I rely more heavily on features that are available only in Berkeley Logo.

Getting Berkeley Logo

Berkeley Logo is available over the Internet, or on diskette from the MIT Press. On the Internet, make an anonymous FTP connection to `anarres.cs.berkeley.edu` and look in the directory `pub/ucblogo`. The relevant files are

`blogo.exe`	Self-extracting archive for DOS machines.

`ucblogo.sea.hqx`	BinHex self-extracting archive for Macintosh.
`ucblogo.tar.Z`	Compressed `tar` archive for Unix.

The files should be transferred in binary (image) mode.

Pointers to these files can also be found on my Web page:

```
http://www.cs.berkeley.edu/~bh/
```

For a diskette, use the order form enclosed with this book.

Within the Logo distribution is a subdirectory (or folder, if you're a Mac person) called `sources`. This contains the C language source files for the Logo interpreter. If disk space is tight, you don't need these files to run Logo; they are provided for people who want to extend the Logo interpreter or implement it for a different computer system.

Berkeley Logo for DOS Machines

If you got Berkeley Logo on diskette, to extract the files you put the diskette in your A or B drive and give the command `a:install` or `b:install`. This will create a directory named `ucblogo` on your C drive. If you got the file `blogo.exe` from the Internet, type the command

```
blogo -d c:\
```

to expand the archive. Don't forget the `-d`.

Berkeley Logo is provided in two executable versions:

`ucblogo.exe` runs on 286-and-up processors, and uses extended memory if you have it, so you can run large Logo programs.

`bl.exe` runs on any PC, but is limited to 640K. That's not big enough for some of the larger projects in the later volumes.

In order to run `ucblogo.exe` you must have the file `zpm.exe` (which is provided) in your DOS path. `Zpm` has to figure out what kind of extended memory interface you have, and in some cases it needs help. You must use the DOS command

`set DOS16M=1`	for NEC 98-series
`set DOS16M=5`	for Fujitsu FMR-60 or 70
`set DOS16M=6`	for ATT 6300 Plus

```
set DOS16M=7          for old Phoenix BIOS versions
set DOS16M=13         for Zenith Z-24X with old BIOS
set DOS16M=INBOARDfor 386 with Intel Inboard
```

Even if UCBLOGO runs correctly for you without any of these settings (which will be the case for most machines) you might try

```
set DOS16M=10         for faster performance on some systems
                      but slower on others – experiment.
```

`Ucblogo` and `bl` also usually figure out correctly what kind of graphics board you have. But for some obscure clones with nonstandard graphics you might have to tell it which graphics mode to use. This is also done with a DOS command:

```
set FG_DISPLAY=xxxx
```

where *xxxx* is the board type and mode, one of the following:

```
CGAHIRES, CGAMEDRES, EGACOLOR, EGAECD, EGAMONO, EGALOWRES,
HERC, ORCHIDPROHIRE, PARADISEHIRES, TOSHIBA, TRIDENTHIRES,
VEGAVGAHIRES, VESA6A, VESA2, VGA11, VGA12, VGA13, 8514A
```

I don't know anything about any of these except that `TOSHIBA` is for a T3100 and doesn't work on my T1200XE. I use `VGA12` on my generic clone.

There are some graphics modes that will work with `bl` but not with `ucblogo`, including `VESA1` for 256 colors of 640x480.

Finally, note that Logo writes directly to the screen and is therefore incompatible with "screen accelerator" TSRs. (For example, my PC comes with one called `pckscrn` and I had to turn it off before running Logo.) The file `ucl.bat` is a sample batch file that I use to disable the screen accelerator, run Logo, then re-enable it. If you have a different screen accelerator you'll need different commands, of course, but the idea is the same.

Ctrl-break or ctrl-Q means stop, ctrl-W means pause.

The Logo `edit` command runs a separate editor, starting that editor with a file containing your selected procedures. Logo will use whatever editor you want, if there is an `EDITOR` variable in your DOS environment. By default, Logo uses Jove, a version of EMACS, which is provided with Logo. This version of Jove is set up so that typing ctrl-C will save the file and return to Logo. You need to put

```
SET JOVERC=C:\UCBLOGO\JOVE\JOVE.RC
SET DESCRIBE=C:\UCBLOGO\JOVE\CMDS.DOC
```

in your `autoexec.bat` or something so that Jove will start up right. `Cmds.doc` is the Jove reference manual, used for its online help.

You also need

```
SET LOGOLIB=C:\UCBLOGO\LOGOLIB\
```

(yes, ending with backslash) in your autoexec.bat so that Logo can find its library files.

The `bl.exe` version of Logo can be run in a DOS window under Windows, but it can do graphics only in full-screen mode. For the larger projects, exit Windows and run `ucblogo.exe` under DOS. (In Windows 95, this can be made automatic if you install `ucblogo` as a "DOS mode" program.) There is an offshoot of Berkeley Logo called MSWLogo, written by George Mills, specifically for Windows. It has a more point-and-click style interface, and doesn't work well with those projects that make heavy use of reading from the keyboard or controlling the position of text on the screen; the Solitaire and Cryptographer's Helper projects in Volume 2 and the finite state machine simulator in Volume 3 are most problematic. But for general use, MSWLogo is a good option for Windows users. The easiest way to get it is from George Mills' Web page:

```
http://www.ultranet.com/~mills/
```

Berkeley Logo for the Macintosh

If you got Berkeley Logo on diskette, insert the diskette in your drive, copy the one file onto your hard disk, and then double-click on it to install the `UCB Logo` folder. If you got Logo from the Internet, you must first convert the BinHex format to an executable file; many file transfer programs do this automatically.

Command-period means stop; command-comma means pause.

On the Mac, Berkeley Logo includes a very simple-minded editor built into Logo itself. It works in the usual Macintosh way; when you have finished editing, you can select "accept editor changes" or "cancel editor changes" from the `Edit` menu.

Macintosh users will find the Berkeley Logo user interface disconcerting, because it was designed to be Logo-like rather than Macintosh-like. For example, you should use the Logo commands `splitscreen`, `fullscreen`, and `textscreen` to rearrange Logo's text and graphics windows, rather than trying to resize them with the mouse.

Berkeley Logo for Unix

Since there are so many different versions of Unix, Berkeley Logo is distributed in source form, and must be compiled for your particular machine. A Gnu Autoconf configuration file is provided, so the compilation process should be reasonably automatic. The X11 library is required for turtle graphics.

Logo uses your system's interrupt character for stop, and your system's quit character for pause.

For the `edit` command, Logo uses whatever program is specified in your `EDITOR` environment variable. If your editor exits with nonzero status (indicating an error) then Logo will not carry out the changes indicated in the edited file.

B GNU General Public License

The following software license, written by the Free Software Foundation, applies to Berkeley Logo and to the Logo programs in this book. I chose to use this license in order to encourage the free sharing of software—my own and, I hope, yours.

GNU GENERAL PUBLIC LICENSE
Version 2, June 1991

Preamble

The licenses for most software are designed to take away your freedom to share and change it. By contrast, the GNU General Public License is intended to guarantee your freedom to share and change free software—to make sure the software is free for all its users. This General Public License applies to most of the Free Software Foundation's software and to any other program whose authors commit to using it. (Some other Free Software Foundation software is covered by the GNU Library General Public License instead.) You can apply it to your programs, too.

When we speak of free software, we are referring to freedom, not price. Our General Public Licenses are designed to make sure that you have the freedom to distribute copies of free software (and charge for this service if you wish), that you receive source code or can get it if you want it, that you can change the software or use pieces of it in new free programs; and that you know you can do these things.

To protect your rights, we need to make restrictions that forbid anyone to deny you these rights or to ask you to surrender the rights. These restrictions translate to certain responsibilities for you if you distribute copies of the software, or if you modify it.

For example, if you distribute copies of such a program, whether gratis or for a fee, you must give the recipients all the rights that you have. You must make sure that they, too, receive or can get the source code. And you must show them these terms so they know their rights.

We protect your rights with two steps: (1) copyright the software, and (2) offer you this license which gives you legal permission to copy, distribute and/or modify the software.

Also, for each author's protection and ours, we want to make certain that everyone understands that there is no warranty for this free software. If the software is modified by someone else and passed on, we want its recipients to know that what they have is not the original, so that any problems introduced by others will not reflect on the original authors' reputations.

Finally, any free program is threatened constantly by software patents. We wish to avoid the danger that redistributors of a free program will individually obtain patent licenses, in effect making the program proprietary. To prevent this, we have made it clear that any patent must be licensed for everyone's free use or not licensed at all.

The precise terms and conditions for copying, distribution and modification follow.

GNU GENERAL PUBLIC LICENSE

TERMS AND CONDITIONS FOR COPYING, DISTRIBUTION AND MODIFICATION

0. This License applies to any program or other work which contains a notice placed by the copyright holder saying it may be distributed under the terms of this General Public License. The "Program", below, refers to any such program or work, and a "work based on the Program" means either the Program or any derivative work under copyright law: that is to say, a work containing the Program or a portion of it, either verbatim or with modifications and/or translated into another language. (Hereinafter, translation is included without limitation in the term "modification".) Each licensee is addressed as "you".

Activities other than copying, distribution and modification are not covered by this License; they are outside its scope. The act of running the Program is not restricted, and the output from the Program is covered only if its contents constitute a work based on the Program (independent of having been made by running the Program). Whether that is true depends on what the Program does.

1. You may copy and distribute verbatim copies of the Program's source code as you receive it, in any medium, provided that you conspicuously and appropriately publish on each copy an appropriate copyright notice and disclaimer of warranty; keep intact all the notices that refer to this License and to the absence of any warranty; and give any other recipients of the Program a copy of this License along with the Program.

You may charge a fee for the physical act of transferring a copy, and you may at your option offer warranty protection in exchange for a fee.

2. You may modify your copy or copies of the Program or any portion of it, thus forming a work based on the Program, and copy and distribute such modifications or work under the terms of Section 1 above, provided that you also meet all of these conditions:

a) You must cause the modified files to carry prominent notices stating that you changed the files and the date of any change.

b) You must cause any work that you distribute or publish, that in whole or in part contains or is derived from the Program or any part thereof, to be licensed as a whole at no charge to all third parties under the terms of this License.

c) If the modified program normally reads commands interactively when run, you must cause it, when started running for such interactive use in the most ordinary way, to print or display an announcement including an appropriate copyright notice and a notice that there is no warranty (or else, saying that you provide a warranty) and that users may redistribute the program under these conditions, and telling the user how to view a copy of this License. (Exception: if the Program itself is interactive but does not normally print such an announcement, your work based on the Program is not required to print an announcement.)

These requirements apply to the modified work as a whole. If identifiable sections of that work are not derived from the Program, and can be reasonably considered independent and separate works in themselves, then this License, and its terms, do not apply to those sections when you distribute them as separate works. But when you distribute the same sections as part of a whole which is a work based on the Program, the distribution of the whole must be on the terms of this License, whose permissions for other licensees extend to the entire whole, and thus to each and every part regardless of who wrote it.

Thus, it is not the intent of this section to claim rights or contest your rights to work written entirely by you; rather, the intent is to exercise the right to control the distribution of derivative or collective works based on the Program.

In addition, mere aggregation of another work not based on the Program with the Program (or with a work based on the Program) on a volume of a storage or distribution medium does not bring the other work under the scope of this License.

3. You may copy and distribute the Program (or a work based on it, under Section 2) in object code or executable form under the terms of Sections 1 and 2 above provided that you also do one of the following:

a) Accompany it with the complete corresponding machine-readable source code, which must be distributed under the terms of Sections 1 and 2 above on a medium customarily used for software interchange; or,

b) Accompany it with a written offer, valid for at least three years, to give any third party, for a charge no more than your cost of physically performing source distribution, a complete machine-readable copy of the corresponding source code, to be distributed under the terms of Sections 1 and 2 above on a medium customarily used for software interchange; or,

c) Accompany it with the information you received as to the offer to distribute corresponding source code. (This alternative is allowed only for noncommercial distribution and only if you received the program in object code or executable form with such an offer, in accord with Subsection b above.)

The source code for a work means the preferred form of the work for making modifications to it. For an executable work, complete source code means all the source code for all modules it contains, plus any associated interface definition files, plus the scripts used to control compilation and installation of the executable. However, as a special exception, the source code distributed need not include anything that is normally distributed (in either source or binary form) with the major components (compiler, kernel, and so on) of the operating system on which the executable runs, unless that component itself accompanies the executable.

If distribution of executable or object code is made by offering access to copy from a designated place, then offering equivalent access to copy the source code from the same place counts as distribution of the source code, even though third parties are not compelled to copy the source along with the object code.

4. You may not copy, modify, sublicense, or distribute the Program except as expressly provided under this License. Any attempt otherwise to copy, modify, sublicense or distribute the Program is void, and will automatically terminate your rights under this License. However, parties who have received copies, or rights, from you under this License will not have their licenses terminated so long as such parties remain in full compliance.

5. You are not required to accept this License, since you have not signed it. However, nothing else grants you permission to modify or distribute the Program or its derivative works. These actions are prohibited by law if you do not accept this License. Therefore, by modifying or distributing the Program (or any work based on the Program), you indicate your acceptance of this License to do so, and all its terms and conditions for copying, distributing or modifying the Program or works based on it.

6. Each time you redistribute the Program (or any work based on the Program), the recipient automatically receives a license from the original licensor to copy, distribute or modify the Program subject to these terms and conditions. You may not impose any further restrictions on the recipients' exercise of the rights granted herein. You are not responsible for enforcing compliance by third parties to this License.

7. If, as a consequence of a court judgment or allegation of patent infringement or for any other reason (not limited to patent issues), conditions are imposed on you (whether by court order, agreement or otherwise) that contradict the conditions of this License, they do not excuse you from the conditions of this License. If you cannot distribute so as to satisfy simultaneously your obligations under this License and any other pertinent obligations, then as a consequence you may not distribute the Program at all. For example, if a patent license would not permit royalty-free redistribution of the Program by all those who receive copies directly or indirectly through you, then the only way you could satisfy both it and this License would be to refrain entirely from distribution of the Program.

If any portion of this section is held invalid or unenforceable under any particular circumstance, the balance of the section is intended to apply and the section as a whole is intended to apply in other circumstances.

It is not the purpose of this section to induce you to infringe any patents or other property right claims or to contest validity of any such claims; this section has the sole purpose of protecting the integrity of the free software distribution system, which is implemented by public license practices. Many people have made generous contributions to the wide range of software distributed through that system in reliance on consistent application of that system; it is up to the author/donor to decide if he or she is willing to distribute software through any other system and a licensee cannot impose that choice.

This section is intended to make thoroughly clear what is believed to be a consequence of the rest of this License.

8. If the distribution and/or use of the Program is restricted in certain countries either by patents or by copyrighted interfaces, the original copyright holder who places the Program under this License may add an explicit geographical distribution limitation excluding those countries, so that distribution is permitted only in or among countries not thus excluded. In such case, this License incorporates the limitation as if written in the body of this License.

9. The Free Software Foundation may publish revised and/or new versions of the General Public License from time to time. Such new versions will be similar in spirit to the present version, but may differ in detail to address new problems or concerns.

Each version is given a distinguishing version number. If the Program specifies a version number of this License which applies to it and "any later version", you have the option of following the terms and conditions either of that version or of any later version published by the Free Software Foundation. If the Program does not specify a version number of this License, you may choose any version ever published by the Free Software Foundation.

10. If you wish to incorporate parts of the Program into other free programs whose distribution conditions are different, write to the author to ask for permission. For software which is copyrighted

by the Free Software Foundation, write to the Free Software Foundation; we sometimes make exceptions for this. Our decision will be guided by the two goals of preserving the free status of all derivatives of our free software and of promoting the sharing and reuse of software generally.

NO WARRANTY

11. BECAUSE THE PROGRAM IS LICENSED FREE OF CHARGE, THERE IS NO WARRANTY FOR THE PROGRAM, TO THE EXTENT PERMITTED BY APPLICABLE LAW. EXCEPT WHEN OTHERWISE STATED IN WRITING THE COPYRIGHT HOLDERS AND/OR OTHER PARTIES PROVIDE THE PROGRAM "AS IS" WITHOUT WARRANTY OF ANY KIND, EITHER EXPRESSED OR IMPLIED, INCLUDING, BUT NOT LIMITED TO, THE IMPLIED WARRANTIES OF MERCHANTABILITY AND FITNESS FOR A PARTICULAR PURPOSE. THE ENTIRE RISK AS TO THE QUALITY AND PERFORMANCE OF THE PROGRAM IS WITH YOU. SHOULD THE PROGRAM PROVE DEFECTIVE, YOU ASSUME THE COST OF ALL NECESSARY SERVICING, REPAIR OR CORRECTION.

12. IN NO EVENT UNLESS REQUIRED BY APPLICABLE LAW OR AGREED TO IN WRITING WILL ANY COPYRIGHT HOLDER, OR ANY OTHER PARTY WHO MAY MODIFY AND/OR REDISTRIBUTE THE PROGRAM AS PERMITTED ABOVE, BE LIABLE TO YOU FOR DAMAGES, INCLUDING ANY GENERAL, SPECIAL, INCIDENTAL OR CONSEQUENTIAL DAMAGES ARISING OUT OF THE USE OR INABILITY TO USE THE PROGRAM (INCLUDING BUT NOT LIMITED TO LOSS OF DATA OR DATA BEING RENDERED INACCURATE OR LOSSES SUSTAINED BY YOU OR THIRD PARTIES OR A FAILURE OF THE PROGRAM TO OPERATE WITH ANY OTHER PROGRAMS), EVEN IF SUCH HOLDER OR OTHER PARTY HAS BEEN ADVISED OF THE POSSIBILITY OF SUCH DAMAGES.

END OF TERMS AND CONDITIONS

How to Apply These Terms to Your New Programs

If you develop a new program, and you want it to be of the greatest possible use to the public, the best way to achieve this is to make it free software which everyone can redistribute and change under these terms.

To do so, attach the following notices to the program. It is safest to attach them to the start of each source file to most effectively convey the exclusion of warranty; and each file should have at least the "copyright" line and a pointer to where the full notice is found.

```
<one line to give the program's name
  and a brief idea of what it does.>
Copyright (C) 19yy  <name of author>


This program is free software; you can
redistribute it and/or modify it under the terms
of the GNU General Public License as published
by the Free Software Foundation; either version
2 of the License, or (at your option) any later
version.


This program is distributed in the hope that it
will be useful, but WITHOUT ANY WARRANTY;
without even the implied warranty of
MERCHANTABILITY or FITNESS FOR A PARTICULAR
PURPOSE.  See the GNU General Public License for
more details.


You should have received a copy of the GNU
General Public License along with this program;
if not, write to the Free Software Foundation,
Inc., 675 Mass Ave, Cambridge, MA 02139, USA.
```

Also add information on how to contact you by electronic and paper mail.

If the program is interactive, make it output a short notice like this when it starts in an interactive mode:

```
Gnomovision version 69,
Copyright (C) 19yy name of author
Gnomovision comes with ABSOLUTELY NO WARRANTY; for
details type 'show w'.  This is free software, and
you are welcome to redistribute it under certain
conditions; type 'show c' for details.
```

The hypothetical commands 'show w' and 'show c' should show the appropriate parts of the General Public License. Of course, the commands you use may be called something other than 'show w' and 'show c'; they could even be mouse-clicks or menu items—whatever suits your program.

You should also get your employer (if you work as a programmer) or your school, if any, to sign a "copyright disclaimer" for the program, if necessary. Here is a sample; alter the names:

```
Yoyodyne, Inc., hereby disclaims all copyright
interest in the program 'Gnomovision' (which makes
passes at compilers) written by James Hacker.


<signature of Ty Coon>, 1 April 1989
Ty Coon, President of Vice
```

This General Public License does not permit incorporating your program into proprietary programs. If your program is a subroutine library, you may consider it more useful to permit linking proprietary applications with the library. If this is what you want to do, use the GNU Library General Public License instead of this License.

Index of Defined Procedures

This index lists example procedures whose definitions are in the text and procedures that you are asked to write in the text. The general index lists technical terms and primitive procedures.

O

P

Q

R

S

T

U

V

W

Y

General Index

This index lists technical terms and primitive procedures. There is also an index of defined procedures, which lists procedures whose definitions are in the text and procedures that you are asked to write.

D

E

F

G

H

I

J

K

L

M

N

O

P

Q

R

S

T

V

W

X

Y